RENEWALS 691-4574
DATE DUE
APR 29
D0786636

# CRITICAL PERSPECTIVES ON IMPERIALISM AND SOCIAL CLASS IN THE THIRD WORLD

# CRITICAL PERSPECTIVES ON IMPERIALISM AND SOCIAL CLASS IN THE THIRD WORLD

**James Petras**

Monthly Review Press
New York and London

*Library of Congress Cataloging in Publication Data*

Petras, James F 1937–
Critical perspectives on imperialism and social class in the Third World.
Includes bibliographical references.
1. Underdeveloped areas. 2. Underdeveloped areas—Social classes. 3. Imperialism. I. Title.
HC59.7.P474 301.44'09172'4 78-13915
ISBN 0-85345-465-5

Monthly Review Press
62 West 14th Street, New York, N.Y. 10011
47 Red Lion Street, London WC1R 4PF

Manufactured in the United States of America

10 9 8 7 6 5 4 3 2 1

# CONTENTS

# ACKNOWLEDGMENTS

These essays reflect readings, discussions, seminars, and political meetings with students, professors, and political activists, as well as my own experiences in the recent period of imperialist wars, revolutions, and counterrevolutions. It would be difficult to enumerate all who at one time or another raised questions and issues which helped me to formulate my ideas more adequately. Some are no longer with us, having died or been killed in the struggle. Discussion and correspondence with Paul Sweezy, Harry Magdoff, Perry Anderson, Peter Limqueco, Maurice Zeitlin, Andrew Zimbalist, Lelio Basso, Terry Hopkins, and Andreas Papandreou were of great value. The intellectual exchanges during graduate seminars at SUNY/Binghamton were another source of ideas—some of the participants eventually collaborated in the writing. Political issues posed by movements were especially important in focusing my intellectual efforts. Discussions and exchanges with members and militants of the Venezuelan, Uruguayan, Argentine, Bolivian, Chilean, and Peruvian Left, with Eritrean revolutionary activists, with Western and Southern European militants, and with members of North American solidarity committees were helpful. Their experiences and insights were especially valuable in helping me to clarify my own ideas. Finally, I greatly appreciate the editorial assistance of Karen Judd and Susan Lowes in the final draft of the manuscript.

# PREFACE

Many of the ideas and conceptions concerning the Third World which have circulated over the past twenty-five years in both conventional liberal academic circles and among Marxist writers have been found wanting. This is not to deny that progress has occurred in some areas in relation to the past: modernization theory challenged the static notions of anthropologists who focused on the "unique" features of the Third World as isolated aspects of "non-Western" societies. The tribe, clan, and village were the loci of study. Beginning in the early 1950s, modernization theorists challenged this conception, and envisioned and promoted "national development"—studying changes in social structure and the state induced by the impact of capitalism (described as the "forces of modernization"), though of course much of this was obfuscated by a rather crusty jargon. By the early 1960s, when "modernization" theorists had conquered most of the major universities, they were, in turn, challenged by a new school of thought; this emphasized the inadequacy of looking at "national societies" and formulated a paradigm that focused on the interaction of metropolitan centers and satellites. This approach, described by some as a "dependency theory," focused on the power relations between regions as the crucial factor in analyzing and understanding uneven development on a world scale—described as development and underdevelopment. By the end of the 1960s and early 1970s the dependency approach clearly had eclipsed modernization theory, although a challenge of sorts emerged from dogmatic Marxist fundamentalists who spend most of their time counting the number of modes of production in a social formation: citations from *Capital* were substituted for historical analysis of the actual processes of capitalist development in the Third World. However, the dependency approach was vulnerable, as it lacked an adequate conceptualization of the class structure and state to accompany its economic analysis.

What I propose in these essays is an effort at synthesis of "dependency" and class analysis which may perhaps lead to a new approach. In some ways, the central concepts reflect an affirmation of Marxist "orthodoxy": the emphasis is on class as the central organizing principle of social analysis. Furthermore, the notions of exploitation, class struggle, and imperialism are the central operating principles that inform the analysis. Having adapted a theoretical approach that closely approximates classical Marxism, however, has allowed me to focus on the specificities within the historical development of Third World societies which have operated to produce state structures, class configurations, and industrial processes substantially different from Western capitalism. Thus, while the basic units reflect classical Marxism, the specific social processes, political regimes, and economic experiences reflect the particular world-historical situation that is being made and unmade in the Third World. "Marxism" is both extremely relevant and irrelevant, depending on the manner and form by which it is applied to the Third World societies.

The essays in this collection attempt to define both the areas in which Marxism is applicable and the directions in which new formulations must be constructed. The problematic is large-scale, long-term change as it is analyzed within specific conjunctures. For the Marxism which I propose is action oriented: not a passive reflection on events, but rather an effort to understand and formulate strategies on the basis of the emergent contradictions present in all capitalist advances, in state or economic activity. In regard to the latter point, the advance of capital, our Marxism rejects economistic interpretations which focus on self-induced catastrophes leading to the demise of capitalism, and focuses on the specific social classes and societal conditions within which political action takes place as the basis for any large-scale transformation of capitalism. Furthermore, we reject stagnationist theories of capitalist development—the idea that "nothing" is happening in the Third World. Massive changes have occurred, transforming economy, society, and polity. Colonial enclaves have become semi-industrial, dependent societies. Peasant oppression and rural unemployment have been increasingly replaced by the exploitation of an industrial proletariat, and an urban underemployed and unemployed labor force. Old-fashioned personalistic authoritarian regimes have been replaced by modern fascist dictatorships. It is not enough merely to note that imperialism has a "new face"; rather, the dynamics of the changes have led to new structures and conflicts. Many of the older issues—nationalization, agrarian reform, industrialization—no longer provide the banner that appeals to millions. Nor are the changes inaugurated under regimes promoting these reforms capable of consolidating their rule. The notion of socialism, as a mass democratic redistributive system, lurks behind every effort to "industrialize," "reform," or "develop" society. The efforts of these essays to examine the nuances and meanings within the "superstructure" (state) and development processes always return to the fundamental issue of which classes rule, benefit from and form society in their image. This method involves an effort to deal with the complexities of contemporary realities from a position which locates the crucial actors within the historically determined class structures. The dynamic interaction between social structures, economic processes, and state forms an ongoing world-historical system that describes a new "totality."

These essays are attempts to clarify the structures and consequences posed by imperialism and class struggle without resorting to ponderous and abstract formulations. The goal is a new Marxist social science which is both rigorous and committed, capable of systematizing data and preparing for revolutionary changes.

# 1

# LIBERAL, STRUCTURAL, AND RADICAL APPROACHES TO POLITICAL ECONOMY: AN ASSESSMENT AND AN ALTERNATIVE

*(with Kent Trachte)*

## Introduction

The growing interest in political economy has led to a proliferation of books and articles reflecting a broad spectrum of interests and approaches. The purpose of this essay is to map some of the major schools, their origins, assumptions, and projections, as well as to examine some of their shortcomings. The study of political economy has a long and respected tradition, dating back to the eighteenth century, and includes the giants of capitalist and socialist thought, notably Adam Smith and Karl Marx. Although the studies of politics and economics have gone separate ways for the better part of a century, especially in the United States, the recent attempts to develop a comprehensive approach which includes state, production, and social relations is to be welcomed.

In our discussion, we distinguish four major schools of thought and propose a fifth. We proceed by outlining their assumptions, specifying the units of analysis, problematics, and modes of analysis, and then critically examine the strengths and weaknesses of each as it has evolved from the narrower perspectives of economics and political science. We conclude by sketching out an alternative approach which shifts the discussion away from growth and development problematics toward issues of class formation and exploitation.

## Liberal, Transnational, Structuralist, and World Systems Approaches

This section presents and critiques several alternative approaches to the study of international political economy. Our analysis is organized with specific reference to the context of the political economy of development and underdevelopment. The analytic points are applicable to other contexts as well, but no explicit attempt will be made to demonstrate that here. That is a task to be taken up at another time.

### *The Intellectual Roots of Liberal Political Economy*

Variants of a liberal theory of international political economy are of relatively recent origin. As late as 1970, it was possible for Susan Strange to lament the absence of general studies of international economic relations where the political analysis predominated over the economic analysis.[1] Her reference was to the fact that the development of neoclassical international economic theory and contemporary international political theory have taken place in relative isolation from one another. The same has been true, for the most part, of theories of political and economic development.

A sociological explanation of this relative isolation is not of concern to us here. Rather, we will proceed by stating some relevant propositions of both neoclassical economic theory and the theory of international politics. It will also be shown how recent efforts within the liberal tradition at formulating a theory of international political economy have been heavily influenced by both perspectives.

The neoclassical model of international development is best exemplified by the writings of Ragnar Nurkse, Gerald Meier, and Gottfried Haberler.[2] For this group of scholars the problems of international development are the stimulation of economic growth and the maximum and efficient use of the world's resources. The units of analysis which are used in evolving solutions to these problems are the nation-state and sectors of national economies. The basic proposition is that international trade, unrestricted by tariffs and other protectionist measures, is the most effective means both for stimulating growth and for efficiently utilizing the world's resources.

This approach is historically linked to the doctrine of comparative advantage that was enunciated by David Ricardo and expanded upon by John Stuart Mill.[3] According to the theory in its original form, each nation should concentrate on producing those products in which it has a relative advantage in terms of its national factor endowments. This concentration will serve as an engine of growth by allowing the underdeveloped economy to overcome the disadvantages of small domestic markets. The additional income gained from this specialization will permit the purchase of new forms of technology and other material goods needed to stimulate development. In addition, specialization is said to encourage foreign investment, thus bringing additional capital, technology, and managerial skills into the economy. In this pure form, the model is based upon an interpretation of the dynamics of the growth of the world economy in the nineteenth century.

More recently, Nurkse has pointed out differences between the nineteenth-century situation and that of the twentieth century and has suggested modifications of the theory.[4] According to Nurske, because of internal barriers limiting the impact of the trade on the growth of the overall economy and because of the demand inelasticity for certain primary products in which underdeveloped nations have a comparative advantage, there is a need to modify the expectation that trade alone can stimulate economic growth. Nevertheless, he is adamant that the case for international specialization remains as strong as ever. Rather, it must simply be recognized that as an engine of growth, specialization is less powerful in relative terms. From this modified theory follow four policy recommendations. First, underdeveloped nations producing primary commodities should continue to produce these commodities up to the level of specialization that international demand will support. Second, resources above this level should be transferred to the areas of the next greatest comparative advantage. Third, it is considered important for the underdeveloped nations to evolve more effective linkages between the export sectors and other sectors of the economy. Fourth, the acceptance of foreign aid and investment is encouraged as a means of filling the remaining gaps. In the final analysis, Nurske feels that the disadvantages of protectionism simply are too great to permit any policy other than specialization.

Like neoclassical economics, the contemporary approach to international politics is distinguished by its emphasis upon the nation-state as the critical, if not sole, actor in world politics.[5] However, there are at least three other characteristic features of which we should take account. First, most theorists of international politics assume that the fundamental problem is the creation of order from the manifold conflicts of interest among various nation-states. Second, it is usually postulated that power is the key element in creating order. Moreover, power is thought of largely as a perceptual phenomenon dependent upon coercive military capabilities. Third, very little attention is normally paid to the linkages between international politics and domestic structures.[6]

It is generally agreed among scholars interested in the area of international political economy that neither the contemporary state-centric model of international politics nor the neoclassical theory of international economics is an adequate framework for studying the problems that have attended the growth of international economic interdependence. Nevertheless, they have been important influences on the two different approaches that have been suggested as alternatives from within the liberal tradition. Some scholars have taken the shortcomings of economists as their point of departure and others have begun by attempting to remedy the flaws of the political theory.

### *The Politics of International Economic Relations as Liberal Political Economy*

Those who depart from the weaknesses of international economics are most concerned with a "certain political naivite" that seems to characterize the literature that economists have contributed to the problems of international political economy.[7]

Most frequently it is said that economists tend to wish away political problems. They are accused of assuming that national foreign economic policies can be derived from a model of rationality that ignores the fact that "political choices on economic policies have seldom been motivated by carefully reasoned assessments of quantifiable economic costs and benefits, but rather by political aims and fears, and sometimes by totally irrelevant considerations and irrational emotions.[8]

What these criticisms have led to is an approach to international political economy that is best captured by the phrase, "the politics of international economic relations."[9] It is really an attempt, as the title of a recent collection of articles indicates, to marry "world politics and international economics."[10] Such a marriage results in a focus on three types of phenomenon. First, an effort is made at the structural level to elucidate how the international political system shapes the international economic system.[11] Second, there is a focus on the ways in which political concerns shape the economic policies of the nation-states and determine the leeway given to transnational actors, such as multinational corporations.[12] Third, specific international economic interactions are treated as international political interactions where actors manage or fail to manage their conflicts of interest.[13]

In reviewing some of the representative studies that this perspective has produced, several factors immediately become clear. First, the primary unit of analysis remains, as it had been for both its intellectual parents, the nation-state. Second, a compromise between the economist's assumption of a harmony of interests and the political scientist's emphasis on conflict has been created.[14] What is argued is that there is a fundamental difference between military and economic competition that is based on the fact that economic gains are sought for their absolute benefit to the nation, while military gains are sought for their relative benefit. Consequently, international economic arrangements that benefit others, even more than oneself, may be approved as long as they tend to maximize one's own gains. In military matters, on the other hand, the question is always whether one is benefitting relative to the other actor. From this second assumption follows a third: economic instruments can be used directly as instruments of power or influence in international politics. This results in a modification of the previous theory of international politics, where the emphasis had been on military capacity and threats of physical violence.[15]

When these scholars turn their attention to the political economy of development, the influence of both world politics and neoclassical economics is apparent. The politics of international development is approached as the resolution of conflicts of interest among national public policies.[16] Its political content is seen to lie in the fact that it is necessary for each of the various nation-states to choose among several competing and often contradictory goals that are advanced by different sectors of the society. Normally these goals are enumerated as economic efficiency, economic growth, full employment, income distribution, price stability, quality of life, and economic security.[17] Both developed and underdeveloped nations must choose to emphasize some of these goals over others. Their different levels of development make it likely that they will choose different goals, and these different choices create conflicts of interest that must be resolved through international politics. Resolution of these conflicts of interest is problematic and may involve a whole range of political tactics, from coercion to coalition-building to reciprocal negotiation.[18] On the other hand, the purely economic processes are not seen as problematic. Once economic efficiency or growth, to take an example, has been chosen as the goal of public policy, it is the theory of neoclassical economics that is considered to offer the right prescriptions for policy. This means that if an underdeveloped nation chooses efficiency, growth, and maximum employment, it is recommended that it pursue specialization, encourage foreign investment, and accept foreign aid.

### *An Evaluation of the Politics of International Economic Relations Approach*

In our view, this approach has made several positive contributions to the evolution of a theory of international political economy. Not the least of these is the momentum toward the rethinking of the separation of economic and political issues and the associated recognition that new tools and categories of analysis are needed. But there are also others. It has become apparent that the processes of international development cannot be treated as simple market operations, but involve political bargaining and choices. The role of the state in both developed and underdeveloped nations as a bargaining unit and as an allocator of resources has been highlighted. At last it has been recognized that economic strength is an instrument of power in international relations, and that the foreign economic policies of states are not susceptible to analysis by rationalistic game theory models. Finally, the scholars who have adopted this approach have contributed to a recognition that international economic issues are not technical problems, but are, as many in the underdeveloped world have been arguing for some years, political problems.

At the same time, we feel that there are some fundamental, if not fatal, flaws involved in the approach. We must ask whether it is really possible to create a new approach on the basis of old concepts. For, despite claims to the contrary, this approach to international political economy has not really created new categories of analysis. Rather, there seems to be a tendency to dress up old concepts in new garb. The danger is that the new clothing may only be serving to conceal the old weaknesses.

This first becomes clear when it comes to identifying the units of analysis. It seems that the concepts of nation-state and system have been borrowed from international politics and combined with the economic sectors of which economists speak. The result is that whereas internation economic transactions have been politicized at the level of the system, there is no adequate unit of analysis for capturing the impact of international political economic relations upon the domestic political economy of underdeveloped nations. The discussion tends to move in terms of imprecise dichotomies, like the north/south system and such euphemistic economic terms as export, industrial, and import sectors. There is no way to account for the interest groups, social classes, and corporate interests whose politics give meaning to these economic sectors.

Relatedly, the approach tends to ignore the processes of transnational linkages and how these affect the development process. When attention is paid to the ways in which political concerns influence national economic policies, this is usually done with an assumption that political concerns involve domestic actors only. Yet the very notion of interdependence suggests the folly of such an assumption. Attention must be paid to multinational corporations, foreign governmental bureaucracies, and other external actors who influence the choice of national economic policy. There is good evidence to the effect that foreign external actors play a crucial role in determining the political choices of underdeveloped nations.[19]

The concept of the state also remains inadequately theorized. Indeed, one can find no indication that any effort has been made to remedy the fallacy of the pluralist understanding of the state as a neutral bureaucratic arbiter pursuing the national interest. While it is doubtful whether such a conception has ever been valid for any historical period or for any state, there is now little doubt that the state in most underdeveloped societies is an instrument of class interests.[20] Any political economy that fails to take account of that fact, even while recognizing the important role of the state as a bargaining unit and an allocator of resources, is bound consistently to confront policies that will seem anomalous. In the final section of this essay we try to show how an adequate theory of the state can enrich the theory of international political economy.

In summary, this approach to international political economy is characterized by a fatal flaw. It is only adequate for conceptualizing the politics of economic relations between nations. It must depend upon the vacuous and imprecise concept of the national interest because it possesses no alternative categories that would allow for its disaggregation.

## *Transnationalism as Liberal Political Economy*

The second approach to international economics and international politics has spawned what Robert Gilpin has called the "sovereignty at bay model."[21] The point of departure in this case is a critique of the state-centric theory of world politics. The main criticism is that this theory is unable to account for economic and political interactions that cross state boundaries, but are not controlled by nation-state governments.[22] It is also argued that the interdependence of the world economy has rendered the concept of national power obsolete.[23] The costs of actions involving the exercise of military power are said to be too high because of the disruption of the world economy that would be involved. Thus, the economic and political struggles are seen to have become moderated. An example frequently used to support this case is East/West detente. Here, as in other arenas of world politics, the nations involved are seen to have recognized that "their efforts to enhance their power and security relative to others are . . . incompatible with an interdependent world economy that generates absolute gains for everyone."[24] The nation-state must adjust and is adjusting to the forces of economic efficiency and rationality.

Effectively, what this school is proposing is a transnational political economy. The nation-state will remain one unit of analysis, but since it is gradually decreasing in importance, there is a need to supplement it with categories that refer to transnational actors. Moreover, it is argued that one of the transnational actors, the multinational corporation, is emerging as the most powerful in global politics.[25] With its massive resources and mobility, a multinational corporation is seen always to have the option of moving its productive facilities. This is said to give it an edge over the national governments with which it may be in conflict and erode the sovereignty of the nation-state. In addition, other transnational actors are seen to have become independent, no longer necessarily subject to the control of national governments.

The transnational perspective generates a specific theory of international development. It is argued that "as the economies of developed nations become more service oriented, and as their labor costs continue to rise, manufacturing will migrate to lesser developed countries."[26] Therefore, rather than seeking to control and limit the operations of multinational corporations as they now are, underdeveloped nations are advised to encourage their growth and expansion. This model of development, like that associated with the other school of liberal political economy, is highly influenced by the neoclassical mode. Again, the mechanism of development is the transfer of capital, technology, and managerial skills from the developed to the underdeveloped world. The difference is that multinational corporations have now become the key actor through which the process of transfer will take place.

### *An Evaluation of the Transnational Approach*

In our view, the strength of this perspective lies in its efforts to supplement the category of nation-state and to highlight the role played by subnational actors in world politics. Its proponents are also undoubtedly right in stressing the significance of multinational corporations as actors in the contemporary world economy. However, there are two basic difficulties with the way in which these insights are presented.

First, the decline of the nation-state is greatly exaggerated. As many have argued from different perspectives, it is state action that has established the global framework within which multinational corporations have been able to grow, and it is state action that is responsible for maintaining situations that are favorable to the continued expansion of the corporations. In fact, periodic interventions of the state are necessary for adjusting and correcting the imbalances of monopoly capitalism.[27]

Second, although transnational theory attempts to locate the multinational corporation at the international level, there is no attempt to locate it within the social structure of either developed or underdeveloped nations. As an organizer of processes of production and distribution, a multinational corporation is a political phenomenon. One cannot understand the interests it represents in international politics unless one has located the interests it represents within national social structures. It is only when this is done for multinational corporations and other transnational actors that progress can be made toward a theory of international political economy that is genuinely transnational.

## *A Final Word on Liberal Political Economy*

One final shortcoming of a liberal political economy should be mentioned. It is common to both of the approaches discussed above and parallels some of the contradictions in Adam Smith's political economy. Both the marriage of international economics and world politics and the transnational approach have failed to anchor the economic processes of production and distribution in a historically specific social system. By this we mean that both approaches have uncritically assumed, just as did Adam Smith, that the capitalist mode of production and the world capitalist market are natural processes. On the one hand, they have failed to historically locate the rise, growth, and transformations of capitalism as a world system and its varying impacts on the problematic of development. On the other hand, they have avoided an analytic understanding of the national political and social foundations out of which the tendencies and structures of that world economy arise. As a result, liberal political economy tends to create abstractions, the lack of historical and analytic grounding of which leads to a tendency to obscure the real social forces at work.

## *The Structuralist Approaches*

A third approach to international political economy is concerned with the elaboration of structures of dependency and dominance on a global scale.[28] As a tradition, it antedates the recent liberal concern to remedy inadequacies of world politics and international economics. Moreover, structuralist theories of international political economy never have been plagued by an artificial separation of economics and politics. By viewing the world from the standpoint of the underdevoped nations, they have been consistently sensitive to the interpenetration of politics and economics in world affairs. Their concern has been with the manner in which those nations located at the center of the global economy created and continue to maintain structures and patterns of exchange that systematically benefit these center nations at the expense of those in the periphery. As such, structuralism stands as a distinctive alternative to the liberal theories of political economy.

### *Galtung's Theory of Structural Imperialism*

A discussion of the structuralist school can begin with the work of Johan Galtung and his effort to develop a structural theory of imperialism.[29] For Galtung, the central problematic of the world economy is "the tremendous inequality, within and between nations, in almost all aspects of human living conditions, including the power to decide over these living conditions; and the resistance of this inequality to change."[30] This inequality is seen to manifest itself in the fact that the world consists of center and periphery nations and that each nation, in turn, has its own center and periphery. The most severe inequality is that between the center in the center and the periphery in the periphery, and the task of the theorist is to conceive of, explain, and counteract the structural violence that ensues from the unequal relationship.

In order to facilitate his project, Galtung further develops the structure of inequality by adding that imperialism as a special system of dominance is characterized by three essential features: (1) a harmony of interest between the center in the center nation and the center in the periphery nation; (2) a greater disharmony of interest within the periphery nation than within the center nation; and (3) a disharmony of interest between the periphery in the center nation and the periphery in the periphery nation. In time, these essential features have given rise to an elaborate set of structural arrangements that have come to replace direct violence as the integrative mechanism of the imperial project. These new integrative mechanisms include: (1) the vertical division of labor and disharmony of interest within the periphery nation, resulting in a general impoverishment of the periphery of the periphery; (2) the way in which the organization and mobilization of the periphery of the periphery nations is prevented by a feudal structure within these nations; (3) the vertical division of labor between nations resulting in an impoverishment of the periphery nation as a whole; (4) the way in which organization and mobilization of the periphery nations as a group are impeded by a feudal interaction structure between nations; (5) the way in which it is difficult to mobilize peripheries both intranationally and internationally because of points one through four above and because the center in the periphery has a monopoly on international interactions; and (6) the way in which the periphery in the periphery cannot appeal to the periphery in the center nation or the center of the center nation because of a disharmony of interests.

Galtung's view of the world political economy is adequately summarized by referring to the three major consequences that follow from the analogy he draws between the global economy and the interaction structure of a feudal society. First, just as the manor lords enriched themselves through their vertical interactions with their serfs, so too do the dominating nations in the world economy enrich themselves as a result of their vertical interactions with the dominated nations. Moreover, in both cases the enrichment is at the expense of the dominated. Second, just as horizontal interaction among serfs was structurally discouraged by feudal society, so too is horizontal interaction among nations in the periphery kept to a minimum. Third, just as serfs were restricted to interactions with one manor lord, so too are periphery nations constrained to one center nation.

### *The Contribution of Raul Prebisch*

Although Galtung's argument contains references to unequal economic transactions between center and periphery nations, this aspect of his argument is not very fully developed. In order to more fully develop the structuralist approach, the work of Raul Prebisch deserves attention.

In the first phase of his work, written during the late 1950s, Prebisch defined the problematic of a political economy of the periphery as stagnation or underdevelopment.[31] His explanation laid particular stress upon a long-term secular deterioration of the terms of trade for the raw materials exported by periphery nations. Data were generated to support the claim that the prices of raw materials had declined relative to the manufactured goods that were imported from the center nations, thus resulting in a net outflow of capital from the periphery to the center and exacerbating the capital shortages in the periphery. Several reasons were advanced to explain these phenomenon. First, it was argued that an inelastic demand for primary products in the center markets has meant that increased peripheral productivity leads to a decline in prices rather than to an increase in consumption. This situation is seen to be reversed for manufactured goods produced in the center; an elastic demand for these goods, particularly in periphery markets, means that increased productivity is absorbed without any decrease in prices. Second, it was suggested that the existence of trade unions and monopolies in the markets of the center nations permitted increased productivity to be retained in the form of higher wages and profits, whereas the lack of effective labor organizations plus the existence of a competitive international market for raw materials led from increased productivity to a decline in prices. Finally, it was pointed out that the price of primary commodities tends to fall because of competition from synthetics and substitutes developed in the center nations. In conclusion, Prebisch's original argument was that because of all these factors together, international trade promotes not growth and development but stagnation and underdevelopment of the periphery.[32]

More recently, in an effort to take account of increasing industrialization and rising growth rates in some peripheral nations, Prebisch has shifted the terms of the discussion away from stagnation to what he now refers to as "the insufficient dynamism of peripheral capitalism."[33] Partly because of the changing needs of capitalism in the center and partly because of a desire to take advantage of the increasing demand for manufactured goods in periphery markets, the center, through its transnational corporations, has initiated a strategy of direct foreign investment in some manufacturing industries in the periphery. What is being created in the periphery is a consumer society, "the conspicuous expression of the imitative capitalism of the periphery."[34] The center is linking up in a combination of interests with the upper strata of the periphery to create the illusion of industrialization. However, this form of peripheral capitalism seems to suffer from an insufficient dynamism and an inadequate rate of capital formation that inhibits real industrialization and genuine development.

How to explain this insufficient dynamism? According to Prebisch, all partners of the alliance between the center and the upper strata are to blame. Power relations within the periphery permit the upper strata to appropriate the primary share of the fruits of increased productivity that flow to the periphery and they utilize it to indulge in excessive consumption. Relatedly, the power of the middle class leads to the absorption of their numbers in spurious and unproductive labor, thus wasting another part of the surplus. Finally, the center nations "have done nothing of consequence to enable the industrialization of the periphery to play an active part in a new international division of labor which will help it make up its historical leeway, nor to resolve the serious problems of primary exports; and the haphazard and stopgap financial cooperation provided is far from what is needed to meet the requirements of development."[35] The strategy pursued by transnational corporations is also seen to limit the dynamism of the periphery. While the desire of transnational corporations to take advantage of increasing demand in the periphery has led them to produce manufactured goods for consumption by the upper strata of the periphery, they are not interested in developing export industries in the manufacturing sector. The reason is that export industries based in the periphery would put them in competition with their parent firms who make the actual production decisions. As a result, peripheral capitalism is prevented from generating the kinds of manufacturing exports that could earn the revenues needed to finance its continuing development.

In summary, what Prebisch is now suggesting is that the center nations and the upper strata of the periphery have forged a common strategy designed to create consumer capitalism in the periphery. This strategy benefits the center and transnational corporations because it allows them to take advantage of the increasing capacity of the periphery to absorb manufactured goods. Foreign investment thus creates a limited manufacturing industry in the periphery, "peripheral capitalism." For various political reasons, however, and because of the unequal distribution of the surplus, both intranationally and internationally, peripheral capitalism generates a very inadequate rate of capital accumulation. Peripheral capitalism thus lacks the dynamism to sustain the kind of integral development a periphery nation needs to "make up for lost time."[36]

### *Structuralist Strategies for Change*

The structuralist analysis of Galtung and Prebisch leads to the recommendation of two basic types of strategies for change.[37] The primary emphasis is on tactics designed to secure a greater degree of control for periphery nations in order to maximize their share of the accumulated wealth of the capitalist world market. Among tactics at this level are included many of the strategies actually adopted by the UN Conference on Trade and Development (UNCTAD): establishment of rules to regulate exchange on more equal terms, self-reliance in the form of import substitution, increase in interperiphery interactions, and the further development of UNCTAD as a viable organization of periphery nations for pursuing their common international goals. A secondary emphasis concerns the articulation of tactics designed to secure a greater degree of control for the periphery within the periphery in order to maximize their share of national wealth. Few of these tactics have yet to receive any ongoing institutionalized status, but they are basically of three types. In one type, one of the centers undertakes to sever their cooperative relationships, either because of a crisis within the center of the center or because of an ideological disagreement over such issues as racism or nationalism. In the second type, the periphery in the periphery undertakes to seize power or to reduce the monopoly of the center of the periphery over international interactions. In an unlikely third alternative, linkages are formed between the periphery in the center and the periphery in the periphery.

### *A Global Dominance System*

One more recent development in structuralist political economy deserves our attention. Departing from Galtung's discussion of the evolution of nonviolent mechanisms of system maintenance, Helge Hveem has suggested the existence of an integrationist impulse that is leading toward a global dominance system.[38] His work envisions the gradual evolution of a hierarchical four-level scheme of production and distribution modeled on the organizational structure of a transnational corporation. At the highest level is the "quartenary level" or "the center of the center where all important decisions concerning the overall functioning and development of the system are taken."[39] The second level is the "tertiary level" where coordination of the activities of control and accumulation takes place. The next level is the "secondary level" where day-to-day management is performed. Finally, there is the "primary level" where day-to-day production of material and extraction of fixed value is performed.

What is distinctive about Hveem's analysis is that he has combined the Marxian problematic of capital accumulation with the Weberian problematic of rationalization at the global level.[40] On the one hand, there continues to exist an international division of labor and an unequal distribution of value that is determined by the needs of capital accumulation in the center. On the other hand, new actors and mechanisms and new types and forms of control are being superimposed over the old hierarchical structures. The process of capital accumulation is thus made more efficient and new modes of legitimation are created.

In Hveem's view, the key to uncovering the nature of the subtle transformation that this effects in the global dominance system is the recognition of the central role played by technocapital—the merger of technology, information, and capital—at the top of the global system of control. He is thus led to agree with those theorists of post-industrial society who have suggested that the ideology of technocapital is leading to a "world that consists of organizations that are built on control, superceding profit as the *raison d'etre* for their existence."[41] Hveem sees this changing impulse toward rationalization and control as an explanation of why center elites are more willing to parcel out shares of wealth to gain the acquiescence of peripheral elites. Moreover, rationalization generates a potent "demonstration effect," which raises the possibility of a perfect system of control and accumulation. With Hveem, the Weberian problematic has been globalized and the structure of domination is complete.

### *An Evaluation of the Structuralist Approach*

The structural approach to international political economy advances the discussion beyond the inhibiting parameters of liberal discourse. One is no longer forced to choose between a reified concept of national interests or to pretend that states are no longer important actors in world politics. Structuralism makes it analytically possible to speak of both the state and the differing interests within the nation. One can analyze both the conflict between center and periphery nations and the conflicts within nations between centers and peripheries. Moreover, it has also been recognized that the center within each nation-state monopolizes national policy in a way that conflicts with the interests of the respective peripheries. Even more importantly, structuralist theorists have revealed some of the processes by which actors within the center of the center penetrate the periphery and influence policy by forming alliances with actors within the center of the periphery. Some progress has also been made in locating the multinational corporation in terms of the social interests that it represents. As Prebisch has pointed out, the presence of a multinational corporation in a periphery is an ambiguous presence; while it is true that they bring with them capital, management skills, and access to new markets, they have little inclination, as representatives of the center of the center, to pursue the kinds of production strategies that are needed to sustain peripheral industrialization.[42] Finally, the structuralist framework has clarified that the international economy does not contain the built-in bias toward development of the periphery of the periphery that most liberal theorists assume.

Paradoxically, the weaknesses of the structuralist approach lie in the same areas as its strengths. While defining the problematic as inequality or underdevelopment reveals many of the dynamics of the political economy of international development that are obscured by the liberal approach, still others are concealed by the failure to come to terms with social relations or production through which value is created in a capitalist economy. Likewise, while the concepts of center and periphery allow us to begin exploring structures of dominance and dependency that are transnational, they suffer from a certain abstractness vis-à-vis the real sources of social change.

Center and periphery are analytically very imprecise concepts. Their abstractness derives from the fact that they are not anchored in the social economic structures of the various nations engaged in the global economy. The concepts fail to specify what concrete social forces fall within their purview, and this makes it impossible to identify whose economic and political interests are being pursued. As a result, structuralists naturally fail to discuss the concrete organizational form that conflicts of interest, or for that matter harmonies of interest, between various centers and peripheries take and how these organization forms can vary historically. In short, a center or a periphery does not act; the terms are merely analytic categories which obscure the real historical actors.

To speak of capitalism as a mode of production is to uncover the most glaring weakness of structuralist political economy. The structuralist approach fails to confront capitalism as a mode of production engendering certain social relations of production. This is reflected in the strategies promoted for changing the unequal distribution of value between and within nations. They approach the problem at the level of patterns of distribution without inquiring whether these unequal exchanges in question might be a product of the capitalist mode of production and the peculiar and specific organization of the market that it entails. In the final section of this essay we hope to show how the fatal moment of error for the structuralist approach occurs when the problematic is defined as "inequality" or "dominance" rather than exploitation.

Similar difficulties are encountered with Hveem's global dominance system. While he is undoubtedly correct in accentuating the rationalizing impulse of monopoly capitalism, he ignores the contradictions that continue to exist on both the national and international level. The recurrence and intensity of violence in Chile, Argentina, Brazil, South Africa, Rhodesia and elsewhere testify to the failure of capitalist rationality to eliminate the contradictions inherent in capitalism as a global system of production. And surely the Vietnamese conflict has not receded so far into our unconscious that we can presume to forget how these contradictions periodically spill over into the international arena in a most explicit way. Even the lack of consensus over a global strategy among the advanced capitalist states is evidence of the incompleteness of capitalist rationality. The project of a global dominance system is real enough, but it must be located as largely a project of the American imperial state. Furthermore, it must be emphasized that it is a project that continues to meet varying degrees and types of resistance from opposing capitalist and anticapitalist forces alike.

### *The World Systems Approach*

The fourth approach to international political economy that we wish to discuss has been designated as the world systems approach.[43] Its intellectual heritage lies in the critique of the developmentalist perspective of liberal political economy that was articulated in the work of Paul Baran, Andre Gunder Frank, Theotonio Dos Santos, and other theorists of *dependencia*.[44] Recently, it has achieved a new status in the attention given to the "unequal exchange" thesis of Arghiri Emmanuel, Samir Amin's discussion of the "accumulation of world capital," and Immanuel Wallerstein's historical interpretation of the rise of a "single capitalist world economy."[45]

The basic framework of a world systems theorist is strikingly elementary. The problematic to be explained is the fact that there exist different stages or levels of national development within what appears to be a unified global economy. The key to explaining this phenomenon, it is argued, is to specify the different political and economic roles which a state or geographic area plays within the overall system. This notion gives rise to the basic categories of analysis: core/semiperiphery/periphery; core/periphery; metropole/satellite.

The real innovation of the world systems approach lies in their choice of the primary unit of analysis—the capitalist world economy. All phenomena are to be explained in terms of their consequences for both the whole of the system and its parts. It is asserted that the internal class contradictions and political struggles of a particular state, like Rhodesia for example, can be explained as "efforts to alter or preserve a position within the world economy which is to the advantage or disadvantage of particular groups located within a particular state."[46]

It is not important that we detail the specific propositions of particular world systems theorists here; indeed, their disagreements over even the number of tiers in the world economy would make that an arduous task. What is important to notice is the direction of generalization in world systems theory, for that is the key to understanding the approach. Specific events within the world system are to be explained in terms of the demands of the system as a whole. Actors are acting, not for their immediate concrete interests, but because the system dictates that they act. As Wallerstein has put it: "Where then in this picture do the forces of change, the movements of liberation, come in? They come in precisely as not totally coherent pressures of groups which arise out of the structural contradictions of the capitalist world economy."[47]

### *An Evaluation of World Systems Approaches*

To conceptualize the issues of the Third World in terms of dependency or as part of a world system is to lose sight of the most decisive *processes* of class formation and *social relations* which beget change and the particular configurations of social forces which emerge on a world scale.

It is not the world system that begets change in social relations, but rather social forces that emerge and extend their activities that produce the world market. The transformations wrought within societies by their insertion in the world market must be seen as an ongoing reciprocal relationship: between the forces and relations of production within a social formation and those that operate through the world market. From the perspective of international political economy, a comprehensive analytical framework must focus on the structural variations and transformations within the capitalist mode of production and the state capacities for exercising hegemony, both within a social formation and on a global basis.

The principal features that characterize capitalist development have varied considerably over time: the process of primitive accumulation, the growth of commercial capital, the expansion and growth of industrial and later financial capital each have their own laws of development, generating their own class structures and appropriate state organization. The class and state variations within core countries are determinants of their relative position in the world capitalist system. Among the capitalist countries (core), the variations in imperial state organization, development of the productive forces, homogenization of the social formation (absence of precapitalist social formation), affect the relative competitive position of each in terms of establishing areas of hegemony. The differentia in class formation contained within each core society are, in turn, essential to understanding the types of class alliances within a social formation and between capitalist countries. Finally, the crystallization of class forces, the degree of polarization within a social formation, outcome of the combined developments of productive forces, external expansion, and internal polarization determine the level and scope of the class conflict—which itself feeds into and influences the worldwide position of a given capitalist class.

The metaphor of a metropole/satellite relation eliminates the most essential factors that account for the specific relations and processes that shape historical development. The focus on the external relationships between social systems leads to an incapacity to differentiate the different moments of capital development, the specific configuration of types of capitals, the particular class relationships and conflicts engendered between capital and labor. This, in turn, leads to overly abstract sets of assertions: core exploits the periphery through unequal exchange or the metropole appropriates surplus. Vague enough to be sure. But not only is the core constantly changing in its internal organization of capital—shifts from merchant to industrial to financial—but the relationships of capitals within the core are in unstable competition; moreover, the social relations of production themselves are changing, creating new sets of demands and crises.

The long-term cycles of capital expansion and contraction on a world scale, the particular forms they take—wars, colonialism, imperialism—are reflections of the unstable relationships between competing and expanding capitals within the core and the crises (depression or stagnation) that are engendered. The notion of core/periphery, especially in the work of Amin, sets up a set of fixed exploitative relations that leaves unexamined the internal crises that disrupt the operations of the mechanisms of expansion and what he describes as surplus appropriation.

Moreover, the general crises of core capital have engendered, in specific but recurring instances, class conflicts and shifts in the axis of state power. Changes of class forces alter the boundaries for the continued reproduction of capital—decisively affecting the global position of the ruling class, i.e., its capacity to appropriate surplus. The indefiniteness of systems analysis before the historic confrontation of classes, the absence of any notion of how the class struggle interacts with the actions of the ruling class—specifically related to its movement in the international arena—substantially weakens the theory's capacity to explain societal change. The conception of the world system remains a static description of national features abstracted from the class realities which produce it.

From the other side of the metaphor, the imposition of satellite status is not a uniform or completed process: the persistence of precapitalist classes and institutions within the restructured peripheral society inserted in the world system suggests a whole complex of social forces that conflict or collaborate in the subordination of peripheral society.

The heterogeneity of precapitalist social formations and the particular ways in which imperialist forces interlock makes notions of dependency and periphery rather vacuous. The internal variations in class development are largely a product of the interface of the original organization of production and the particular moment of imperialist domination. The social relations of production that emerge from and shape the further development of the subordinated peripheral society cannot be encapsulated in any vague and amorphous notion of "underdevelopment."

The pivotal unit which facilitates core subordination of peripheral society is the existence within the latter of collaborator classes whose function is to organize the state and economy in accordance with the core definitions of the international division of labor. The creation of an international political economic order based on the inequalities of nations is rooted in the existence of an expanding center of capitalism and a set of classes within the periphery whose own expansion and position is enhanced in the process. The insertion of particular social formations within the world capitalist market and division of labor is largely the product of classes which combine a double role—exploitation within the society and exchange outside the society. This dual process leads to the expansion of production relations and antagonistic class relations within peripheral society, growing exchange relations, and competition with the core.

The political economy of world systems analysis emphasizes the aggregate economic and technological levels of societal development as the decisive features in defining roles and conflict in the world order. This approach understates the centrality of conflicts between social systems—Zaire/Angola, Mozambique/South Africa, Eritrea/Ethiopia—and the fundamental contradictions within social systems, i.e., conflict between classes, the capital/labor conflicts in Italy and France, for instance.

Obviously all societies participate in the world capitalist system at different levels and, depending on the development of their productive forces, with differing degrees of influence within it. Nevertheless, what is more important is the organization of production, the class relationship, and the class character of the state which differentiates societies and ultimately provides meaning to their insertion within the world system. In understanding the processes of world historic change it is not as important to know that Zaire and Mozambique are peripheral societies as it is to recognize the profound class transformations that affect one and not another. The same could be said for Cuba and China in comparison to the Dominican Republic and India: both are peripheral countries (or perhaps one or the other is semi-peripheral), but their participation in the world capitalist market is informed by a different set of class interests which act decisively to effect the character and shape of the development of the productive forces within society and to contribute to undermining the organizing principles of the world capitalist system in the larger historical perspective. Thus, the decisive factors differentiating societies are found in their internal class relationships and struggles; the external articulation (between the class structure/world market) of these internal changes influences and shapes, but in no decisive sense develops and initiates the basic changes that mark the scope of the transformation and the direction of the transition. Insofar as imperialist forces act, they operate within the class formation and cannot be conceptualized as the impersonal forces of the market; but rather they must be marked as part of the internal class alignments.

Having stated the above, however, it is important to recognize that the capitalist world market does have a profound effect in shaping the developments within a social formation: obviously, the lower the level of productive forces within a transitional society the greater its vulnerability to forces operating through the market. In the case of revolutionary societies this increases the chances of distortions and aberrations from the original class project. This contest between internal class developments and the operation and demands of antagonistic class forces acting through the world market is one of the central issues to be confronted by socialist theorists; but it is not dealt with adequately simply by looking at the fact of insertion in the world market in isolation from the decisive shifts and changes in class formation. Without a clear notion of the antagonistic class interests located in the interior of a social formation, there is a tendency among world system theorists to dissolve the issue into a series of abstract developmental imperatives deduced from a static global stratification system which increasingly resembles the functional requisites and equilibrium models of Parsonian sociology. The purpose of social revolution is not development; nor is the development of the productive forces an instrument of mobility toward higher levels in the world stratification pyramid (shifts from periphery toward core). The problematics of social revolution are focused on transforming social relations of production in order to create the bonds of class solidarity (internationalism in the world sphere) to transform the world social order. The analysis of world system through its use of formal stratification criteria of differentiation *subsumes* specific class differences into general developmental categories; *subordinates* notions of class conflict to mechanisms of (international) social mobility; and *amalgamates* social transformations with their opposite, by abstracting power relations from their historic class context. Here the notions of system-convergence are buttressed by an analysis in which structural position in a system of (world) stratification leads to internal homogenization: all peripheral countries as they ascend the ladder become more and more like the core states which, in turn, are increasingly alike because of their common position within the world capitalist system, and so on. The great revolutionary conflicts then are reduced to becoming merely one of several instruments to a common outcome: Russia becomes like the United States, China like the Russians, Cuba follows China, Vietnam, etc.; the functional imperatives of the world system demand conformity to its operating principles as the price of ascent.

The general weakness of this theory, of course, is that it explains everything and explains nothing: why the particular collectivist, revolutionary forms of struggle? Why the egalitarian aspirations? And why the profound efforts to transform capitalist society? This is a roundabout way of becoming part of the world capitalist system—to say the least.

Whereas one can conceive analytically of a world capitalist system, in historical experience it is made up of specific imperial and revolutionary societies that enter into conflict precisely over its existence. Herein lies the contradictory phenomena: of anticapitalist societies which both participate in and struggle against the forces within the capitalist market. The form and outcome of that struggle depend on the organization and consciousness of the classes within the anticapitalist society. The manner in which the fundamental contradiction (between anticapitalist social formations/capitalist world market) will be resolved depends on the evolution of class forces within the country and the proliferation of revolutionary forces in other societies. The capitalist world market thus must be demystified from a set of static institutions/factors and described essentially for what it is: a series of class relationships that have their anchorage and instrumentation in the imperialist states. The world market operates through the class-directed institutions that impose the exploitative class relationship throughout the world. The world capitalist system can best be analyzed by examining the hegemonic class relationship and imperialist state and the conflicting class relationships that emerge in each social formation.

## Class Analysis and World Historical Perspective: An Alternative

Expansion on a world scale has been characteristic of our epoch—although the process has not been as smooth as some commentators would have us believe. In fact, recurring crises—recessions, depressions, and fluctuations—are indeed the very mechanisms through which the economic system has sought to recover its dynamic.[48] The problem then is not one of absolute stagnation but of examining the conditions under which the process of capital accumulation takes place and its impact on the class structure. The issue in debate has been over "underdevelopment" and the focus has been on which social system is more conducive to growth and "development" to overcome "underdevelopment." While of late some attention has been paid to income distribution and inequalities,[49] the sources of those inequalities, their roots in social relations and state control, have been passed over. The issue of exploitation, rooted in capitalist social relations or in bureaucratic collectivistic forms of statism, has hardly been analyzed; even less so have class relations served as a point of departure within which to locate the problem of capital accumulation and expansion.

The conditions under which accumulation takes place include: (a) the nature of the state (and state policy); and (b) class relations (process of surplus extraction, intensity of exploitation, level of class struggle, concentration of the workforce). The impact of capital accumulation on class structure includes: (a) class formation/conversion (small proprietor to proletarian, or kulak, rural proletarian to urban subproletarian, landlord to merchant, merchant to industrialist, national industrialist to branch plant manager of a multinational corporation—these are just some examples of the processes under this rubric); (b) income distribution (concentration, redistribution, reconcentration of income); and (c) social relations: labor market relations ("free" wage, trade union bargaining), semicoercive (market and political/social controls), coercive (slave, debt peonage).

Production expands, growth does occur in cyclical patterns, largely as a function of external decisions ("demand") and internal conditions (externally linked classes, alienated state, repressed social movements). Accumulation is characterized by uneven development, reflected in the particular product areas integrated to the external world and sharp income inequalities derived from the external class linkages, control over state revenues, and coercive controls over working class and peasantry.[50]

Unlike dependency studies, which center on the growth of productive forces and how the external ties block growth, the focus on conditions of accumulation and its impact on class relations allows us to focus more concretely on the nature of the state ultimately involved in both accumulation and class formation, as well as internal class relations as they emerge from, as well as shape, capitalist development.

A discussion of imperialism that focuses on its expansionary/stagnationist tendencies overlooks its essential character as the international expression of capitalism's historical mission to develop the forces of production in accordance with the logic of capital accumulation, a process that is, by its nature, uneven, exploitative, and contradictory.

### *The Old and New Contradictions*

In the period prior to neocolonial type of peripheral exploitation, the political and social forms of domination were largely extensions of metropolitan institutions. The exceptions were mostly colonial-settler regimes that, in the first instance, developed autonomist tendencies as wedges to open up political space and commercial opportunity; the existence of preimperial social formations and traditional political authorities (chieftaincies, high-caste functionaries) mostly served as surrogates of imperial authority largely delegated to tribute collecting functions. The process of surplus extraction was, therefore, relatively direct. The colonial official inside was the foreign officer outside. The essential concentradiction was between imperial capitalism extracting surplus value from colonized classes; the national struggle was, in large part, unmediated by internal class and political conflicts.

In the neocolonial phase, national independence and the formation of the national state led to the creation of social strata between imperial capitalism and the labor force. Drawn from a variety of sources, including political movements, the university, the army, the civil service, this social strata is representative of the propertyless "intermediary" groups; rooted in the state bureaucracy, it has access to powers of the state, including revenues and expenditures. The impulse to personal property ownership and affluence through derivative "ownership" via association with metropolitan enterprises or through directorships in state enterprises creates the basis for negotiated conflict between imperial/nationalist social strata on the one hand and on the other hand by enlarging the scope of the class relationship, heightening tension within the periphery between these intermediary strata and the labor force. Imperial capital exploitation mediated by internal class forces creates and multiplies contradictions and disguises them. Imperial policy is oriented toward manipulating national "intermediaries" as a protective covering, whereas the dominant national strata struggle to increase their social preponderance, vis-à-vis their own labor force.

### *Class Alliances and Capital Accumulation in the Periphery*

A number of strategies emerge for the national intermediaries dominant in the peripheral countries. But before discussing the principle options open to the dominant national strata, it is worthwhile to briefly survey three interrelated issues: the social basis of nationalist predominance over socialism during the independence struggle, subsequently in the post-independence period, and the political, social, and economic possibilities opened by independence to nationalist regimes.

Nationalism emerged largely as a result of the low degree of social differentiation within the colonies, leading to the amalgamation of various class and preclass forces. The existence of subsistence farmers and their general isolation from political life contributed to making the land question less pressing than the national question. As a result, political organization was confined to the urban petty bourgeoisie, products of commercial and administrative expansion. The predominance of the petty bourgeoisie, the small size of the proletariat and its relative isolation from the peasantry created circumstances in which the tradition of class struggle was much weaker than nationalist politics. The large concentrations of urban petty capitalists and state employees over and against the industrial proletariat set the tone and direction of independence politics.

Nationalism sustained itself in the post-independence period, in part because the slowness of industrial expansion did not favor the growth of social classes that might be more receptive to class politics. As a result of the relatively weak position of the industrial proletariat, the trade unions were, in many cases, absorbed in the state apparatus, further undermining the socialist option. In addition to these organizational measures, the national state ironically has resorted to communal mystifications and regional loyalties to sustain its power, thus at the same time disintegrating the source of its legitimacy, as well as undermining class divisions. Parallel to national disaggregation, the nationalists have followed a policy of external integration—grafting on to the police and military apparatus the ideology and orientation of the metropole. These structural adaptations and policies have been reinforced by specific changes in the mode of political activity: demobilization of the population and bureaucratization of political life. Legitimate political action is confined largely to competition over employment in the expanded state sector. While nationalism in power has not led to the demystification of oppressive class relations, control over the *government* has led to a number of economic openings or possibilities: the national intermediaries can bargain over terms of dependency, diversify the sources of dependency, increase revenues, create a framework for the development of internal markets through social expenditures and (state) investments, promote diversification of production, create the basis for the expansion of the national bourgeoisie—anchored in either the state or private sector or both—and the petty bourgeoisie (mainly public employees), and open up opportunities for statist development policies. These possibilities are, in large part, contingent upon the type of international and national class alliances that are formed, as well as the bargaining strength of the classes within the alliance.

The post-independence national regime can choose among at least three strategies or types of class alliances for capital accumulation. In the first instance, it can join with imperial firms and regimes in intensifying surplus extraction from the labor force through a variety of post-independence working relationships outlined under the abovementioned rubric of dependent neocolonialism. An alternative strategy for the national regime involves extracting the surplus from the labor force and limiting or eliminating the share going to the imperial firms, thus concentrating it in the hands of state and/or private national entrepreneurs. This approach, which can be referred to as a national developmentalism without redistribution, leads to concentration of income at the top of the national class hierarchy.

A third alternative is for the national regime to ally itself with the laboring population, extend the areas of national control (through nationalization), reinvest the surplus of the national economy, or promote a redistribution of income within the national class structure.

The type of class alliance on which the national regime rests and the strategy for capital accumulation directly affect the distribution of income. Capital accumulation from above and outside (what can be called the "neocolonial" model) results in an income structure that resembles an inverted pyramid—with wealth and power concentrated in the hands of foreign capital. The national bourgeois developmental approach, which capitalizes on the foreign elite and the national labor force, concentrates income among the intermediary strata (in the form of the governing elite of the periphery), leading to income distribution along the shape of a diamond.

The alliance between national intermediaries and the labor force, what can be referred to as a "national-popular" strategy, leads to a broader based society in which income is more diversified, spreading downward and taking the shape of a pyramid.

As the above indicates, the struggle against imperial domination is now mediated through a class structure which itself contains contradictions, i.e., is itself a source of exploitation. The *pattern* of exploitative relations varies from one development strategy to another. In the neocolonial model, the national bourgeoisie serves as a means of heightening imperial exploitation in order to extract a share of the surplus for itself; examples of this regime include Brazil, Chile, Indonesia, Iran, Taiwan, South Korea, and South Vietnam. Policy is characterized by coercion, and a demobilized population, open access to raw materials, tax and other incentives to foreign investors. The forms of joint exploitation vary greatly, expressing the differences in bargaining power between the national and imperial bourgeoisie. Under conditions of total foreign control of the economy, the national bourgeoisie obtains tax revenue. Under conditions of partnership in which majority ownership and management prerogatives are in foreign hands, the national bourgeoisie obtains a minority share of earnings plus tax revenues. Whatever the specifics, the foreign component is clearly dominant in internal, as well as external, relations.

In the developmental model, the bourgeoisie dominates foreign capital and exploits the national labor force. In this case, the national bourgeoisie serves as a means of national capitalization, but at the expense of the labor force—reconcentrating capital in its own hands. This type of elite nationalism is difficult to identify as a pure type, apart from the neocolonial/populist models, because the national bourgeoisie generally is in a weak position, numerically and socially. The initiatives for this form of capital accumulation usually come from outside of the bourgeois class and its parties, most often from the military. Only under dictatorial conditions can this narrow and weak strata resist the pressures from below and from the outside, and then not usually for any duration of time. Moreover, national bourgeois developmentalism overlaps considerably with the neocolonial approach in some cases; in other instances, it approximates the national popular approach. Some possible examples of this type of regime would include Mexico (under Echeverría), Venezuela (under Pérez), Peru (under Velasco), Argentina (under the second Perón regime and the earlier Frondizi regime). The developmental model ostensibly gives the state the role of maximizing national bourgeois interests. In this context, it has a double function: anti-imperialist gesturing and disciplining the labor force. In practical terms, the national developmental state attempts to redefine the terms of dependency to favor national capitalist strata and contain labor demands. The forms for capitalizing the national bourgeoisie include:

1. increasing tax revenues to include the majority of earnings;
2. extending ownership to majority shares, including management rights;
3. limiting foreign capital activities to the external sector (commercialization), fragmenting their operations (exploration rights, management contracts), limiting exploitation to specified time periods, limiting access to local capital, directing foreign industry to export markets, etc.; and
4. selective nationalization: expropriation of particular enterprises by the state, in many cases to provide cheap services to private sector.

The developmentalist approach, however, while squeezing the foreign sector, also shares with the foreign sector an interest in maximizing exploitation of the labor force: maintenance of production, labor discipline, and popular demobilization. The success of this type of "establishment nationalism" depends on the avoidance of confrontations with foreign sectors and the labor force. Threats from either side may cause the national bourgeoisie to seek alliances: with populists if threatened by foreign interests, or with imperial groups if threatened by the left. While the rise of establishment nationalism may have been influenced initially by radical nationalist pressures, the usual tendency has been for it to dissolve in a series of external agreements which erode the original national developmental project.

The national-populist alliance, composed of bourgeoisie/petty bourgeoisie, workers and/or peasants, attempts to capitalize the economy on the basis of nationalist measures directed at foreign firms, state financing and stimulating national-populist regimes, including Argentina (under the first Perón government, 1945–1955), Bolivia (under the National Revolutionary Movement, or MNR, 1953–1956), Brazil (under Goulart), Mexico (under Cárdenas). The striking characteristics of this type of regime are the frequency with which it has appeared in the periphery, its short duration as a national-popular regime (usually it is overthrown or evolves into one of the two other variants), and the special conjunctural conditions which favor the formation of this alliance, such as, for example, the windfall earnings that accrued to Argentina during World War II. One of the basic weaknesses of this type of regime as a vehicle for capital accumulation is found in its efforts to eliminate foreign exploitation without developing adequate substitutes: after the initial redistributive measures and after the initial euphoria over the reduction of the foreign presence, the issue arises as to which of the two national social classes will capitalize the economy, the national bourgeoisie or the workers/peasants. The national bourgeoisie, without its external sources of finance, must seek, in and through the state, means to promote the accumulation of capital, at the expense of the working class. On the other hand, the workers' participation in the populist alliance is not based on a change in the mode of production but on increases in consumption: to restrict consumption is, by definition, to terminate the populist aspect of the alliance. The continuation of populist measures beyond the initial period, or the extension of nationalization beyond the foreign sector to encompass national bourgeois strata, alienates the bourgeoisie and leads to an alternative non-capitalist model of capital accumulation.

The initial impetus to class formation, mainly externally directed capital accumulation based on simple surplus extraction, gave way to a more complex process where an internal ruling class with its own state apparatus emerged to mediate the process of exploitation and accumulation. Capital accumulation in the periphery has had a varied experience: the least durable and expansive regimes have been the most popular and nationalist; the least popular have been the most expansive and least national; and the regimes which have been national but not popular have eventually evolved into one of the other two approaches.

Recent historical experience suggests that among capitalist countries in the periphery the most effective instrument of capital accumulation and growth is precisely the least national and most exploitative model, the neocolonial, or "from above and outside," approach. The historical conditions, more specifically the political preconditions, for this growth have in fact been nonpopular, externally oriented regimes resting largely on alliances between military elites and property classes whose incapacity to accumulate capital leads them to rely on foreign capital. The imperial state plays a crucial role in changing the balance of forces in favor of dominance by externally oriented developmental regime. The device has been the coup carried through by military and civilian officials, in large part socialized, trained, and/or financed by agencies of the state apparatus of the imperialist power, dominant in its region. The property-based political-military regime functions to create conditions that permit externally induced industrial growth without danger of nationalization, wage demands, or autonomous trade unions.

### *Development Strategies, Social Regimes, and the Role of the State*

The intensification of exploitative relations inherent in the neocolonial and national (bourgeois) developmentalist approach accelerates the growth of economic inequality and social polarization. Where a modicum of political freedom exists, the bourgeois drive to accumulate capital gives rise to new social forces, those which provided the base for national-popular or socialist movements and regimes with their commitment to redefining class relations. These new forces thus provide the basis for a new development strategy based on redistributive reforms, a reversal of previous approaches.

In this context of latent and overt class conflict within peripheral societies, imperialist relations are central in sustaining or destabilizing the two polar types of social regime. When a neocolonial regime is replaced by a national-popular government which makes serious inroads on foreign corporate capital's exploitative capacity, the imperial response is to effectively collaborate with national political and social forces and end the national popular regime. The new orientation is based on a restructured state apparatus, whose initial function is to eliminate the obstacles to externally based capital accumulation ("discipline labor," denationalize firms, demobilize the populace, etc.).

The crucial instrumentality in this process of reversing regimes, reconcentrating income, and reopening economic channels is the state.[51] The state is the critical unit in the process of converting class alliances into development strategies. The social and political nature of the state in the periphery is best understood through its relationship to the imperial state—whose role and activities in the formation of imperial networks include shaping the state in the periphery. The imperial and the bourgeois state in the periphery can be studied from at least two dimensions: (1) the central role of the imperial state in creating conditions for neocolonial capital accumulation; and (2) the role of the imperial state in state formation in the periphery. The latter includes state-building in the neocolonial context and disaggregating the state in the context of national-popular or even national developmental regimes.

The focus on private investment, trade, the multinational corporation in the study of imperialism is useful but not adequate, for these economic activities and organizations operate within a universe which is not explainable by the behavior and activity of these units. To understand where, when, and how capital expanded into the periphery in a period of substantial political upheavals and class conflict one must look to the role of the imperial state. Three moments in the movement of capital are profoundly affected by imperial state activity: initial entrée, expansion, and survival.

At each point the imperial state plays a decisive role in creating the conditions for capital expansion and accumulation. In the initial period the imperial state is heavily involved in a number of activities, including (1) "state-building," creating the formal machinery of government to secure the groundwork for effective exploitation; the creation of an imperially sound army and police force is crucial; (2) eliminating or containing internal dissidents; (3) minimizing external competition; and (4) creating the economic infrastructure through loans and "aid."

Whereas these activities do not always achieve maximum success, without them it is quite doubtful that private enterprise, even on the scale of monopoly corporations, would have risked the financial resources and manpower that led to their becoming multinational corporations.

The initial thrust of the state laid the basis for long-term, large-scale movements of capital. The relationship between the imperial state and the multinational corporation, however, was not confined to this initial effort, but was continuous and comprehensive. The process of expansion and accumulation necessitated the elaboration of worldwide financial networks to finance a great diversity of activities in a variety of locales; alongside state-building, the imperial state assumed the much more complex task of fashioning a world monetary system, financial agreements, development banks, credit agreements, and so on, that provided the multinationals with mobile capital to facilitate and accelerate the accumulation of capital and intensify the extraction of surplus. The decisions of corporate heads to extend their conglomerates was based on the financial networks organized and directed by the imperial state.

Yet the extension of imperial ties to the new states and the subsequent expansion of imperial capitalism throughout the periphery led to the simultaneous transformation of the class structure and polarization of society. Small proprietors and subsistence farmers became rural laborers, sharecroppers, or urban migrants; urban masses were converted into day laborers or concentrated as unemployed/semiemployed slum dwellers. The neocolonial state (the product of imperial state-building), whose prime function was facilitating externally induced capital accumulation, isolated itself from a mass constituency. The petty bourgeoisie (including military officers) and other socially mobile or aspiring bourgeois classes, not having direct access either to imperial or state revenues, became potential or actual detonators of a national-popular upheaval. It is out of this context then that the third function of the imperial state, what might best be described as the enforcer role, emerges: the use of direct and indirect military and economic pressure to ensure the survival of the multinational corporation and the conditions necessary for accumulation and reproduction. This imperial state enforcer function has manifested itself in a great variety of ways, from direct military intervention and financing of mercenary troops to economic blockades and credit squeezes. Imperial state power has been utilized against nationalist social movements out of power, as well as governments in power. It has been used against populist as well as democratic socialist governments; against elected governments as well as nonelected governments. The critical issue for the imperial state is not the formal structure of government but access to the internally generated surplus and the creation of class relations which facilitate access.

The targets of imperial state intervention have been those regimes and movements that attempt to alter substantially the conditions for imperial capital accumulation, limit the access points which the imperial state possesses within the periphery, and create conditions for national capital accumulation. The isolation of the neocolonial state, the vulnerability of the bourgeois development state, and the porosity of the national-popular regime provide a great number of opportunities for imperial state activity: to buttress the former and to destabilize the latter.

## *The Imperial State as State-Builder*

In its broadest terms, imperialism in the periphery has been involved first and foremost in the creation of a new social order, one in which social relations are tied to the dynamic of externally induced expansion and accumulation. The foremost problem for the imperial state is to prevent political decay or disintegration through the creation of a durable political order, one in which social control over the labor force permits the continuous flow of capital and the reproduction of exploitative social relations. At the operational level, a number of imperial agencies, ranging from military missions to university advisory teams, have been involved in shaping the counterpart agencies, personnel recruitment programs, as well as forging converging perspectives within the state bureaucracy as it evolves. The technical skills, such as budgeting, planning, and project elaboration, are imparted within an ideological framework that reinforces external bonds. Imperial state-building, however, does not merely involve piecemeal administrative block-building (imperial agency insertion in distinct administrative areas), but the integration of the commanding heights of the peripheral state into the overall politicoeconomic project of the imperial state through long-term development agreements, including trade, financial, and technical assistance. The imperial strategy is directed largely toward influencing elites, described euphemistically as "leadership training." The apex of the state pyramid is the central target; and within that pyramid the army and police have a central position. The astronomical sums of military aid during the post-World War II period into the periphery are, in large part, efforts to create and later maintain the external allegiances of peripheral state apparatuses. Independently of social origins and within the context of technical preparations (professionalization), the military and police are pivotal groups in imperial state-building in the periphery. Out of these foundations of state-building, a whole series of other administrative programs have emerged, linked to the imperial project. Tentative and isolated instances of neocolonial parliamentary governments have been spawned, although the boundaries within which social and ideological competition takes place are sharply limited and transparent to those who aspire to participate.

The origins of the neocolonial state are not always vested in elite transfers of power (from colonial to national). Moreover, national political leadership meshed in neocolonial networks are not always lacking a certain legitimacy derived from their role in the national struggle. Nevertheless, the process we are discussing concerns the formation and orientation of institutions of the post-independence national state, which does not preclude conflict in the period prior to national independence. In sum, the process of imperial state-building can be schematically considered in the following manner:

1. Securing ties with the political leadership, including, at a minimum, the heads of the police and military, but not necessarily limited to these areas.
2. Extending influence to budgeting, economy, planning, public works—administrative areas that directly affect specific economic opportunities for foreign enterprises, as well as general conditions for capital accumulation.
3. Training programs and technical missions to promote efficiency and ties with middle levels of the bureaucracy and research institutes which can provide inexpensive sources of information and effective implementation.
4. And creation of new state power centers, including the development of special forces in the military, regional military alliances and economic authorities, international banking officials with project supervisory powers.

The whole point of imperial state-building is to provide a variety of access points to shape policy priorities and agendas in order to avoid the use of "external pressures," to avoid having to act from the outside. Within the periphery, the alienated state articulates the interests of imperial capital by promoting growth on the basis of the exploitation of national classes. Only sustained and continuous inflows of capital and an elaborate political police/military apparatus and surveillance provide this state with durability.

### *The Imperial State as State Disaggregator*

Social polarities and political mobilization frequently have accompanied the exploitative social relations characteristic of imperial capital expansion. Equally important, the socially exclusive and economically constricting effects of externally directed accumulation has set in opposition numerically and strategically important strata in the periphery. The process of imperial accumulation leads to concentration of wealth and opens opportunities to petty-bourgeois strata for national capitalization through control over the state and its revenues. The emergence of national movements, and eventually governments, sets the stage for redefining relations with the imperial power. Yet, in most instances, controlling the government is not identical with controlling the state: the critical means of production, as well as important fractions of the army/police/state bureaucracy, remain, at least initially, still tied to the metropolis and serve to countermand the orders of the national government. In this context, the imperial power may seek to renegotiate terms of dependency or disarticulate the national regime's development project through a variety of measures, and through agencies located outside or inside the national state. The more decisively the national government challenges the process of external accumulation, the more likely efforts will be made by the imperial state to undermine the regime. Unlike the circumstance of a neocolonial regime, where state-building is the key, with a national regime the imperial state operates to disaggregate the state: the rhetoric speaks to destabilizing, not stabilizing, society.[52] The incomplete transformation from a neocolonial or national development regime to a national popular state provides several opportunities for reversing changes. The imperial state utilizes the financial networks and military-administrative apparatuses that were elaborated earlier to promote imperial-capital accumulation in order to coerce the national-popular state. Financial and credit constraints lead to disarticulating the economy and alienating the national bourgeoisie. External links with the military are reinforced in the process of disintegrating the state. Alienated from the national-popular project of the government, the proimperial segment of the military serves as the instrument for overthrowing the government, reversing changes, and reconstituting a state to promote imperial capital accumulation.

State formation and disaggregation are then two crucial processes for imposing exploitative class relations located in imperial induced economic expansion. Without the intervention of the imperial state, the neocolonial state would be difficult to sustain; without the neocolonial state, the conflicts generated by imperial-capital accumulation would become unmanageable. Without the strong state, the polarization of class forces would be skewed toward the left; and the alternative of a petty bourgeois-led popular-national alliance would either limit the capacity of imperial capital to extract surplus from the labor force or lead to a more profound transformation of society.

## Conclusion

The political economy of the periphery is moving in a new direction which involves redefining the problematic, reformulating the key concepts, and developing a more dynamic and inclusive analytical framework. In the preceding section, we outlined what some of these issues and problems encompassed. We will restate our position in summary form:

1. The previous problematic, which focused on development, abstracted from the social relations of production and emphasized to a great degree the extension and increase in productive forces. The result has been to downgrade the degree to which labor is the creator of value and the source of wealth. The focus on social relations of production allows us to focus on the issue of exploitation and on the forms and techniques by which labor is degraded, as well as to understand the forms by which exploitative relations of production can be transformed.

2. By redefining the problematic of political economy from development to exploitation, we thus are required to reformulate the key concepts with which we analyze the new problematics. Notions, such as dependence and modernization, that operate to

explain or discuss development are inappropriate. Rather, our focus should be on the class relationships, both at the internal as well as the international level, and the types of class relationships that are engendered in the process of accumulation.

3. These class relationships, however, are evolving phenomena, products of changes in the level and forms of capitalist development in the core; the impact of these changes in the core on the productive systems and class forces in the periphery in turn produce impacts back on the core from the class forces in periphery, modifying or transforming the relationship. The notion is one of reciprocal interplay between conflictive and collaborative classes, which reproduce or refashion the economy and state structures through which they operate.

4. This approach rejects aggregate notions of national interest in defining the critical actions between or within productive and state systems and focuses instead on the idea of class differentiation. In the periphery, this means that the problem is one of identifying the location of core capital within the class structure of peripheral societies and its relationship to the peripheral state and dominant classes. The implication here is that class cleavages are less confined to national boundaries and more involve class units which cut across national boundaries.

5. Thus, this approach locates the process of capital accumulation within the framework of class/state relationships. It is within this schema, based on the determination of class coalitions and hegemonic influence, that studies of income distribution and types of regimes could be fruitfully analyzed.

6. The problem of accumulation is not, however, local or national, but global; moreover, the source of accumulation has become dissociated from the locus of accumulation, thus creating the problems associated with movements of capital and the activities of the multinational corporations. We emphasize, however, that these movements and activities can best be understood through the notion of the imperial state, the worldwide political network which facilitates the growth and expansion of capital. Moreover, the overly economistic arguments put forth (mainly by economists) concerning the multinational corporations fail to account for the significant role of the imperial state in establish-

ing the prior and essential conditions for the flows of capital. Imperial state activity is essential to determining the scope, direction, growth, and survival of the multinational corporations. The concerns of U.S. political scientists with a foreign policy advisory orientation, with political order, stability, and institution-building in this context are piecemeal intimations of the centrality of the imperial state in creating the conditions for long-term, large-scale expansion. Unfortunately, these policy notions are not anchored in the economic process, nor are the policy prescriptions linked to a central organizing principle that can account for the multiplicity of contexts in which the same problematic is posed, nor is there any effort to account for the coincidence between the forms of economic development (large-scale, long-term movements of core capital) and the need for authoritarian government. The facile acceptance of an authoritarian state-developmental strategies syndrome is rooted in a recognition of the inequalities and exploitation that result from foreign based capital accumulation and concomitant social tensions. Lacking an anchor in the social relations of productive systems, developmental social scientists have obscured the centrality of exploitative social relations through general references to "systemic strains," or "development imperatives," or have derived the authoritarian attributes from vague cultural and historical determinations within peripheral society.

## Notes

1. Susan Strange, "International Economics and International Relations: A Case of Mutual Neglect," *International Affairs* 46 (April 1970):304–15.
2. See, for example, Gottfried Haberler, *International Trade and Economic Development* (Cairo: National Bank of Egypt, 1959); Ragnar Nurkse, *Equilibrium and Growth in the World Economy* (Cambridge, Mass.: Harvard University Press, 1961); Gerald Meier, *The International Economics of Development* (New York: Harper and Row, 1968); and for a survey and summary, see John Pincus, *Trade,*

*Aid and Development: The Rich and Poor Nations* (New York: McGraw-Hill, 1967).

3. For a discussion, see Pincus, *Rich and Poor Nations*, and Hla Myint, "The 'Classical Theory' of International Trade and the Underdeveloped Countries," *Economic Journal* 68 (June 1958):317–37.
4. See Nurkse, *Equilibrium and Growth*, particularly the essay, "Patterns of Trade and Development."
5. The classic works in the state-centric tradition include Hans J. Morgenthau, *Politics Among Nations* (New York: Alfred A. Knopf, 1960); Morton Kaplan, *System and Process in International Politics* (New York: John Wiley and Sons, 1957); Richard Rosecrance, *Action and Reaction in World Politics* (Boston: Little, Brown & Co., 1963); and Richard Rosecrance, *International Relations: Peace or War* (New York: McGraw-Hill, 1973).
6. As always, there are exceptions. See, for example, James N. Rosenau, ed., *Linkage Politics: Essays on the Convergence of National and International Systems* (New York: Free Press, 1969); and Horst Menderhausen, "Transnational Society vs. State Sovereignty," *Kyklos* 22, no. 2 (1969):251–75.
7. The argument is one of the central themes in Strange, "Case of Mutual Neglect," and is presented as a piece of accepted wisdom in Joan Edelman Spero, *The Politics of International Economic Relations* (New York: St. Martin's Press, 1977).
8. Strange, "Case of Mutual Neglect," p. 310.
9. We refer to Spero, *Economic Relations*.
10. C. Fred Bergsten and Lawrence B. Krause, eds., *World Politics and International Economics* (Washington, D.C.: The Brookings Institution, 1975).
11. See, for example, Robert Gilpin, "The Politics of Transnational Economic Relations," in *Transnational Relations and World Politics*, ed. Robert O. Keohane and Joseph S. Nye, Jr. (Cambridge, Mass.: Harvard University Press, 1973); C. Fred Bergsten, Robert O. Keohane, and Joseph S. Nye, "International Economics and International Politics: A Framework for Analysis," in *International Economics*; David H. Blake and Robert S. Walters, *The Politics of Global Economic Relations* (Englewood Cliffs, N. J.: Prentice-Hall, 1976); and Spero, *Economic Relations*.
12. See, for example, Stephen D. Cohen, *The Making of United States International Economic Policy* (New York: Frederick A. Praeger, 1977); Edward L. Morse, *Foreign Policy and Interdependence in Gaullist France* (Princeton, N. J.: Princeton University Press, 1973);

Susan Strange, *Sterling and British Policy: A Political Study of an International Currency in Decline* (New York; Oxford University Press, 1971); Peter J. Katzenstein, "International Relations and Domestic Structures: Foreign Economic Policies of Advanced Industrial States," *International Organization* 30, no. 1 (Winter 1976):1–46; and Ronald I. Meltzer, "The Politics of Policy Reversal: The U.S. Response to Granting Trade Preferences to Developing Countries and Linkages Between International Organizations and National Policy Making," *International Organization* 30, no. 4 (Autumn 1976): 649–58.

13. See, for example, Richard N. Cooper, *The Economics of Interdependence* (New York: McGraw-Hill, 1968); Bransilav Gosovic and John Gerard Ruggie, "On the Creation of a New International Economic Order: Issue Linkage and the Seventh Special Session of the U.N. General Assembly," *International Organization* 30 (Spring 1976):309–45; Roger D. Hansen, "The Political Economy of North-South Relations: How Much Change?," *International Organization* 29 (Autumn 1975):922–47; Isebill V. Gruhn, "The Lome Convention: Inching Towards Interdependence," *International Organization* 30 (Spring 1976):240–62; Karen Mingst, "Cooperation or Illusion: An Examination of the Intergovernmental Council of Copper Exporting Countries," *International Organization* 30 (Spring 1976):263–88; Robert E. Baldwin and David A. Kay, "International Trade and International Relations," in *International Economics*.
14. See Bergsten, Keohane, and Nye, "International Politics," pp. 21–22.
15. The contrast can be seen by comparing with Thomas C. Schelling, *Arms and Influence* (New Haven: Yale University Press, 1966).
16. This approach is characteristic of, among others, Gosovic and Ruggie, "International Economic Order"; Bergsten, Keohane, and Nye, "International Politics"; and Hansen, "North-South Relations."
17. See Bergsten, Keohane, and Nye, "International Politics," pp. 22–36.
18. In particular, see Gosovic and Ruggie, "International Economic Order"; and Gruhn, "Lome Convention."
19. On the influence of multinational corporations, see Richard J. Barnet and Ronald E. Muller, *Global Reach: The Power of the Multinational Corporations* (New York: Simon and Schuster, 1974); on the effect of transnational organizations on everyday decisions, see Leon Gordenker, *International Aid and National Decisions: Development Programs in Malawi, Tanzania, and Zambia* (Princeton, N.J.: Princeton University Press, 1976); for a more critical perspective that links international organizations to the nation that domi-

nates them, see R. Peter DeWitt, Jr., *The Inter-American Development Bank and Political Influence* (New York: Frederick A. Praeger, 1977); on how private banks can determine the parameters of decision-making, see Don Oberderfer, "U.S. Banks Impose Conditions, Set $240 Million in Loans for Peruvian Government," *Washington Post*, August 29, 1976, p. A10; for critical perspectives that link foreign influence to the theory of imperialism, see Teresa Hayter, *Aid as Imperialism* (New York: Penguin Books, 1971); and James Petras and Morris Morley, *The United States and Chile: Imperialism and the Overthrow of the Allende Government* (New York: Monthly Review Press, 1975).

20. See, for example, Hamzi Alavi, "The State in Postcolonial Societies," in *Imperialism and Revolution in South Asia*, eds. Kathleen Gough (Aberle) and Hari P. Sharma (New York: Monthly Review Press, 1973); Colin Leys, *Underdevelopment in Kenya: The Political Economy of Neo-colonialism* (Berkeley: University of California Press, 1975); Colin Leys, "Post-Colonial State," *Review of African Political Economy* 5 (1978):39–49; James Petras, "State Capitalism in the Third World," *Development and Change* 8, no. 1 (January 1977):1–18.
21. Gilpin, "Three Models of the Future," in *International Economics*, p. 39.
22. Some scholars take part in both this approach and the previous; others conceive of them as totally antagonistic. Works that depart from this criticism include Keohane and Nye, *International Relations;* Karl Kaiser, "Transnational Politics: Towards a Theory of Multinational Politics," *International Organization* 25 (Autumn 1971):790–817; Robert Keohane and Joseph S. Nye, Jr., "Transgovernmental Relations and International Organizations," *World Politics* 27 (October 1974):39–62; and Samuel Huntington, "Transnational Organizations in World Politics," *World Politics* 25 (April 1973):333–68.
23. In addition to the above, see Richard N. Cooper, "Economic Interdependence and Foreign Policy in the Seventies," *World Politics* 24 (January 1972):159–81; and Edward L. Morse, "The Politics of Interdependence," *International Organization* 23, no. 2 (Spring 1969):311–26.
24. Gilpin, "Three Models of the Future," in *International Economics*, p. 41.
25. In addition to most of the above, see Raymond Vernon, *Sovereignty at Bay: The Multinational Spread of U.S. Enterprises* (New York:

Basic Books, 1971); and Charles P. Kindleberger, *American Business Abroad* (New Haven: Yale University Press, 1969). For a well-argued counterargument, see David Leyton-Brown, "The Nation-State and multinational Enterprise: Erosion or Assertion" (paper presented at International Studies Association Convention, Washington, D.C., 1978).

26. John Diebold, "Multinational Corporations—Why Be Scared of Them?," *Foreign Policy*, no. 12 (Fall 1973):79–95.
27. See Paul Baran and Paul Sweezy, *Monopoly Capital: An Essay on the American Economic and Social Order* (New York: Monthly Review Press, 1966); James R. O'Connor, *The Corporations and the State* (New York: Harper and Row, 1974); Ralph Miliband, *The State in Capitalist Society* (New York: Basic Books, 1969); and Jürgen Habermas, *Legitimation Crisis* (Boston: Beacon Press, 1973).
28. Some of the important works in the structuralist tradition include Johan Galtung, "A Structural Theory of Imperialism," *Journal of Peace Research* 8, no. 2 (1971):81–119; Helge Hveem, "The Global Dominance System," *Journal of Peace Research* 10, no. 4 (1973):319–40; Dieter Senghaas, "Conflict Formations in Contemporary International Society," *Journal of Peace Research* 10, no. 3 (1973):163–84; Klaus Jurgen Gantzel, "Dependency Structures as the Dominant Pattern in World Society," *Journal of Peace Research* 10, no. 3 (1973):203–15; and Volker Rittberger, "International Organization and Violence," *Journal of Peace Research* 10, no. 3 (1973):217–26. For reviews and discussions of this corpus of scholarship, see Harry Targ, "Global Dominance and Dependence, Post-Industrialism, and International Relations Theory: A Review," *International Studies Quarterly* 20, no. 3 (September 1976):461–82; Harry Targ, "International Feudalism, Dialectics and the Quest for Autonomy" (paper presented at International Studies Association convention, Washington, D.C., 1978); and Herbert Reid and Ernest Yanarella, "Toward a Critical Theory of Peace Research in the United States: The Search for an Intelligible Core," *Journal of Peace Research* 13, no. 4 (1976):315–41.
29. Galtung, "Theory of Imperialism."
30. Ibid., p. 81.
31. The important works from this stage of Prebisch's development are Raul Prebisch, *Towards a New Trade Policy for Development* (United Nations, UNCTAD E/Conf. 46/3), February 12, 1964; and Raul Prebisch, "Commercial Policy in the Underdeveloped Countries," *American Economic Review* 44 (May 1959):251–73. For a summary, see Pincus, *Rich and Poor Nations*, chaps. 2 and 4.

32. Both H. W. Singer and Gunnar Myrdal agree with Prebisch on the essentials: see H. W. Singer, "The Distribution of Gains Between Investing and Borrowing Countries," *American Economic Review* 40 (May 1950); H. W. Singer, *International Development: Growth and Change* (New York: McGraw-Hill, 1964); Gunnar Myrdal, *An International Economy* (New York: Harper and Row, 1956); and Gunnar Myrdal, *Rich Lands and Poor* (New York: Harper and Row, 1957). For a survey of the "neoprotectionist" thesis, see Margaret DeVries, "Trade and Exchange Policy and Economic Development: Two Decades of Evolving Views," *Oxford Economic Papers* 18 (March 1966):19–44. For critiques and assessments of the limitations of the thesis, see M. J. Flanders, "Prebisch on Protectionism," *Economical Journal* 74 (June 1964):305–26; Meier, *Economics of Development;* and Kathryn Morton and Peter Tulloch, *Trade and Developing Countries* (New York: John Wiley and Sons, 1977).
33. See Raul Prebisch, "A Critique of Peripheral Capitalism," *CEPAL Review* (First semester 1976), pp. 9–76.
34. Ibid., p. 11.
35. Ibid., p. 61.
36. Ibid., p. 15.
37. These are most coherently presented in Galtung, "Theory of Imperialism," pp. 107–09.
38. Hveem, "Dominance System;" and for a summary, Targ, "Global Dominance" and "International Feudalism."
39. Hveem, "Dominance System," p. 323.
40. This effort to synthesize Weber and Marx places Hveem within the Western tradition of critical thought that is represented in the work of Lukacs, Horkheimer, Marcuse, and Habermas. See Georg Lukacs, *History and Class Consciousness: Studies in Marxist Dialectics* (Cambridge, Mass.: MIT Press, 1971); Max Horkheimer, *Eclipse of Reason* (New York: Seabury Press, 1974); Herbert Marcuse, *One-Dimensional Man* (Boston: Beacon Press, 1964); Jürgen Habermas, *Legitimation Crisis* (Boston: Beacon Press, 1973); and Trent Schroyer, *The Critique of Domination* (Boston; Beacon Press, 1975). In our estimation, Hveem fails in his effort at synthesis, ultimately opting for the Weberian problematic and losing touch with the centrality of capital accumulation.
41. Targ, "International Feudalism," p. 9.
42. Prebisch, "Peripheral Capitalism," pp. 67–72.
43. It was so designated by one of its major practitioners, Immanuel Wallerstein. See Immanuel Wallerstein, "The Present State of the Debate on World Inequality," in Immanuel Wallerstein, ed., *World*

*Inequality: Origins and Perspectives on the World System* (Montreal: Black Rose Books, 1975), p. 16.

44. Paul Baran, *The Political Economy of Growth* (New York: Monthly Review Press, 1957); Andre Gunder Frank, *Capitalism and Underdevelopment in Latin America* (New York: Monthly Review Press, 1967); Andre Gunder Frank, "The Development of Underdevelopment," in Andre Gunder Frank, ed., *Latin America: Underdevelopment or Revolution* (New York: Monthly Review Press, 1969); Theotonio Dos Santos, "The Structure of Dependence," in *Readings in U.S. Imperialism*, eds. K. T. Fann and Donald C. Hodges (Boston: Porter Sargent, 1971). For a recent review and effort to defend the dependency perspective, see Fernando Cardoso, "The Consumption of Dependency: Theory in the United States," *Latin American Research Review* 12, no. 3 (1977):7–24.
45. Arghiri Emmanuel, *Unequal Exchange: A Study of the Imperialism of Trade* (New York: Monthly Review Press, 1972); Samir Amin, *Accumulation on a World Scale* (New York: Monthly Review Press, 1974); Immanuel Wallerstein, *The Modern World-System* (New York: Academic Press, 1976); Immanuel Wallerstein, "Dependence in an Interdependent World," *African Studies Review* 17 (April 1974):1–26; and Immanuel Wallerstein, "The Rise and Future Demise of the World Capitalist System," *Comparative Studies in Society and History* 16, no. 4 (1974):387–415.
46. Immanuel Wallerstein, "The Present State of the Debate on World Inequality," in *World Inequality*, p. 16.
47. Ibid., p. 26.
48. M. C. Tavares and José Serra, "Beyond Stagnation: A Discussion on the Nature of Recent Developments in Brazil," in *Latin America: From Dependence to Revolution*, ed. J. Petras (New York: John Wiley & Sons, 1973).
49. Irma Adelman and Cynthia Taft Morris, *Economic Growth and Social Equity in Developing Countries* (Stanford, Calif.: Stanford University Press, 1973); José Serra, "The Brazilian Economic Miracle," in *Latin America*.
50. For an informative discussion on accumulation, see Samir Amin, *Accumulation*.
51. For an interesting discussion of one agency of the imperial state, see NACLA, "The Eximbank, Exports for Empire," *Latin American and Empire Report* 8, no. 7 (September 1974):17–32.
52. See James Petras and Morris Morley, *United States and Chile*.

# 2

# ASPECTS OF CLASS FORMATION IN THE PERIPHERY: POWER STRUCTURES AND STRATEGIES

## Introduction

Several dimensions in the study of the transformation of peripheral societies warrant special consideration because of the specific historical experiences that differentiate them from Western Europe and the United States. The problem of analysis of class structures in peripheral societies has been complicated by the tendency to derive universal theoretical constructs from particular historical experiences, both in terms of "locus" in the world system and of "timing" in the development of the world-capitalist system.[1] The problem of world-historical change has been further complicated by the narrow empiricist style of research that reaches no deeper than the level of personages and institutions, delving into the intricate details of decisions without any sense of the origins, dynamics, and direction of the large structures which inform the behavior of institutions and of the personages who occupy the positions and make the decisions.[2]

Beyond those theoretical and methodological problems, numerous other issues of great importance have also hindered the understanding of peripheral societies. Among these are the capital errors of conceiving the social structures either as autonomous entities[3] or as mere extensions of "metropolitan classes."[4] An adequate reformulation of the problem must depart from a notion of an "external/internal" division which cuts across the most salient feature of peripheral societies; what is crucial is the manner in which class structures "cross" each other and the various combinations of class symbiosis and interlock. The problem of conceptualizing the class structure leads to a related issue, that of identifying the essential features of peripheral societies and determining the viability of different political strategies for structural change. The common procedure here has been to extrapolate the product of Western experiences and to prescribe it as the process for the periphery.[5] Hence parliamentary forms of political activity (and their "derivatives"), largely the historical products of capitalist hegemony and limited class struggle within core countries in the world system, have provided the models for analyzing political change, as well as providing measures of political "suitability," "maturity," and numerous other expressions of the ideological preferences and prescriptions of the social "scientists.[6]

The fundamental problem to consider in discussing the political formulas for transformation is not one of simply transferring one set of institutional end products to another, nor is it merely a problem of locating the historical experience of one set of countries in a time sequence or world setting,[7] but rather of dealing with the very special problem of the inequality of power on a world scale and of the tendency for those "inequalities" to manifest themselves with peripheral polities. More specifically, the issue of transition from one social system to another through electoral processes and within a class society assumes that the events and forces within a country are in "free and equal" competition—independently of the existence of exogenous classes and institutions—an assumption that hardly captures a major facet of political-economic life in the late twentieth century.

If the notion of free and equal electoral competition in peripheral societies is flawed, its extension into the "transitional" period has similar problems: the notion of an open society of competitive forces assumes that the unitary principles overarch the social divisions, that representation of all classes is compatible with structural change, that open intercourse with opposition governments and social classes is compatible with the growth and security of the new society. For some, these propositions can be boiled down to a couple of simple formulas: the "peaceful transition to socialism" and the "coexistence of different social systems."[8] The positive virtue of that set of ideas is its evasion of the central issues involved in any discussion of transition in peripheral societies: the problem of survival and consolidation in the face of overt and covert threats. Against that, the ideologists extrapolate the end products of a consolidated revolution (peaceful coexistence, routinization of change) and transfer them as prescriptions to countries beginning the transition in situations in which changes are still reversible. Political forms and external relations in the period of transition are dictated by the needs of survival and consolidation under conditions of intense internal and external pressures by interlocked classes: the problems of political representation and development strategies are located within these central considerations.

Beyond the period of transition, peripheral countries face the issue of "development;" but that issue (including questions of priorities, direction, etc.) can be confronted only indirectly or by answering a prior question: What is the nature of the class structure and relations within which development will take place? Class transformation and the subsequent "weighting" of different classes will give shape and substance to development, as will development, in one form or another, shape the emerging class structure. The pivotal institution shaping both the class structures and serving as its instrument in the development process is the state, initially the revolutionary force (army, movement, party), later its politico-administrative organization. The problems posed for revolutionary society are not merely those of taking over the state, nationalizing the monopolies, and in general socializing the established order, but of uprooting and transplanting a decomposing social order—from its value system and recreational facilities to its occupational structure—which served another social system. A general process of demodernization, and in many cases delumpenization, is essential to create the conditions and classes for effective socialist development. The alternative form of state-capitalism, while exhibiting many of the common external features of socialist development, is in reality the imposition of new forms on old structures, leading to a socioeconomic impasse in which the older "structures" increasingly inform the newer forms.

## Modes of Production and Social Relations in the Periphery

The capitalist mode of production may have different social relations if we define a capitalist mode of production by the creation of surplus value—the amount above and beyond subsistence reinvested by capital in commodity production.

Within similar modes of production, social relations differ according to the availability of labor and alternative modes of production. Where labor is scarce and alternative economic activity is readily available, labor is recruited and bound to production by coercive means. For example, in the periphery capitalist firms in mining and agriculture were organized around forcible labor recruitment, and the ties were based on noneconomic factors.[9] In England, where economic processes (the enclosure movement) led to the "freeing" of laborers from the means of production (land) and preempted alternative forms of economic activity, labor flows toward the industrial centers and the subsequent "contractual" basis of employment defined capitalist social relations in terms of the free-wage capitalist prototype.[10]

The conversion of a particular set of social relations in Europe, reflecting particular historical circumstances, into the universal and defining characteristics of capitalist production is an error of historical proportions.

The growth and expansion of large-scale, multifarm agro-enterprises in the periphery led to greater labor needs and increased the spread of "coercive" forms of labor recruitment.[11] In the periphery, wage labor was inversely related to the growth of surplus production. Only in areas of petty-bourgeoisie production—small-scale producers of commodities—was a modified form of wage labor introduced as the principal form of social relationship. Even the experience of the West itself suggests that where capital fully controlled the state, extraeconomic measures of coercion were utilized to force workers to be free-wage laborers.[12] In many cases, where labor recruitment was a serious problem, nonwage payments were as important (if not more so) in securing a stable or captive labor force.[13] Only with the expansion of capitalist enterprise on a worldwide or continentwide basis and only after a large enough pool of labor was available without alternative forms of economic activity was free-wage labor the predominant social relation of capital. The process of bringing together labor, capital, and machinery to produce surplus value defines the capitalist mode of production, not the particular forms within which the relations of production are organized. In the periphery, social relations were coercive and payments were in kind because, in most instances of primitive accumulation, the transfer of money payments may be less possible or profitable and because labor has yet to accept the harsh discipline of capitalist exploitation. Subsistence agriculture in the periphery was, in many cases, preferable to subsistence employment in the mines and plantations of European entrepreneurs.

In the colonial period, the locus of power was in the hands of the imperial state, which recruited labor, transferred capitalists, and distributed the means of production (land, mines); the subsequent relative autonomy and eventual independence of the colonial settlers was a product of the growth and expansion of production located in the agro-mineral enterprises. The growth of production, the increase in exports, the extension of markets, banking, and transport were all products of the transformation of surplus value from "coerced labor" into merchant capital and banking capital, which in the periphery were products of capital generated in the agro-mineral productive sectors. The expansion of capital to diverse sectors was indeed facilitated by the nonwage character of labor, which was denied "mobility" through various political-social contrivances—from debt peonage to vagrancy laws and informal blacklisting.

## Economic Diversification and Political Power

For many social scientists the shift from a predominantly enclave-based export economy to a predominantly semi-industrial dependent society signalled a shift in the organization and structure of power. According to Frank Bonilla and José A. Silva Michelena, the diversification of production led to power becoming "diffuse, precariously held, compartmentalized, and in conflicting concentrations."[14] What the above formulation confuses is the study of particular moments and transitory configuration with the more essential dimensions of society. The study of power in the periphery requires us to distinguish the essential from the secondary. Power is to be understood first through an analysis in the following sequence:

A. Modes of production, social relations of production, and the resultant process of accumulation and expansion define the parameters within which "policy" is formulated and discussed.
B. The "foundation" of society is the crucial moment in which control over the mode of production is defined; the class structure which emerges—class-formation—is implicit in any discussion of "foundations."[15]
C. The new capitalist social formation possesses certain imperatives (dynamic) to which state activity is directed: facilitating the accumulation of capital while safeguarding the "foundations."
D. Policy decisions reflect the efforts by different social interests within the class structure to shape specific allocations of state resources to improve their relative position.
E. Policy studies within a decision-making framework focus on the relative influence of different social interests in the allocation of marginal increments at a certain moment in a social system. The problem of state power cannot be tested by examining derivative phenomena historically and structurally removed from the foundations and organizing principles of a society.

A common mode of production unites the owners of capital in essentials: maintenance of the foundations, state promotion of the dynamic (accumulation) and support for the class structure (especially at the upper ends and among "support groups"). Within those boundaries, individual owners and factions embodying a variety of political, social, and economic orientations can be found competing for influence within the state power. It makes little sense to discuss the plurality of competing groups without first understanding the unitary basis of their involvement.

In peripheral societies, power is cumulative: status, wealth, contacts, access, and communication networks add up to and generate "power." Furthermore, interests overlap: media, industry, and bureaucrats converge to defend and propagate policies and values tending in the same direction.

The organization of power does not begin with the formation of a party, faction, or interest group, but rather those forms embody pre-existing and more fundamental units of power (classes), which organize and control the factors and relations of production (codified perhaps in a constitution), which are directed by a bureaucratic-military apparatus (government) that embodies the foundations and propels its expansion.

The peculiarity of political action in the periphery is that the ruling class does not usually seek out mediating structures but is directly represented in the state, and in some cases the state-classes are combined features of society (the members of the highest state bodies are the ruling class). The rather weak position of parties, interest groups, and the like is not a product of the "underdeveloped nature" of society. The lack of influence of this institutional configuration is an expression of a more fundamental weakness of the ruling classes, the lack of "legitimacy" of the ideology or values of the dominant class within which parties and narrow-focus interest groups can grow. It is specifically in the West, where ruling class ideas circulate generally within the society and where the capitalist mode of production and class divisions are taken for granted, that narrowly focused parties and interest groups have the legitimacy to bargain and compete. Power in peripheral society, then, is located in the structures of production, and policy is largely derivative: the interest groups that emerge and compete for power (short of revolutionary classes, parties, or movements) are expressions of the consolidation and institutionalization of the ongoing structure of power. The terms under which ruling class power is exercised are subject to the class struggle. Therefore, the power of the capitalist is rarely absolute, except in cases of totalitarian dictatorships, under which the class antagonism becomes latent, and rulership appears total. The dominance of a mode of production defines the prerogatives of the ruling class and the role of the state. However, the state, while subject to the laws of development of that mode of production, is also subject to the level of the class struggle. Economic development is, in the first instance, informed by the class struggle; hence, in the capitalist periphery the central problems for imperial and national capital (and its academic apologists) are "stability" or control and subordination of the labor force where possible, segmentation and nonpolitical bargaining activity where necessary. Modes of production and their laws of motion are, in the final analysis, class relations and are thus determined by the capacity of each class to impose its terms of control over production, including the disposition of the surplus. Nevertheless, distribution appears largely as market relations—the behavior of the capitalists apparently being ruled by the demand and supply of market forces.

The crucial difference between the above discussion as it applies to the overall social and political configurations within the periphery and to the imperial countries is the existence of liaison groups, which link the class structures of both peripheral and metropolitan societies. The process of capital accumulation "from the outside" led to the growth of internal classes, which grew in proportion to their capacity to extend and develop their external linkages. The peripheral bourgeoisie expanded, not with the growth of an internal market, but with the expansion of the external market.[16] The periphery is composed of interlocking classes, which integrate and organize production and structure political activity toward facilitating the free flow of capital and goods between areas.[17] The peripheral nation contains classes of double nationality: state rule is shared with economic "subjects" with external political allegiances. An "open" political system is then necessary to facilitate the interlock of classes and the free flow of capital. The "liaison groups" within the periphery (landowners, industrialists, military, etc.) provide the "access" points for economic entry and political influence.[18] This pattern of class formation provides for a skewed political pattern in which great concentrations of capital on a worldwide scale enter into competition with locally anchored class forces—a problem that seriously cripples the notion of political competition.

## Electoral Competition, Unequal Power, and External Intervention

The uneven development of capitalism on a world scale has led to the formation of capitalist states with a worldwide network of organizational and financial resources and a politico-military apparatus that sprawls across continents, permeating and interlocking with the emerging military-administrative apparatuses of the periphery. Economic expansion through multinational corporations stimulates and is in turn propelled by the worldwide imperial state network. The combined inputs of the imperial state and the multinational corporations weigh heavily on the side of ruling commercial-agro-industrial classes in any electoral contest.[19] The balance of class forces within the periphery cannot simply be deduced from the relative economic power of local classes, but is related to their capacity to draw on external support and the willingness of outside forces (both state and multinational) to contribute. Electoral contests in the periphery are particularly susceptible to results predetermined by large influxes of outside funding; hence, the electoral results may best be viewed as measures of how much impact exogenous forces have on electoral competition. In recent years, documented accounts reveal U.S. corporate and government involvement in the elections of Bolivia (Gulf), Chile (ITT and Anaconda), and many other countries, including Venezuela, where such influence has not yet been acknowledged.[20] In addition, U.S. government loans have been frequently disbursed just prior to election campaigns to aid conservative candidates; this was the case in Eduardo Frei's successful campaign in Chile in 1964 for example.[21] Under those circumstances, the notion of elections as expressions of the popular will is hardly convincing. The crucial factors that determine an election, including public exposure, image, mass perceptions, and organization, are all heavily influenced by the amount of financial resources available. Even in the "core" capitalist democracies, the issue of one man/one vote has been seriously challenged by those who point to the vast economic inequalities and political repression.[22] To that criticism, some have argued that the organization of the masses counterweights the economic power of the elite—that the numerical superiority of workers counterbalances the influence of capital.[23] But even here, the notion of the influence of "numbers" is based on the unfounded assumption that those counted have a common set of purposes and a political organization that acts in concert with their goals, thereby posing a political alternative; in a word, workers become influential when they are class-conscious and therefore act in their own interest. The mere existence of a majority of workers within an electoral setting, as Marx pointed out long ago (and as Lichtheim, Lipset, and others have deliberately distorted),[24] is not adequate to defend their self-interest. Only where a tradition of class struggle and organization exists can the workers utilize the electoral approach with any effect.

Furthermore, as the cases of Chile under Salvador Allende and Cheddi Jagan in Guyana indicate, even where class organization and consciousness do lead to electoral victories, those results can be reversed through nonelectoral means. The nature and structure of electoral processes are heavily biased against structural change; nonelectoral paths become the more meaningful mode of correcting the imbalances and distortions caused by interclass linkages and external intervention.

## Structural Transformation and Political Representation

The two prime concerns of regimes attempting structural transformation are survival and consolidation. Threats to the regime emanate from the interlocked ruling classes, which by their nature can draw on resources from the internal, as well as international, political arena. External economic blockades and financial squeezes can be combined with internal subversion, boycotts, sabotage of production, and the like. In response, the regime, in order to survive, may choose an autochthonous development strategy,[25] which closes off all relations with hostile forces for a period of time—a necessary precondition for taking stock of national resources, reorienting the values of population sectors alienated from national realities by their imperial life styles, and preparing labor mobilizations for infrastructural development. The initial period of "closure to the outside" creates the institutional security and national commitments that permit a subsequent return to selective outside relationships.

In response to the internal destabilizers, the institutionalization of popular power requires a period of nondemocratic forms of representation.[26] The combined resources of interlocking ruling classes and the "open" nature of the polity create a great deal of vulnerability to economic disruption and social dislocation, which could undermine the regime if political channels were not selectively closed. The institutional channels through which interest groups and parties linked to the ruling classes act may be closed or their activities sharply delimited. In a period of "foundation-building," when the social order is being transformed, nondemocratic forms of representation are necessary for the consolidation of the new property relations. The reemergence of reciprocity and civility is a postrevolutionary phenomenon bound up with the degree to which mass participation and solidarity replace indirect representation.[27] Without the transitional period of nondemocratic representation, structural changes could not be defended, and the possibility of a later period of popular participation would be difficult to envision. Without the conversion from indirect representation to direct participation, a new class society could emerge. The forms of political representation become increasingly important as a society moves beyond the initial period of structural transformation. Furthermore, within the period of transition, the more profound the transformation and the greater the opposition, the more likely it is that the early forms of nondemocratic representation will persist and perhaps develop separate and distinct organizational interests apart from the original constituents. Nevertheless, profound changes also require a greater intensity of mass participation, which, while at first finding expression in centralized leadership, at last finds in its own activity the basis for converting the system from indirect to direct rule.

## Demodernization and Development

Modernization in most peripheral countries was initiated and directed by the imperial countries as part of their overseas expansion.[28] The notion of "modernization," as has been pointed out, has been given as many definitions as there are writers who use the terminology.[29] I use the term to describe the conversion of an autonomous agro-subsistence economy to a dependent nonindustrial society whose major characteristics include a class structure with a preponderance of bureaucratic, commercial, and "low-paying service" occupations linked to the metropolitan ruling class and its military-administrative institutions. Imperialism has exploited the periphery and financed the expansion of a series of bureaucratic roles, which in turn have generated a series of satellite services. Likewise, the selective insertion of Western advanced technology within the periphery has created a new stratum of industrial workers but has undermined the crafts and subsistence farmers, driving them into cities and suburban slums as migrant laborers. The implantation of imperialist industry has incorporated a segment of workers into the labor force but, at the same time, has converted a larger layer of the population from productive to nonproductive labor.[30] In large part, that process of incorporation/ejection has been caused by the nature of imperial investment: capital inflows employ few workers, whereas capital outflows prevent the reincorporation of workers ejected from preimperial economic pursuits. The interlocking classes (national bureaucratic/foreign corporate) have channeled the residual surplus remaining in the country toward "modernization," the multiplication of bureaucratic, commercial, and service occupations. The productive resources have been concentrated in foreign corporate investments, and the state is in charge of the distribution of consumption. Through imperial-directed modernization, wide social strata have been incorporated into a hierarchical society of subordination and consumerism; the entourage of clients has been tied to the lifestyle of the imperial patron and largely earns the residual surplus by performing nonproductive work, i.e., policing the local population and providing recreational facilities. Civil servants, small and large business people, bankers, peddlers, prostitutes, personal servants, message boys, cab drivers, hotel workers, restaurant workers, barkeepers, military officers, pimps, and procurers gain part or all of their livelihoods through their relationship with the imperial capitalist class and its apparatus.[31] Increasingly, the size of the productive sectors has shrunk, while the tertiary occupations have grown: the long list of services belies the fact that most are concentrated in the lowest ends of the income scale. Production has been increasingly concentrated in a small number of economic activities; the countryside, either because of mechanization, military assaults, or capital transfers, has been increasingly abandoned. External markets or their surrogate—the external consumer within the national economy—have defined the nature of effective demand. And as capital has flowed from the countryside, so too has the population followed it in pursuit of employment. Population movements in the periphery can best be understood in terms of the flow of capital: from areas of surplus appropriation to areas of surplus disposal—from hinterland to capital city, from periphery to core.

Imperial-induced modernization has radically transformed not only the class structure, and market, but also the value system of broad layers of the population. The top-heavy commercial and service sectors play an increasingly important role in defining the lifestyle of the society, since they dispose of an increasing share of national income. The emphasis of those strata is heavily skewed toward individual services, luxury goods (especially foreign imports), commercial enterprises, specialty shops, and personal indulgences. Even in the lowest levels of the society, the notion that hustling for the foreigners beats working in a factory has taken hold. Consumerism and nonproductive, low-paying services define the modernized version of imperial-dominated peripheral societies.

A basic prerequisite for socialist development is the demodernization of society: substantial transfers of population from the "service," or tertiary sector—especially low-paid personal service workers and government employees—to productive employment in agriculture and industry. That occupational shift, in turn, involves a series of other basic changes: a shift in investment from capital-intensive to labor-intensive projects; a shift in the products produced from specialty and luxury items for foreign patrons to products for popular consumption; a shift from catering to the "external" market to producing for the internal market. More important, large-scale infrastructural development and social services replace the heavy emphasis on imports of luxury goods and the elaborate and sometimes bizarre personal services provided to the rich. All of those changes, in turn, are accompanied by the society's drive to resocialize adults: individual mobility and exploitation are replaced by collective mobility through social solidarity. The values of production, mass participation, national pride, and manual labor replace consumerism, hierarchical decision-making, deference, xenophobia, and leisure-class lifestyles.[32]

The efforts to change structure, lifestyle, and values lead to massive attempts to redirect investment from the capital city to the countryside: both from the perspective of the new development strategy and the resocialization process, the notion of decentralization makes good sense. The great urban concentration of service, lumpen, commercial, and bureaucratic strata simply reinforces the ethos of the previous regime: the new forms are accepted, but the old values and routines reassert themselves. The issue of social transformation, then, is not merely the socialization of existing production, but the uprooting of old economic activities and the creation of new ones: rural decentralization, paralleled by investment and population shifts, accompany the transformation of ownership and provide the class basis for continuing the revolutionary transformation. To merely socialize the modernized society would lead to a rapid degeneration of the new society, ending with a state version of a highly bureaucratized, elitist society that replicated the values and norms of the previous society.

Demodernization is a prerequisite for the development of socialized productive forces in peripheral society and substantially guarantees the process of transformation without major reversions.

*Revolutionary Transition in the Periphery*

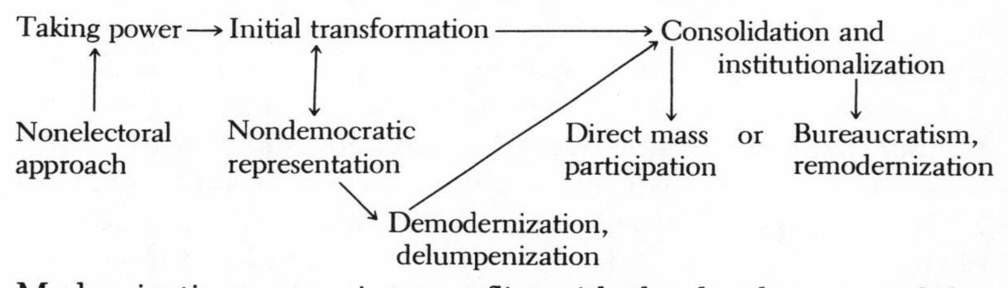


Modernization comes into conflict with the development of the productive forces, forcing an increasing share into nonproductive activities as well as facilitating the outflow of capital and importation of nonessential goods. Rather than being considered a prerequisite for "development," "modernization" should be seen as a mjor obstacle to the rational allocation of resources and manpower involving gross class, regional, and sectorial imbalances.

## Delumpenization: A Special Case of Demodernization

In countries that have been invaded by U.S. military/administrative forces or that have served as recreational reserves for metropolitan leisure activities or both, a process of delumpenization must necessarily accompany structural change; through retraining, relocation, and resocialization, a substantial stratum in a vast array of occupations, licit and illicit, which depended on metropolitan patrons and in some cases owed allegiance to them, must be integrated into the working class (or offered exit visas). The transition from lumpenproletariat to working class works from two sides: social and class specific. Besides being a class position, being "lumpen" involves a way of life, a social situation. Lumpenization is the other side of a society in which the affluent upper class regards lumpen services more than productive labor as long as they serve its interests.* To transform the lumpen, society itself must be transformed, because the lumpen's values are only the mirror image of the consumerism of the upperclass, but without the means to achieve it. Nevertheless, the structural transformation of society does not necessarily lead to the conversion of lumpen to worker. Within the revolution, a concerted effort at cultural transformation and the application of specific measures that provide incentives for productive work and deny the physical facilities for lumpen subsistence are needed. Peripheral cities which have been heavily occupied by imperial military forces (such as Bangkok, Saigon, Phnom Penh) or engage a substantial tourist clientele (prerevolutionary Havana and the capitals of the Caribbean) have experienced the growth of a whole series of ancillary occupations, which service the foreign occupation and which foster within the lower class the lifestyle and consumer wants of the foreign bourgeoisie.[33] The older rural values are disdained. Factory work is scarce. The possibilities of securing "something," a windfall gain, illuminate the consciousness of the huge army of hustlers forcibly uprooted from the countryside by military terror or corporate expansion. No doubt, the loss of working-class or peasant status, the lingering doubts about self-worth of those relegated to dubious occupations, and the desire to accumulate capital to enter business, as well as personal ties to the patron, all influence the lumpen in a reactionary or conservative political direction. But other factors mitigate against that rightist orientation. Some lumpen develop a clientele among workers out of which may emerge a sense of solidarity as part of a working-class community. Family ties with peasants and workers may continue to influence the outlook of the lumpen, especially when the family is located within a class-anchored trade union or political

* When lumpen violence exceeds recognized bounds and, say, affects tourism, it is, of course, harshly repressed. During the early 1970s, Jamaica and other Caribbean islands applied severe sanctions, including the death penalty, to crimes affecting tourists.

tradition. In other words, stratification within the lumpenproletarian class might lend itself to the following division:

*Lumpen Political Orientation and Class Situation*

| *Social situation* | Class Composition<br>*Working or peasant class* | <br>*Middle or upper class* |
|---|---|---|
| Milieu | x | x |
| Clientele | x | x |
| Political mobilization | x | x |
| | Left | Right |

Left-wing lumpenism, however, is only a tendency, which requires for its development an external pole to "orient" it; otherwise the "natural" course is to prey on the surrounding community in search of capital to advance from the lumpen to the petty-bourgeois world, the ideal of the bulk of the lumpen.

The processes of autochthonous development, nondemocratic representation, demodernization, and delumpenization have accompanied the Cuban, Chinese, and now the Cambodian revolutions as efforts to transform the class structure into the basis for the reorganization of the economy during the initial period of transition from neocolonial to socialist society.

## Notes

1. The notion that capitalism can be reduced to the existence of wage labor and that nonwage payments define a "feudal" or precapitalist society has been central to a good many mistaken scholars, who unfortunately have theorized from the particular aspects of Marx's historical analysis. See Ernest Laclau, "Feudalism and Capitalism in Latin America," *New Left Review* 67 (May-June 1971): 19–38.
2. Samuel Huntingdon, *Political Order in Changing Societies* (New Haven: Yale University Press, 1968); and Szymon Chodak, *Societal Development* (Oxford: Oxford University Press, 1973).

3. W. W. Rostow, *Politics and the Stages of Growth* (Cambridge: Cambridge University Press, 1971).
4. Andre Gunder Frank, *Capitalism and Underdevelopment in Latin America* (New York: Monthly Review Press, 1967).
5. Reinhardt Bendix, *Nation Building and Citizenship* (New York: Doubleday & Co., Anchor Books, 1969).
6. Rostow, *Stages of Growth*.
7. Alexander Gerschenkron, *Economic Backwardness in Historical Perspective* (Cambridge, Mass.: Harvard University Press, 1962).
8. Soviet social theorists and their colleagues in the Italian, French, and Chilean parties are among the leading exponents of this viewpoint.
9. Stanley Stein and Barbara Stein, *The Colonial Heritage of Latin America* (Oxford: Oxford University Press, 1970).
10. Karl Marx, *Capital*, 3 vols. (New York: International Publishers, 1967), vol. 1.
11. Charles H. Harris III, *A Mexican Family Empire* (Austin, Tex.: University of Texas Press, 1974).
12. Thomas More, Introduction to *Utopia* (New York: E. P. Dutton & Co., 1973).
13. The widespread use of company stores in mining areas of the United States throughout the nineteenth and early twentieth centuries are examples of nonwage forms of social relations of production.
14. Frank Bonilla and José A. Silva Michelena, *A Strategy for Research on Social Policy* (Cambridge, Mass.: M.I.T. Press, 1967).
15. Borrowed and modified from Hannah Arendt's use of the term in *The Human Condition* (Chicago: University of Chicago Press, 1970).
16. Caio Prado, Jr., *The Colonial Background of Modern Brazil* (Berkeley and Los Angeles: University of California Press, 1967); also Celso Furtado, *The Economic Growth of Brazil* (Berkeley and Los Angeles: University of California Press, 1963).
17. See Maurice Zeitlin et al., "New Princes for Old? The Large Corporation and the Capitalist Class in Chile," *American Journal of Sociology* 80 (July 1974): 87–123.
18. James Petras, "Sociology of Development or Sociology of Exploitation?," *Tiers Monde*, September 1976.
19. Richard J. Barnet and Ronald E. Müller, *Global Reach: The Power of the Multinational Corporations* (New York: Simon and Schuster, 1975).
20. James Petras and Morris Morley, *The United States and Chile:*

*Imperialism and the Overthrow of the Allende Government* (New York: Monthly Review Press, 1975).

21. See *Latin America*, May 16, 1975, p. 146; and Petras and Morley, *Overthrow of Allende*.
22. Michael Parenti, *Democracy for the Few* (New York: St. Martin's Press, 1974); Alan Wolfe, *The Seamy Side of Democracy* (New York: David McKay, 1973); G. William Domhoff, *The Higher Circles* (New York: Random House, Vintage Books, 1971).
23. Robert Dahl, *Who Governs?* (New Haven, Conn.: Yale University Press, 1961).
24. George Lichtheim, *Marxism*, 2d ed., rev. (New York: Frederick A. Praeger, 1966), p. 99. Lichtheim and Lipset, both conveniently omit the last part of the sentence below that they quote from Marx.

    Seymour Martin Lipset and Lichtheim, like Dahl, ascribe political power to mere numbers and the vote. In his introduction to T. H. Marshall's collection of essays, *Class, Citizenship and Social Development* (Doubleday & Co., Anchor Books, 1965), Lipset makes Marx a forerunner of his position:

    > On the left, Karl Marx himself became an early exponent of the proposition that in a political democracy the right to vote means a significant share in power. As he put it in discussing Britain in 1852, for the "working class, universal suffrage means political power, for the proletariat forms the great majority of the population . . ."

    What is revealing about Lipset's quote from Marx is what is left out. In the full passage, Marx wrote:

    > But universal suffrage is the equivalent of political power for the working class of England, where the proletariat forms the large majority of the population, where in a long, though underground civil war it has gained a clear consciousness of its position as a class, and where even the rural districts know no longer any peasants but only landlords, industrial capitalists (farmers) and hired laborers.

    In that passage, Marx reveals a much clearer and sophisticated notion of the conditions for working class power than either Lipset's or Dahl's simpleminded ideas about the vote and "numbers." For Marx, workers with an understanding of their interest as members of a collectivity, and sharing and expressing that common understanding, are the basis of power.
25. Autochthonous development is similar to what Mao describes as self-reliance. It essentially involves depending largely on natural

resources and labor within national boundaries and minimizing external trade and substantial imports of technology. This policy is not a form of xenophobia but an effort to avoid entering into compromising negotiations to secure these resources before the new state is consolidated. The position and demands of the imperial countries in this period are largely centered on political demands, namely, reversing structural changes and destabilizing the economy. The choices of the periphery revolve around the need to avoid external relations which facilitate those circumstances.

26. Nondemocratic representation can take various forms, some less democratic and more centralized than others. The notion here is that political power is drawn from, based on, and responsible to a particular configuration of classes, but is not subject to its direct control through elections. It may take the form of a party, movement, or popular army.
27. Maurice Zeitlin, *Revolutionary Politics and the Cuban Working Class* (Princeton: Princeton University Press, 1967). James Petras and Hugo Zemelman Merino, *Peasants in Revolt* (Austin, Tex.: University of Texas Press, 1972).
28. *Encyclopaedia Britannica*, 15th ed., s.v. "Colonialism" (by Harry Magdoff), reprinted in Harry Magdoff, *Imperialism* (New York: Monthly Review Press, 1978).
29. Dean Tipps, "Modernization Theory and the Comparative Study of Societies: A Critical Perspective," *Comparative Studies in Society and History*, January 1973.
30. Philip McMichael, James Petras, and Robert Rhodes, "Industry in the Third World," *New Left Review* 85 (May-June 1974): 83–104; María Tavares and José Serra, "Beyond Stagnation: A Discussion of the Nature of Recent Developments in Brazil," in *Latin America: From Dependence to Revolution*, ed. James Petras (New York: John Wiley & Sons, 1973); Glaucio Soares, "The New Industrialization and the Brazilian Political System," in *Latin America: Reform or Revolution*, eds. James Petras and Maurice Zeitlin (Greenwich, Conn.: Fawcett Publications, 1968).
31. On Puerto Rico, see Morris Morley, "Dependence and Development in Puerto Rico" and Mary K. Vaughn, "Tourism in Puerto Rico," in *Puerto Rico and Puerto Ricans: Studies in History and Society*, eds. Adalberto Lopez and James Petras (Cambridge, Mass.: Schenkman Publishers, 1974).
32. These processes are best illustrated by the Cuban and Chinese examples. On Cuba, see Richard R. Fagen, *The Transformation of*

*Political Culture in Cuba* (Stanford: Stanford University Press, 1969); Arthur MacEwan, "Equality and Power in Revolutionary Cuba," *Socialist Revolution* 4, no. 2 (October 1974): 87–108. On China, see William Hinton, *Fanshen* (New York: Monthly Review Press, 1966); John Gurley, "Capitalist and Maoist Economic Development," in *America's Asia*, eds. Edward Friedman and Mark Selden (New York: Random House, Vintage Books, 1971).

In revolutionary Cambodia and Vietnam, the processes of demodernization and deurbanization proceeded at a fairly rapid pace. In those countries, "forced urbanization" (during the massive terror bombing by U.S. warplanes) swelled the city populations to several times their original sizes in a period of less than a decade. The massive and rapid return of rural refugees to productive activity has unfortunately been distorted by the U.S. media, including the *New York Times*, into some sort of forced death march for soft city dwellers. Likewise, the *New York Times's* account of the loss of gay Saigon is reminiscent of similar complaints about Havana and Shanghai after their revolutions. The enormous dislocation caused by the United States in uprooting masses of peasants and transplanting them into unproductive urban activity servicing the "fun-loving" Americans is described as the norm; the return of peasant refugees to productive activity and their homes is described as abnormal. The feats of distortion performed by U.S. journalists in the service of governmental policy are truly astonishing, but no less so than those performed by social scientists. Vietnam, like China and Cuba, is an exemplary case of a revolutionary process in which nondemocratic representation, first embodied through the popular revolutionary army, serves as the basic instrument to safeguard the social transformation against hostile internal and external forces. In Portugal's case, the revolutionary socialist elements in the Portuguese Armed Forces, as the process of transformation deepened, found that nondemocratic forms of representation (popular militias and the military high command) were the only adequate institutional forms for carrying out a thorough going transformation against the "obstructionist" Western European-style Socialist Party and the sectarian Communist Party. The degree of "external political leakage" through the electoral process (April 1975) was evidenced by the heavy inflow of funds to both parties from the East and West.

33. See Fagen, *Political Culture in Cuba*, and Vaughn, "Tourism in Puerto Rico."

# 3

# STATE CAPITALISM AND THE THIRD WORLD

## Introduction

Among certain writers on the Third World, the notion has been popularized that the class structure can be understood as a simple dichotomy between ruling classes and masses, and that development will take one of two forms: neocolonial exploitation (leading to expansion or stagnation, depending on the school of thought) or revolutionary socialist development. Some writers on dependency are more like "theoreticians of the conjuncture," possessing a facility for developing sweeping theoretical perspectives within a very narrow historical time frame. Within the neocolonial paradigm the national bourgeoisie—weak, vacilating, dependent—is assigned the role of forward shield of imperial capital, hence it has been dubbed a "lumpen bourgeoisie." While in long-term, world-historical perspective it is probably correct to view Third World prospects in dichotomous terms (socialism or neocolonialism), over the short and medium run it grossly oversimplifies events and developments, underestimates the political and social capacities of nonsocialist forces, and seriously distorts the actual class structure in formation in the Third World. Because Third World private capitalist and classical petty-bourgeois classes have shown little inclination or capacity to develop dynamic national economies, it does not follow that there exist no other forces which are capable of tackling the job. The early stages of capitalist development, especially for countries beginning their industrialization after 1850, have always involved large-scale state investments in most if not all of the essential areas of the economy for varying periods of time.

In the last quarter of the twentieth century, faced with the mighty power of the multinational corporations, whatever "national" effort in the Third World is forthcoming, requires a vastly expanded role on the part of the state. If indeed nineteenth-century Japan required massive state investments to alter the balance of power between national and imperial capital, how much more so is this the case in the underdeveloped economies of contemporary Africa, Asia, and Latin America. Under mounting international pressures from the imperial centers, with their voracious appetites for raw materials and growing capacity to absorb local markets, the nationalist state remains the last barrier to total subordination and fragmentation in the new international division of labor.

Indeed, in recent years a number of Third World countries have experienced one form or another of industrialization for varying periods of time. While most of the industrialization has been directed from the outside, thus fragmenting the process of industrialization, there have been a few comprehensive efforts attempting to incorporate most of the ingredients of industrialization within the nation-state. Externally induced effort limits industrialization in the Third World to particular "moments" of the process—whether it be assembly plants, light industry, or capital goods (without the technico-research capacities). Despite the high growth rates which a minority of dependent countries have experienced in recent years, the qualitative aspects, the scope and depth of industrialization have been far from acceptable. In many cases one finds that the greater the degree of externally induced industrialization, the more fragmented becomes the economic activity (the more immersed it becomes in the world capitalist division of labor), and the greater its vulnerability to external fluctuations. For these reasons, among others, the externally directed industrial effort is becoming increasingly rejected in the Third World in favor of a national state-capitalist model. Such a model attempts to devise a different pattern of industrialization linking the various phases of the industrial effort, from technological innovation through assembly, within the bounds of the nation-state. The key strata initiating and seeming to direct the conversion from neocolonialism (externally induced expansion) to state-capitalism—via evolution, coup, popular uprising, or some combination of the three—are the state sector employees, civil and/or military. This last possibility of capitalist development in the Third World then borrows "socialist forms"—political (one-party state, socialist rhetoric, etc.) and economic (state ownership, planning, etc.)—to accomplish capitalist ends, namely, the realization of profit within a class society.

The perplexing problem of national-capitalist development remains. What are the agencies for nonsocialist "national development"? What social strata will occupy the crucial positions and direct the "nationalist state," and from whence do they emerge? What promise do they hold for the future? The social strata which directs national capitalist development does not fit any of the classes described by Marx in the development of capitalism in Europe. They are not bourgeois or petty bourgeois because they do not own property; they are not workers because they are not directly linked to the productive process, although they may sell their labor power as salaried employees. Even if we grant a certain overlap with workers or petty bourgeois in our description we must consider the fact that a significant new social force—what I will call an "intermediary stratum"—has defined a new capitalist development project tying the expansion of capitalist market relations to the expansion of the state. The problem is not, through definitional acrobatics, to redefine this stratum so that it can be accounted for within the classical class schema, but to understand its peculiar social characteristics in order to explain the specific way it goes about the process of capital accumulation.

Over a prolonged period of time imperial-directed economic expansion of agro-mineral exports has left a residual amount of its earnings in the "host" country. The cumulative impact has been to expand the "service" sectors of the dominated society. As a result, the governmental (civil and military), commercial and banking, bureaucracies have expanded far beyond industrial activity, forming a relatively large, concentrated (in urban centers) intermediary cadre group whose conception of the world is shaped largely by the administrative milieu in which they are located. Concentrated in the large metropolitan centers, relatively better organized than other groups in the society, with developed lines of communication, the bureaucratic stratum provides the politicized cadres that coopt political and social movements that emerge elsewhere in the society as well as preempt those activities, in the case of the military, through sharp and decisive action at strategic historical moments. The notion of a petty bourgeoisie "vacillating" between the big bourgeoisie and the proletariat obviously is inadequate to account for the behavior of a stratum that seizes power and imposes its own imprint on society. Nor does it explain the relative durability of these regimes or the frequency of their appearance. Only if there is a significant mobilized proletariat/peasantry with a class-conscious leadership confronting an organized and coherent bourgeoisie would the problematic of the fragmentation or the demise of the petty bourgeoisie be on the agenda. Lacking those conditions, it is possible to conceive of a class-conscious stratum vertically and horizontally linked functioning as an independent class (apart from workers and bourgeois) with its own political-economic project. Hierarchical order and functional interdependence, the two characteristics of the bureaucratic order, lend themselves to a political ideology that embraces collectivism without redistribution. What is transparent in the egalitarian claims of the state-capitalist regimes that emerge from these intermediary strata is the sharp differentiation in political power which sooner or later translates itself into equally pronounced socioeconomic inequalities, despite subjective protestations to the contrary. The bureaucratic milieu of the intermediary stratum in the final analysis decisively influences and shapes its vision of the new social order.

The early cases of state-capitalist regimes, Turkey and Mexico in the 1930s and 1940s and Bolivia in the 1950s, allow us to put their contemporary counterparts in historical perspective. I am referring now to Libya, Algeria, Ethiopia, Peru, and Venezuela (among others) where the state has recently taken the initiative in wresting control over the major productive facilities. Past and present experience with Third World state-capitalist regimes suggests three areas of socioeconomic change: (a) major efforts at transforming an agro-export society through national industrialization, (b) the creation of an internal market through agrarian reform which concomitantly limits or eliminates the political power of the landlord class, and (c) nationalization or control over natural resources and harnessing of the surplus to national development projects.

These broad similarities between earlier and contemporary state-capitalist regimes should not blind us to some important differences, however. For one, the contemporary state-capitalists can count on the active support of the collectivist economies in the noncapitalist world to a far greater extent than was true in the earlier period. The early state-capitalist regimes were forced to promote national growth largely because the Western capitalist countries, undergoing the world crises of the 1930s or World War II, were not in a position to expand economically abroad. Present state-capitalist expansion is a product of active support from a major sector of the world economy, whereas the earlier versions of state-capitalism grew for the opposite reasons, namely because of the "neglect" of the imperial centers. The earlier versions of state capitalism confronted with the reemergence of imperial capitalism, especially after World War II, largely capitulated: the influx of multinational corporate investment in the manufacturing sectors occurred subsequent to the early industrialization and redistributive efforts in the larger post-statist regimes. The internal markets, national industries, and infrastructure investments were ideally suited to the profit-maximizing proclivities of the multinationals. Today's state-capitalist regimes, by contrast, begin with the expropriation of the multinationals which have pre-empted national industrialization and go beyond the import-substitution efforts of the earlier state-capitalist regimes, attempting a more comprehensive "integral" form of industrialization. Finally, the earlier state-capitalist regimes provided a greater leeway for private firms within the national economy. It was not unusual for private sector employers to take over state enterprises and turn them to private gain, establishing a plethora of related and unrelated private firms. Among the contemporary state-capitalist firms the tendency is for the state managers to devise administrative and legislative measures that heighten the "autonomy" of the firm or development corporation, i.e., transforming it into a private fiefdom while maintaining the juridical forms of public enterprise.

The historical experience of state-capitalism suggests, however, that whatever the initial dynamic and innovation, over the long term stagnation, privatization, and external dependence are recurring phenomena. Insertion into the world capitalist market on unequal terms and increasing indebtedness leads to a crisis that proceeds toward the dissolution of statism as a mode of expansion. What is also different today from the earlier period is the extent to which state-capitalism has become increasingly commonplace, attractive even to the most retrograde type of political rulers (especially in the oil countries). What in an earlier period (in Turkey, Mexico, and Bolivia) appeared as specific sociopolitical formation reflecting national peculiarities and revolutionary impulses has recently become the dominant mode of nationalist capitalist development in the Third World, with its own patterns of redefining imperial relations and setting forth *new* sets of contradictions between exploiters and exploited. The long-term trend is toward the emergence of new patterns of differentiation and conflict, between state bureaucrats and workers, between peasant-kulak organizers of agro-coops and rural workers. In this context the old clichés that evoke the rhetoric of "uniting the many to defeat the few" give few clues to disentangling the new national and international class alignments.

## The Contemporary Historical Conjuncture

Throughout the Third World there is a new type of political-social regime emerging, rooted in control of the state apparatus, which extends control over the economy through nationalization of imperial enterprise. The failure of privately induced nationalist-capitalist industrial expansion is a fact that characterizes most of the Third World in the post-World War II period. The lack of capital, competition from imperial firms, "liberal" economic policies promoted by states controlled by agro-export sectors, small internal markets, stiff competition in international markets, the low level of technology and the long maturation period for profits relative to nonindustrial investments have all militated against large-scale, long-term investments in industry by indigenous capitalists. In addition, national capitalists have frequently sought out foreign capital, selling total or part ownership of the firm in exchange for market outlets, technology, access to credit, or immediate access to cash. In general, private national capital has been confined to slow-growth consumer industries (textiles, food processing, shoes, etc.) oriented toward internal markets, the size and growth of which is constricted by the low level of effective consumer demand and vast social inequalities, both products of exploitative social relations.

On the other hand, foreign-financed industrial expansion has resulted in heightened social inequalities, long-term decapitalization of the economy, and, in many cases, enclave economies which fail to absorb the increasing number of urban underemployed and unemployed. In addition, external debts and political influence of foreign-owned firms call into question the sovereignty of the state. The efforts at neocolonial development or national private accumulation then present serious problems from the point of view of national independence and economic expansion. Countries in which foreign investment-induced expansion occurs are usually nations, such as those in the Middle East, and Nigeria, that contain strategic raw materials of great demand in the "center." In other cases, such as Hong Kong and South Korea, they tend to be assembly-plant and commercial centers which have a controlled labor force, exploited at subsistence wages. Finally, imperial industrial capital also has invaded local economies following a national-populist regime which has created a substantial internal market. Imperial industrial expansion is directed in this case to capturing the internal market, as it has in Mexico, Brazil, and Argentina.

State-capitalism emerges in part as a response to the unfavorable economic fortunes of private national capital and the high political and social "costs" of foreign-induced economic expansion. State-capitalist oriented social strata lack an independent socioeconomic base of any importance. Whatever "property" they own is incidental to their political and social power. Their key weapon is political capacity: their ability to take hold of the state machinery, alter the distribution of social power, and reorganize economy. For civilian and military employees in and around the administrative centers, the concentration on the "state" is a necessity, not only in the sense that it is the only means of obtaining a livelihood but because it holds the key to their own and (in their eyes) their countries' futures. Given the monopoly control over land, commerce, industry, and banking, the probability of advancing through pure private economic activity is quite low. The only available vehicle through which capital accumulation can take place is the state, but only insofar as the principal sources of profits can be taken over or out of the hands of their current benefactors. The expropriation of imperial firms is both an economic necessity to state capital-induced accumulation and a source of political legitimacy: by integrating the resources and capital formerly controlled by foreign firms into a "national" development effort through the process of nationalization, one of the essential elements of the bourgeois-nationalist revolution is confronted, the formation of a national economy. The incapacity of the state-capitalists to sustain their national economic project, the tendency to disarticulate the public sector—to sell out profitable enterprises first to national and then to foreign capital—suggests that even the "nationalist" component of the bourgeois revolution is not consummated by this strata over the medium or long run.

The state-capitalist attack on imperial firms has several economic and political dimensions. Imperial firms are the principal source of the economic surplus and thus the basis of any sort of development push, but their expropriation does not call into question the fundamental issues of capitalist property relations. The transfer from imperial to state ownership occurs without any radical shift in the social relations of production (including wage/salary differentials, managerial prerogatives and/or the hierarchy of authority), market determination, or profit calculations. State ownership does not in any fundamental way transform the conditions of exploitation of labor, but rather reflects a shift in the source of exploitation and perhaps a change in the disposition of the surplus (a greater percentage is reinvested in productive facilities within the nation instead of in the metropolis). From the political vantage point, striking at imperial firms avoids serious internal conflicts as fractions of the state-capitalist ruling class might maintain direct or indirect ties with indigenous property groups. The maintenance of a national private sector allows state capitalists who accumulate at the expense of imperial capital to branch out at a later period in private ventures. The sequence in some state-capitalist regimes is for state-capitalists to accumulate private wealth through salaries and other perquisites, to open opportunities for investment through the state, to finance private investments through private savings and public loans, and to eventually "reinvite" foreign capital for joint ventures. The Mexican experience is illustrative. The existence of "private economic space" allows this option to remain available even if latent during the initial period of a state-capitalist regime. In summary, the principal characteristics of state-capitalist regimes are statism, economic nationalism, and capitalist-social relations. In the present conjuncture, national state capitalism appears as a rising social formation displacing the traditional neocolonial regimes and confronting the socialist aspirations of the masses.

## International and National Setting for State-Capitalist Power

Within the present conjuncture there are several crucial international and national factors that facilitate the formation of state-capitalist regimes. The rise of national state-capitalism occurs in a period of the relative declining power of U.S. imperialism, the growth of interimperialist rivalries, the decay of the nationalist vocation of the national private bourgeoisie, and the relative weakness of the newly politicized and mobilized mass movement of workers and peasants. In assessing the relative strength of the United States and its significance for countries in the Third World, it is important to keep in mind that in the post-World War II period, Washington was the principal gendarme of the Third World, frequently intervening to crush popular governments and social movements. Having lost its monopolistic position within the capitalist world, the U.S. imperial state is in a weaker position in dealing directly with the Third World, no longer holding all the cards of diplomacy, finance, and trade within the noncapitalist world. When we speak of a relative decline of U.S. imperial power, we are drawing a comparison with the recent past. Today U.S. trade and investment represents a declining proportion of total foreign trade and investment in and between the Third World and the rest of the world. Europe, Japan, and the communist countries have increasingly eroded the previously unchallenged U.S. position. Just as the United States benefited from the demise of European colonialism through the neocolonial period, the rest of the industrialized world may take advantage of the disintegration of the U.S.-dominated neocolonial networks, developing new ties and "advanced relationships" (management and service contracts) with the new state-capitalist regimes whose anti-imperialism will adversely affect principally U.S. interests. The possibility of diversifying external sources of finance as well as trade relations and avoiding U.S. economic retaliation (trade boycotts, financial blockades) in response to economic nationalist measures will enhance the chances of state-capitalist development strategies. The opportunities are great, the risks minimal when national state-capitalists can pick and choose trading partners and financial sources among imperial rivals. As each imperial center expands in search of new markets and investment outlets, it may, when perceiving relatively durable regimes, offer more favorable terms to the Third World countries than if there were one sole dominant imperial country. The diversity of external sources encourages a range of development choices to the competing power centers within Third World countries. The neocolonial elites tied to a single metropole no longer dominate the political scene.

Henceforth, dissident segments within the governmental apparatus grasp at the external opportunities, to break with the existing pattern of internal-external domination and to redefine the terms of dependency, choosing new sets of "partners" and achieving a degree of autonomy relative to the previous set of imperialist interests.

One may ask why the national private bourgeoisie has not played this role of fashioning an independent economic policy. The answer cannot be provided by simple ideological deductions from sacred texts. The notion of a "progressive national bourgeoisie" is largely derived from a misreading of French revolutionary history in which the bourgeoisie supposedly led the struggle against the "feudal" ancient regime. Historical accounts tell a different story: even during the eighteenth century, the bourgeoisie did not lead the social revolution (more often it collaborated with the feudal elite), although nothing prevented it from taking advantage of the new revolutionary situation once it was consolidated. The worldwide expansion of imperial capital into the remotest societies has incorporated the national bourgeoisie largely into its network: through "joint ventures" (investment associations), patent and licensing agreements, loans, credits, trade, the private national bourgeoisie has become integrated into the imperial system, although it fights rearguard battles to avoid complete displacement. Today, the national private capitalist class requires and supports foreign capital, and financial and technical support even as it fears some of the consequences. At the same time as national capital has become incorporated into the imperial system, it has lost the basis for internally directed development projects: the greater the external ties, the less likelihood that "nationalist" revolutions will be organized and promoted by the national private bourgeoisie. As imperial capital spreads outward to the Third World, national capital moves inward into agriculture and commerce, at once "capitalizing" agriculture and creating the economic and social links that prevent the bourgeoisie from initiating agrarian reform. Nevertheless, once state-capitalists promote nationalist measures it is probable that the bourgeoisie will seek ways and means of benefiting from them.

The third factor which facilitates the emergence of state-capitalism is the relative weakness of the workers and peasant movement. Under conditions of severe repression during the period of neocolonialism, the masses had a few opportunities for political experience. Scarce membership in cadre organizations, sparse membership in class organizations (peasant or trade unions) and political parties make it difficult for the masses to intervene directly into the political struggle. Spontaneous outbursts and general strikes weaken the old power and undermine its authority, but do not provide an alternative leadership. The low level of social differentiation, a product of stagnant economies, further inhibits the growth of class-based combative organizations.

In these circumstances, the military emerges as the best organized political force to take advantage of the political disjuncture. Through its nationalist-populist ideology, it attempts to lay claim to the allegiance of the masses. More important, upon assuming political power, the military-national-state-capitalist regime attempts to substitute itself for the absence of a coherent capitalist class, and through the state it attempts to perform the tasks of the bourgeois revolution. A precondition for the creation of a national-capitalist economy is the nationalization of imperial firms; the basis for creation of an internal market is the agrarian reform. Hence the state-capitalist regime is characterized by extensive efforts at nationalization and land reform. The manner through which these radical reforms are implemented and their political and social consequences, however, clearly distinguish these efforts from a socialist revolution: the state bureaucracy replaces the imperial investors and indigenous landowners as the organizers of production and, of course, the appropriators of the surplus.

In the latter half of the twentieth century, the propertyless intermediary strata—professionals, employees, military, university groups—located between the workers and peasants on the one hand, and the native property groups on the other, are the only possible social force which lacks direct ties to the landlords and imperial firms and is therefore capable of directing a bourgeois national revolution. But given its specific position in the social structure, it will do so only through the instrumentalities at its disposition—the state. Unlike the earlier bourgeois revolutions which led to the incorporation of greater and greater sections of society to private market relations, in the present period, market relations and capitalist production are extended through the expansion of state enterprise: first through expropriation of imperial firms, later through direct state investments. Unlike other experiences in which the state expropriates unprofitable private enterprises, or operates firms at a loss to provide cheap services for the private sector, in state-capitalist societies, the expropriated firms are profitmaking and are looked at as the "engines" of development.

## Relationship of Military to Class Structure

As was pointed out above, the state-capitalists do not eliminate the national private sector, nor do they alter the position of the working class in the productive system. In fact, the very origins of the regime are based on social and political "stalemate": when internal conflicts, mass pressure, and imperial domination undermine the rule of the traditional landed and commercial strata and when the mobilized working and peasant classes, for lack of a revolutionary party, political consciousness, and/or revolutionary leadership are incapable of taking power, the military may appear on the scene as the "arbiter" of society. Through its control over the state apparatus it attempts to "mediate" between the masses and the national bourgeois classes. The "nationalist" ideology serves to mystify the essential socioeconomic differences which continue to divide the classes and especially the specific class interests of the newly emerging state-capitalist class. A crucial factor facilitating the rise of the intermediary strata to power are internal divisions within the traditional ruling class.

Within the traditional ruling class, conflicts emerge over the sources and expenditures of government revenue, as each fraction (landed, commercial, industrial, both national and imperial) tries to minimize its payments and optimize its subsidies. State-capitalism should not be confused with state intervention, which is a frequent occurrence in many types of liberal or neocolonial regimes. In the latter, the state functions as a handmaiden of the private sector, not as an active competitor, providing credits, subsidies, and cheap services at a loss. In state-capitalist regimes the state as the owner of productive and profitable firms is a substitute for the private sector.

The second level of conflict (but related to the first) concerns the type of "development" policies that will be pushed by the neocolonial state: while the various fractions of the ruling class overlap, different kinship groups are anchored primarily in one or another economic sector. Hence there is competition to shape government policy in favor of agriculture, commerce, or imperial capital. In normal times, this "particularistic" orientation among ruling-class fractions is manageable within the bounds of the neocolonial state. But in times of societal crises—because of famine, prolonged economic stagnation, blatantly odious agreements with imperial firms, or whatever—the state appears to be abandoning its most elementary functions, such as, for example, control over its people or the survival of the nation.

As a result of delegitimization of the regime and the absence of a governing class capable of formulating a coherent national policy which aggregates the interests of the diverse fractions of the ruling class, spontaneous mass outbursts and/or discontent within the armed forces becomes pronounced. The long-term effects of external dependency, leading to the absence of financial reserves, further undercut efforts by regimes to offer ameliorative measures to contain the discontent. In these circumstances, a mass upsurge, or the threat of it, may precipitate military intervention. The declining authority of the old ruling class and the rising power of the masses incline the military initially toward measures favoring the rural populace and against the ruling class, especially its imperial fractions. In order to avoid internal divisions and to consolidate political power, the military regime appeals to nationalist sentiments, thus attempting to unify potentially conflictive forces in society. Because its original social base is so narrow, state-capitalism as the political-economic project of intermediary strata requires a military regime and/or a one-party state to sustain it. At one and the same time it opposes imperialist property interests and attempts to discipline the labor force. The national state-capitalist class directs and controls the process of capital accumulation but at the expense of the labor force, reconcentrating capital in its own hands. The state-capitalist regime attempts to redefine the terms of dependency and to contain labor demands to favor nationalist-capitalist accumulation.

The forms of national state-capitalist accumulation include a variety of policy instruments: initially it can involve increasing tax revenue from the earnings of imperial firms; extending ownership to include management rights; limiting foreign capital activities to the external sector (commerce); fragmenting their operations (exploration right, management contracts); limiting exploitation to specified time periods; limiting access to local capital; directing foreign-owned industries to export markets. It culminates in measures involving varying degrees of nationalization that have allowed the state-capitalists to capture the bulk of the surplus. Nevertheless, while squeezing out imperial capital, the state-capitalists share with imperial capital an interest in maximizing exploitation of the labor force: the slogans and goals include maintaining production, labor discipline, and popular demobilization. The success of state capitalism depends on the avoidance of confrontations with imperial capital and the labor force. Threats from either side may cause the state capitalists to seek alliances: with the masses if threatened by the right, with the imperialists if threatened by the left. While state-capitalist regimes may be influenced initially by radical nationalist pressures, the usual tendency has been for economic nationalism over the long run to dissolve in a series of external agreements which erode the original national developmental project. The cases of Mexico, Turkey, and Egypt are rich in material on the trajectory of state-capitalist development and are instructive regarding the essential limitations and failures of such a regime. The political and social conditions for national state-capitalist expansion—

requiring limitations on imperial influence while retaining the conditions of capitalist exploitation—create explosive contradictions.

The class position of the intermediary stratum allows it to play an anti-imperial role and favor agrarian reform: product of the administrative structures emerging from agro-commercial and/or mineral expansion but not tied to the big property holding elites, it reflects the interests of all those submerged salaried groups in search of an industrial formula. Receptive to working-class support against the traditional ruling class, it hopes to subdue and harness its energies to the new state-capitalist development effort. Hence the zigzag political course, the ambiguities, "contradictions," and "crises" in day-to-day affairs. The effort to create a political base independent of imperialism on the one hand, and "above" the working/peasant masses on the other, leads to a vulnerable political situation, one in which divisions within the junta can easily lead to reversion to a proimperial regime.

The polyclass euphoria and mass appeals that accompany the initial period of state-capitalist power and the foreclosure of the imperial option are inevitably followed by repressive measures against the trade unions and autonomous working-class mobilization. Without its external sources of finance, the state-capitalist class must seek in and through state ownership means to promote the accumulation of capital at the expense of the working class. On the other hand, the workers' support—to the degree that it exists—is not based on any change in the relations of production but on promises of increases in consumption: when the state-capitalists restrict consumption they terminate the "populist" aspect of their politics—and henceforth must rely on coercion. Hence in its social origins and social ties, the state-capitalist regime represents a break with the neocolonial system but remains unintegrated with its potential mass constituency. Structural changes and ideological appeals without mass participation become the hallmarks of the transition from neocolonialism to national state-capitalism. The initial impetus to class formation in the Third World, mainly externally directed capital accumulation based on simple surplus extraction, is increasingly giving way to a more complex process where in some cases an internal ruling class with its own state apparatus has emerged to dominate rather than mediate the process of exploitation and accumulation.

## Contradictions in the State-Capitalist Regime

The emergence of a state-capitalist formation cannot be considered a "historical" stage in the development of the productive forces, but rather a transitional regime, a phase between one type of exploitation and another, or a moment in the struggle for socialism. A historical stage presumes the consolidation of social power by a new ruling class and the expansion of the productive forces over a period of decades—eventually giving way to new social forces emerging from the new productive relations. There is no historical basis to conceive of this outcome from the new state-capitalist regime: the sharpest contradictions emerge from the very inception of the regime. The very basis of the regime, drawn from a narrow stratum of public functionaries (civilian and military), clashes with the "public" nature of the productive forces: social ownership based on capitalist social relations is inherently an unstable and conflictive circumstance. Short-term trends toward public ownership conflict with the long-term conversion toward new forms of integration into the world capitalist system. The reentry by the new ruling class into the world capitalist system is preceded by the re-creation of a class-based society: new forms of social differentiation within state-capitalist society are in part products of differential political power rather than "overt" ownership of property. Within stratified property, class relations and class struggle reemerge on a higher level in which the central issue becomes who controls the state. The centralization of property ownership in the state, the narrow social basis, and exploitative social relations result in the emergence of the "coercive" state: the state performs its essential duty of disciplining the labor force, hence appearing to the labor force as an alien power.

Finally, just as the initial anti-imperialist declarations are later confined to maximizing the surplus that accrues to the state bourgeoisie, the original articles of faith in "national liberation" can in some countries become transformed into instruments of ethnic domination. Ethnic expropriation has served as a mechanism for creating cross-class bonds and peasant loyalties toward the ruling class. In a number of African countries, in colonial settler regimes, and in Turkey and Israel large-scale ethnic expropriations have created durable long-term alliances between reactionary elites and segments of peasants or farmers pertaining to the dominant ethnic group. Here we confront the essential limits of bourgeois nationalism: unable to transcend the framework of the nation, the bourgeois nationalists, relying on ethnic allegiances, convert the nation into a prison for oppressed nationalities. Struggles that begin as authentic popular national liberation efforts are transformed by the state-capitalist bureaucracy into wars of national oppression. The case of Ethiopia in Eritrea is instructive in this regard. From being a movement of liberation of the people from imperialism, it ends up using the weapons of imperialism against the people.

The political consequences of the struggle between the state-capitalist regime in Ethiopia and the Eritrean masses are clear: the continuance of the war against the Eritrean people drains the national resources of the Ethiopian nation, thus preparing the way for the return of imperial dependence, dependence which can only in the final analysis compromise the initial anti-imperialist impulse. In denying the national independence of the Eritreans, the Ethiopian regime will end up losing its own national identity. The fate of the Ethiopian national liberation movement depends on ending the war of conquest in Eritrea: the continuance of the war can only heighten U.S. influence and ultimately sap the nationalist effort. New social forces are emerging within the nationalist revolution. These new social forces in Ethiopia, the students, workers and peasants, embrace the internationalist perspective of revolutionary socialism, recognize the national rights of Eritrea, and create the basis in the future for a socialist confederation freely arrived at by equals.

In the last quarter of the twentieth century, the world-historical process has been enormously speeded up. In the past, whole centuries separated the period of progressive bourgeois nationalism from its imperialist expression. Today, in the course of a brief period, we witness the way in which the class and national consciousness of the oppressed people press forward, forcing even the most radical of bourgeois nationalists to confront their ultimate reality: the oppressive class-exploitative side of bourgeois society.

## Conclusion

The political consequences of the rise of state-capitalism in the context of a growing mass struggle in the Third World are manifold. First, we can expect a state-capitalist regime to redefine the terms of dependency, shifting the sources of external finance from private investment to bank loans and government-to-government loans. Efforts to diversify trade and import technology signal the outer limits of the new independent foreign policy. The long-term effects could lead to a new international division of labor that circumscribes the scope of industrial activity to light and consumer goods sectors. Through licensing and patent agreements the technological transfers from the imperial center could lead over the long-run to the preemption of innovative capacities in the state-capitalist countries and their reintegration into the imperial system, paying an increasing share of their earnings on the premiums for technological borrowing. The class struggles emerging from the new class structure will have as their target the unified political-economic structure of state-capitalist society, and the state will become the target of even the most minimum wage demands. Class struggle under state-capitalism becomes immediately and directly "political," in the double sense that the masses directly confront the state as their employer, and the state confronts the workers as the source of capital expansion. As the class struggle deepens, there arises the possibility of further differentiation between nationalist and "socialist" sectors within the regime, leading directly to the struggle for socialism and state power.

# 4

# INDUSTRIALIZATION IN THE THIRD WORLD
*(with Philip McMichael and Robert Rhodes)*

## Introduction

The 1970s have witnessed a major retreat among writers who, a decade ago, were considered in the vanguard of Marxist thought. In recent issues of *New Left Review*, for example, Régis Debray has come out as a stout defender of French bourgeois nationalist tradition, in much the same fashion as any ordinary de Gaullist—absentmindedly forgetting two centuries of class struggle, repression, and colonialism embedded in that "tradition."[1] Eric Hobsbawm's favorable commentaries on the Italian Communist Party's "permeationist" approach to the state can be read in much the same fashion as Fabian writings about the British state seventy years age: the same conception of the permeable state, the same notion of struggle through education (only the intellectual clutter of Gramscian quotes about "ideological hegemony" are absent).[2] Nicos Poulantzas, with his usual ponderous rhetoric, follows in the same way: the class struggle is now located in state structures—the class nature of the state is dissolved by a series of socialist appointments.[3] Arghiri Emmanuel and Bill Warren follow suit. For Emmanuel, Lenin's notion of imperialism, or what he quaintly refers to as "investment imperialism," does not exist—unequal exchange accounts for underdevelopment, itself subject to the "bargaining position" of

Third World countries.[4] Warren continues this line of thought and argues that imperialism has created the conditions for rapid and sustained independent capitalist development in the Third World.[5]

In brief, a group of influential European Marxist scholars (and there are others who follow this drift) have abandoned the fundamental ideas that inform Marx's and Lenin's writings, including the coercive nature of the capitalist state, the centrality of class relations and class struggle in advanced capitalist societies over and against nationalism, and the centrality of productive relations to imperialist exploitation (not trade). It would be important to trace out the sociological reasons for the shift from Marxist to conventional social democratic and liberal notions of state, society, and international development. However, it is more important in evaluating the soundness of that change to critically examine those scholars' theoretical and empirical arguments to determine whether they sustain their new perspectives. For indeed, if the theoretical and empirical basis of Marxist thought is unsound, then "revisions" are in order. On the other hand, the followers of intellectual fashion in the late 1970s European "theory" circles seem to begin by rejecting Marxist postulates, then assume the premises of neoliberal views of the state, society, and international relations (with occasional "Marxist" terminology spliced in to ease the transition), citing isolated bits and pieces of empirical data to substantiate their preconceptions.

The purpose of this essay is not to discuss all the neoliberal trends among ex-Marxists, but rather to critically examine the writings of one writer, Bill Warren, in one area—imperialism and industrialization. We will proceed by briefly locating the discussion in the general debate over underdevelopment and proceed to a theoretical and empirical critique.

Throughout the 1950s and early 1960s, Marxist writings on the Third World focused on the problem of underdevelopment and the incapacity of capitalism to develop the productive forces because of the dependent relations established by imperialism. Socialism was presented as the only force capable of liberating the productive forces and enabling countries to industrialize. Beginning in the early 1970s, a number of writers, including

Warren, began to question those conclusions, arguing, in effect, that a form of dependent development was possible—in which industrialization occurs under the aegis of foreign capital. Extending that line of reasoning, Warren argues that political independence, interimperialist rivalries, regional blocs, the presence of the communist countries, and popular demands have increased the bargaining power of Third World countries and created the basis for Third World industrialization, which is increasingly independent and gradually reducing inequalities between the imperial centers and the Third World. He concludes by arguing that the obstacles to development in Third World countries are mostly internal.

Our criticism focuses on the approach theory and data that Warren presents. We will argue that Warren's method of observing "sectors" in isolation from each other severely flaws his analysis; his failure to examine the political and social structures that inform "growth" vitiates his efforts to identify the limitation and impediments to long-term, large-scale industrial growth. At the theoretical level, there is an inadequate statement concerning the key relations between imperialism and capitalist development in the Third World. Related to that is the failure to specify the relationship between industrial growth and imperialism. For us, the issue is not the presence or absence of industrialization, but its nature, which in turn requires an understanding of the class relations, state forms, and class struggles imposed by international capitalist expansion.

## Third World Industrialization According to Warren

As a reflection of the direction of some socialist scholarship away from stagnationist theories of underdevelopment, Bill Warren's article, "Imperialism and Capitalist Industrialization"[6] addresses an important issue. The ambiguities and lack of theoretical sophistication of such concepts as "underdevelopment" and "dependency" indeed beset current Marxist analyses of the world capitalist system. However, Warren's recent contribution to that subject, rather than advancing the analysis of international political economy, has temporarily mystified and redirected it.

Warren's argument is based upon the proposition that some capitalist industrialization in the Third World has been realized and that the prospects for sustaining the process are indeed quite good. The most significant phenomenon responsible for this, Warren asserts, is the loosening of dependency ties as national capitalisms develop in the Third World—evening out the distribution of power in the postwar capitalist world economy. Any obstacles to the industrialization process are internal to the Third World countries and no longer reside in current relationships between imperialist countries and the Third World. In fact, according to Warren, "imperialism declines as capitalism grows." That is, the original "international system of inequality and exploitation called imperialism" has "created the conditions for the destruction of this system by the spread of capitalist social relations and productive forces throughout the noncapitalist world."

To substantiate these far-reaching claims, Warren correctly warns the reader that empirical observations will be the burden of his article. And a burden they are, not only in their incapacity to support his claims but also because the conclusions Warren draws from his data follow the logic of isolating, and considering in isolation, only one element of a structured whole. Indeed, Warren's method of analysis is to isolate sectors of Third World economy from the rest of the economy, as well as from the political and social structures which condition and result from the circumstances of enclave growth. Imperial-induced fragmentation in the Third World economy is reflected in the author's fragmented approach in studying "capitalist industrialization." This creates several problems.

First, one looks in vain for a theoretical justification of the *separation* of imperialism and capitalism: the essential point of dispute is never confronted—that is, that imperialism is the expression of the inherent tendencies of capital to universalize itself, to expand across national boundaries simultaneously with its internal concentration in the imperial centers. Second, the *dynamic* of this system and how it is organized is similarly not addressed (whether the multinational embodies the drive or is merely an "organizational form" is a discussion for another time). Once that dynamic is identified, the problem then shifts to the *direction* and *types* of economic orientation that the outward expansion manifests: regions (industrial, semi-industrial, agro-mineral) and economic areas (minerals, food stuffs, industries, etc.). Only then can one reasonably address the conditions internal to the target region or country. Yet Warren avoids this problem also.

In short, it appears that Warren discusses somewhat inadequately the manifestation on outward forms and expressions of imperialism within conjunctural situations. Imperialism is treated neither systematically nor in the time frame adequate for a historical analysis. The "facts" strung together are not linked to any theoretical conception, nor are actions and events connected and explained by any notion of the directions of *historical* change. Historical instances, all of them reversible, are not capable of providing the benchmarks that define a new historical epoch. The problem is not merely one of looking for the "agencies" of change, revolution, or whatever, but of understanding that at their base economic activities are carried out by human beings who enter into social relations.

## Warren's Theoretical Muddle

Before investigating Warren's construction of evidence, we must first elaborate and examine what may be regarded as his theoretical muddle. An unsystematic theoretical and conceptual foundation clears the way for the most vulgar empiricism—that is, the arrangement of various discrete "facts," *fragmenting* the particular totality and *redefining* it on the basis of the mistaken assumptions behind the selection and presentation of those facts.

### *Imperialism*

The thrust of Warren's treatment of imperialism lies in his conception of it as a temporary historical phase of capitalist expansion, which is now in decline due to "a major upsurge of national capitalisms." We learn that the "historical mission" of imperialism was to "spread the capitalist system and advance the productive forces throughout the world," and that upon completion of that process imperialism is destroyed by its progeny: "national capitalisms." Such a homogenizing view of capitalist expansion—a universalist image of a kind of reversible domino theory—assumes away the structural-historical process through which capitalism universalizes itself in an increasingly integrated world market. Such an image is not one to which Marx, Lenin, Luxemburg, or Bukharin would lend their weight (as Warren modestly suggests), particularly since Warren misunderstands the forces of destruction inherent in the imperialist system; namely, the socioeconomic crises and the development of the class struggle precipitated by the structural contradictions in the capitalist mode of production.

Thus, on the one hand, Warren presents an undifferentiated notion of "the advance of productive forces," and, on the other, he chooses to historicize imperialism as an expendable feature of the capitalist epoch. What is missing from Warren's thesis is any attempt to address the process of capital accumulation that bears directly upon the *character* of the development of productive forces and gives rise to imperialism as a specific form of the process at the level of international socioeconomic relations. Warren's view of imperialism as a temporary phenomenon is an inadequate formulation. Rather, imperialism is the international expression of *capitalism's* historical mission to develop the forces of production, in accordance with the logic of capital accumulation, which is by nature an uneven and contradictory process. Accordingly, imperialism does not simply preside over an undifferentiated spread of the capitalist system throughout the world, and then, when the task is done, politely withdraw in the "nonantagonistic" environment that Warren imputes to current imperialist-periphery relationships. Imperialism is an integral condition and consequence of the nature of the accumulation process, whose tendency to concentration and centralization of capital is the determining element in the structure and distribution of the forces of production and international relations. It is not an ultimately independent variable to which "indigenous capitalisms" are temporarily "tied."

Warren speaks of imperialism as a "system" without ever attempting an explanation of the origins or mechanisms of such a system, other than to assert that it is one of "inequality, domination and exploitation." Without any clue to the mainsprings of imperialism, we have no way of understanding why imperialism should appear, and then disappear. If there is no theory of imperialism, there can be no comprehension of its historical development such that its contemporary manifestations can be analyzed.

Warren's amorphous conception of imperialism ultimately stems from his apparent lack of a theory of capitalism. He tautologically defines "successful" capitalist development "as that development which provides the appropriate economic, social and political conditions for the continuing reproduction of capital, as a social system representing the highest form of commodity production." No theoretical guidelines are advanced, and no historical analysis is provided that suggests under what conditions capital reproduces itself (ad infinitum?) and, more specifically, what character that reproduction imparts to the accumulation process (undifferentiated units of capital?). No mention is made of the social relations of production that are produced and reproduced as the condition of capital accumulation—and therefore no element of conflict or contradiction is introduced, in accordance with the harmonious image of capitalism that Warren projects in his thesis of "national capitalisms" undermining imperialism. Furthermore, there is no discussion of the *sphere* of this "successful capitalist development," other than an implicit assumption that "appropriate" conditions are to be realized at the national level, specifically in the Third World. If one is setting up a model of this sort and alluding to a system "representing the highest form of commodity production," then it is insufficient to isolate the manufacturing sector as one aspect of capitalist development. Such a model requires, for instance, attention to the transformation of agriculture into a capitalist enterprise, as part of the general development of the home market, which is a necessary condition for the realization of the highest development of the commodity form. An analysis at the level of the national unit disintegrates the structure of international capitalism and, therefore, assumes away the very totality whose character determines the social relations of production and the uneven sectorial configurations within each Third World country.

### *Industrialization*

Warren's conceptualization of industrialization suffers from similar disabilities as his notion of "successful capitalist development." Specifically, he makes no attempt to delineate the character of "capitalist industrialization" in the Third World, which can become meaningful only within the international dimension that Warren, for analytic purposes, ignores, or at best holds constant.

Warren's notion of "industrialization" assumes that a "single" comparable type exists, thus losing sight of the significance of the different experiences, with their correspondingly different meanings, of the various Third World countries. Industrialization, at this level, *exists in many forms*, for instance: (a) assembly plant operations; (b) low-level industrial technology (complementing highly technical industrialization in the imperialist countries); (c) the establishment of import-substitution industries—essentially confined to short-run efforts; and (d) the establishment of capital-intensive industry with little positive, and sometimes negative, impact upon the domestic labor force in the long run. Moreover, another form pattern relates to the cyclical character of industrialization, which often, is expressed in sequences of political crises, such as those in, for example, Brazil and Indonesia, where the pattern has been one of stagnation, giving rise to social challenge, followed by repression. Warren's notion of industrial-capitalist progress is vague enough to embrace both the stagnation and destruction of the forces of production and totalitarian control, as well as the production of goods and services. An undifferentiated notion of manufacturing progress in the Third World countries is completely removed from specific experiences.

The term "industrialization" can cover a number of processes: (a) simple elaboration of raw material; (b) the transformation of processed raw material into parts; (c) assembly of parts; (d) creation of machinery (capital goods) to sustain the process of industrialization; (e) consumption of a substantial proportion of industrial output; and (f) research and design of products and machinery (patents, licenses). Under the aegis of the multinational corporation, this process has been fragmented: each "industrializing" colony or semicolony partakes of a part of the industrial process, but not the whole. Much of what Warren has euphemistically referred to as "industrialization" has been in large part "assembly plant" operations. Hence, to assume the equivalence of capitalist industrialization within imperial centers and within the Third World is to overlook essential differences in the structure of industry, as well as the rather significant differences that each has on class structure. To equate the fragmented, externally integrated, and technologically dependent industrialization of the Third World with that of Western imperial countries is also to ignore the vast qualitative differences in the levels of development of productive forces, as well as the tentative and vulnerable nature of the industrial efforts in the Third World.

### *Independence/Dependence*

As a consequence of Warren's linear image of the global spread of capitalism under the aegis of "imperialism," his allusions to independence and dependence are divested of any operational meaning within the structure of the international capitalist economy. A geographical representation of world capitalist expansion obscures structural relationships established in the historical process of the internationalization of capital—relationships that determine the character of the forces of production and class formations within Third World countries.

Warren's thesis is that formal, political independence in the Third World has been directly responsible for fostering industrialization, the effect of which has been to alter the character of inequality between imperialist and Third World countries. Warren does not analyze the basis of that inequality and its modification, except in terms of statistical comparisons showing relative levels of industrial growth between imperial and Third World nations. We have already noted that this procedure confuses externally induced (primarily) industrial expansion with its physical location, making this sort of empirical consideration of "inequality" a rather more complicated exercise. More seriously, the mystification inherent in Warren's conceptualization of imperialist relations of "inequality, domination and exploitation" as being determined at the level of *national* relationships is an expression of the very "Third Worldism" he purports to oppose. That is, the conceptual implications of "underdevelopment" under imperialism, as matched against an unstated ideal criterion of development, obscure an understanding of the historical and contradictory process of international capital accumulation, whereby elements of outlying societies have necessarily developed a specific structural relationship, and not a linear relationship, with the centers of world capitalism.

The confusion of the structure of international capitalist economy with its constituent societies gives rise to Warren's facile discussion of independence. The amorphous view of unequal and exploitative relationships between nations is an ideological formulation that removes the dimensions of inequality and exploitation from their basic sphere: the social relations of production of capitalism. Warren's discussion, conducted in terms of undifferentiated Third World nations, makes no attempt to analyze the internal and external relationships of classes in an international economy dominated by the capitalist mode of production. It is these relationships, and their concrete political manifestations in the experiences of Third World countries, that should constitute the point of departure for any historical analysis of the nature of independence and dependence. Certainly, as Warren argues, "independence" is not completely chimerical, but he must complete the dialectic: independence/interdependence. The ultimate question is not whether Third World countries are politically independent, but is: How do these states mediate capitalist expansion according to their class composition and their structural links within the international economy?

Warren abstractly states that "formal political independence gives underdeveloped countries a degree of manoeuvre and initiative which, over time, must inevitably come into play, and which is conducive to economic advance." He does not discuss the *limits* or *confines* of the bargaining power of Third World countries, the *limits* of playing off foreign powers, the problem of backsliding, limited gains, and regressive processes—he only cites specific gains. He makes no systematic attempt to summarize the experience of a *variety* of countries *over time* to provide an evaluation. Each example of gain can be refuted with cases of loss. For example, Chile's and Bolivia's bargaining positions changed drastically within two years. Peru's nationalization of oil was matched by the extension of new oil concessions. And there are many others. Obviously, the politicoeconomic process is much more complex than one of totaling up points on a scoresheet. The problem is one of *basic approach*—decisions, tactics, or conjunctural occurrences take place within a world economy, and the distribution of power is such that resources are quite concentrated, while the forces of production and control are quite unbalanced. To reduce the problem to isolated measures of particular regimes is to substitute a discussion of episodes for a global structural-historical analysis of the Third World.

## *Trends*

Generalizing on a tricontinental scale, Warren projects the following trends: "rapidly advancing industrialization" (with a "sustained momentum"); "burgeoning economic nationalism"; "growing sectoral diversification"; and "the development of capitalist social relations in the more primitive sectors." His evaluation of trends, conducted in simple *ceteris paribus* fashion from a selection of empirical "evidence," proceeds to interpretive assertions such as prediction of "a major upsurge of national capitalisms"; "the balance of power has shifted . . . towards a more even distribution of power"; and "imperialism declines as capitalism grows." To leap from statistical patterns (which are not significant in terms of Warren's thesis, as we shall see) to the assumption that they reflect the scenario of a transformation of international political economy constitutes a questionable use of empiricist methodology. Abstraction from political and structural processes and projection of linear trends from statistical tables provide no grounds for the theoretical conclusions that Warren advances.

The summary of trends that Warren describes are gross descriptions that contain distortions (uneven development, cyclical patterns, fragmented processes), omissions (overthrow of economic nationalists, reversal of trends, rise of pro-imperialist regimes in the major Third World centers such as Brazil, Indonesia, Iran, South Africa, and Israel), exaggerations (diversification is still primitive), and, most important and underlying the trend analysis, a misreading of the essential imperialist dynamic underlying "industrial expansion" and "the development of capitalist social relations." This dynamic involves the sweeping expansion of imperial capital from the dynamic imperial centers.

Warren misreads the imperialist dynamic, which involves the sweeping expansion of capital from the imperial centers, the takeover of marketing operations, and the import of technologies that form the base of the Third World's social-economy, combined with the increasing penetration of all aspects of the superstructure (the state and its administration, civilian politics, and the military). The unequal interpenetration of national and imperial enterprises has been matched by the increasing and unequal interdependence of Third World states (increasingly militarized) with the imperial state and multinational corporations. Rather than witnessing a major upsurge of national capitalisms, we are seeing the establishment of nondurable (Chile), faltering (Argentina, Egypt), or erratic (Peru, Libya) national capitalisms in the midst of postnational societies (Black Africa, East Asia, Central/South America) increasingly integrated into the imperial network through regional subimperialist powers (Brazil, Iran, Indonesia), which manifest the dual characteristics of colonized and expansionist nations. Warren's simplified "homogenizing" description of the Third World is a poor substitute for a concrete historical analysis of the contradictory trends within each area. The complex and varying relationship between Third World countries and the imperial countries, and between certain Third World countries with special relationships to imperial centers and the rest of the Third World, undermines the basic interpretative assertions that inform Warren's essay.

## Warren's Evidence and Interpretation

Following his arrangement of sections, we must now consider the evidence Warren presents to support his predictions.

### *Undifferentiated "Growth"*

Warren's argument that "substantial" and "sustained" progress has been made in Third World industrialization is based on absolute figures of manufacturing output over time. The exercise is essentially one of *comparing* manufacturing growth rates and occupational distribution (the manufacturing labor force as a percentage of the total active population) in the Third World countries with those statistics for the developed countries. Whereas Warren sees a tendency for Third World manufacturing growth to outpace that in the developed countries, comparison by occupational distribution (which indicates to him the extent of an economy's construction of "modern productive forces") presents a less cheerful picture; nevertheless, he finds "progress [being] made in some important Third World countries." Such a comparative exercise suffers from two primary defects: (1) Warren artificially separates the Third World from the developed capitalist countries when considering the locus of industrial expansion; and (2) the exercise assumes that what is being compared, namely Third World and developed economies, have similar historical and economic experiences subsumed under the statistical concept Gross Domestic Product.

We have already drawn attention to the conceptual difficulties underlying Warren's use of the term "industrialization." The basic problem with his measurement of growth is that he considers industrial expansion purely on the basis of its geographical location, with no attempt to assess whether and to what degree the expansion is internally or externally derived. How much of what he describes is "Third World industrialization," how much is due to or linked to foreign capital, and how much is for its benefit (profits, market expansion and control)? For the purposes of his argument ("upsurge of national capitalisms"), it is insufficient to include in statistical accounts expansion on the basis of physical location—separating such expansion from any external linkages. In fact, if we wish to engage in counting exercises, then the industrial expansion of firms abroad is an additional measure of the expansion of imperialist countries, a process which tends to limit the area of national capital in the Third World. Warren ignores these implications, apparently not only because they are concealed in statistical tables, but also because his geographical image of the linear growth of "national capitalisms" fostered by independent governments precludes confronting the issue of external/internal expansion. One expression of this is Warren's comment that Third World manufacturing output grew at a faster rate between 1960 and 1968 than did that in the advanced capitalist world "*despite* the fact that during the 1960s industrial growth in the developed capitalist world has been exceptionally high by historical standards." (Emphasis added.)

On a comparative basis, in countries with a low base line of industrialization, the rates of growth of manufacturing are less important than volume—and here the gap between imperial and Third World countries is growing enormously. Taking figures from Warren's table showing the world production of manufactures by continent, we can observe the difference in volume between 1937 and 1959:

| | (1937) | (1959) |
|---|---|---|
| Imperial countries | 103 | 244 |
| Third World countries | 12 | 35 |
| | 91 | 209 |

Warren's attempt to buttress his optimism about Third World manufacturing growth rates by citing annual average rates of manufacturing growth for selected countries is nonsense, since he includes no data on the base lines from which this procoess began in each country. Again, his presentation leaves aside the question of whether subsidiary firms anchored in the metropolises can be classified as "Third World." As a concept, GDP may be somewhat useful in measuring the expansion of services and products in the imperial centers, but in the Third World what is being measured is not usually "domestic" product, but expansion by and for imperial enterprises which happen to be located there. The most modern "dynamic industries" in the Third World—which are the fastest growth sectors—are controlled by metropolitan conglomerates.

From his presentation of the average annual growth rates of manufacturing, Warren argues that the "unique feature of the postwar Third World, taken as a whole, is its sustained momentum over a period longer than any previously recorded." Such a remark cannot be sustained if time series data revealing a cyclical pattern of industrial expansion interrupted by crises is included. For example, growth conditions in Brazil alternated between a boom in the 1950s, stagnation in the early and mid-1960s, and boom again in the late 1960s. To average out growth conditions is to conceal the specific problems of industrial expansion in the Third World, and thus to abstract from the particular social configurations and the structure of the economies, which vitally affect the character of industrial expansion. One consideration ignored by Warren is the phenomenon of internal colonialism; by citing *industrial growth* apart from overall growth, he avoids dealing with the size of the sector affected and its relationship to and impact upon the Third World's economy. In Latin America for instance, the overall growth rate between the mid-1950s and mid-1960s was low, yet industry expanded. Excluding the various conditions of industrial expansion allows Warren to project quite unqualified and optimistic assertions, devoid of any direct recognition of the contradictions accompanying that phenomenon. The thesis of cyclical industrial expansion within a generally stagnating economy is more accurate than his account.

Warren claims from his observations of absolute growth rates that there has been a significant "redistribution of world industrial power." To measure distribution of world industrial *power* by "growth rates" of industry, which encompasses economies starting from the barest minimum of industrial production and covers a generation, is delightful simplicity. The volume of production, the level of technology, the research capabilities, the allocation of resources, the development of education, and the use of manpower are at least equally relevant to measuring the historic capacity of a country to become a significant industrial power. Indeed, in the past Third World countries manifested "industrial expansion" (India in the eighteenth century, Paraguay and Argentina in the nineteenth, for instance), which, however, could not be sustained against the influx of foreign capital, with its greater productive capacities and military capabilities. Warren claims to be able to prove "redistribution" of industrial power, but, for scarcity of data or lack of conceptual lucidity, he scrapes up the notion of a 1 percentage point difference in the industrial growth rate between the imperial centers and the Third World—a very slender reed upon which to hang such a weighty theoretical claim!

In fact, the growth of the proportion of industry to GDP is in part accounted for by the stagnant nature of nonmanufacturing sectors in the Third World; and in the imperial countries the expansion of agricultural production and skilled services account for a greater proportion of GDP. Likewise, if one is to compare *within* Third World economies the expansion of low-productivity and low-paying services with high-growth industries, over twice as many workers are entering the former, compared with the latter. Warren's undifferentiated chart of manufacturing growth in the Third World obscures this phenomenon. The use of percentages of GDP does not tell us anything about the interrelationship of sectors, which conditions industrial growth, and hence has little to say about the elimination of the conditions of underdevelopment. Manufacturing in Mexico, Argentina, Chile, and Iran depends on exports of raw materials to sustain it; the principal market is external; and the few lines of manufacturing exports are foreign owned. The industrialization process in these cases is subject to considerable external constraints, which fetter the internal expansion and development of the capitalist mode of production. Warren's method of comparison is misplaced—particularly when he fails to take account of the imperial centers' highly developed and mechanized agricultural sectors, which should be considered as part of their industrial growth and one condition of it. Including agriculture in his comparison would greatly heighten the differences between the proportions of the industrial sector and the GDP of the two areas.

### *Independence and Industrialization*

Warren's characterization of the economic consequences of formal independence is that it releases both external constraints upon and internal forces compelling industrialization. With respect to the latter, he claims: "Independence has been a *direct cause* (not just a permissive condition) of industrial advance in that it has stimulated popular pressures for a higher living standard where these have been a major internal influence sustaining industrialization policies."

Such a characterization again fails to differentiate among politicoeconomic conditions. "Independence" by itself has not been the direct cause of "industrial advance"; rather, industrial advance has taken place in some countries as a result of *particular* mass struggles, mobilizations, and national leadership. On the other hand, one could say that the Third World countries with the "greatest advance," in Warren's terms, have been those least independent of foreign controls, for example, Brazil, Indonesia, and Zaire. Moreover, if we measure industrial expansion by the nationality of the capital rather than its geographic location, then these dependent countries do not show the same "advances." By shifting his argument between "industrial advances" and "national capitalism," Warren obscures any distinction by subsuming foreign-induced industrial expansion under the category of "national." Contrary to Warren, "popular pressure" in the high-growth dependent countries has been the least effective stimulus to expansion. In the cases of Brazil, Indonesia, and Zaire, the conditions for what Warren chooses to describe as "industrial advance" have been massacres and repressive forms of mass control. And since industrial growth is largely foreign induced, the *sine qua non* of large-scale foreign involvement has been the reduction or elimination of popular pressure.[7] Warren, in fact, makes passing reference to the nature of the political regimes in

Brazil and Iran as a brand of "economic nationalism," which he then proceeds to lump together with "dependence on and alliance with U.S. imperialism," and by so doing reveals the contradiction in his own argument.

Indeed, Warren's analysis of the conjunctural aspects of international and internal politicoeconomic forces during the Cold War period leaves a lot to be desired. The relationship of the intensive political and economic integration of the international capitalist economy in this period (particularly by the United States) with the internal policies of Third World states is an issue to which Warren pays little attention in his discussion of independence. What he has done is amalgamate the periods of popular mobilization leading to national independence with the post-independence *demobilization* of those popular forces that created the conditions for dependent industrialization—for instance, in countries such as India, Algeria, Indonesia, Nigeria, and Kenya.

With respect to the Third World's domestic economic policy, Warren argues that such institutional measures as "control banks, export-import and currency controls, taxation and expenditure systems, and new para-state policy-making agencies . . . can have a decisive effect on growth." In fact, those agencies cited as increasing "institutional control," while purporting to direct national efforts have not infrequently been agencies for channeling national resources to foreign interests: providing investment funds to foreign capital, offering low-cost infrastructural facilities and services, meeting foreign interest payments, encouraging branch-plant penetration of domestic markets, and so on.* Warren then argues that the effects of such institutional measures, and the resulting circumstances he attributes to them,

* Moreover, Warren's style of argument in itself characterizes his general tendency to frame his discussion as conditional. This mode of arguing is theoretically and operationally irrefutable, and hence proves nothing. The time and conditions of fulfillment not being specified (or being forecast for an undisclosed future) allows the author limitless speculation. Not infrequently he shifts (without warning and without providing the missing data) from the "conditional" to the assertive; from being a possibility, in some time and place, the said results are then asserted to have taken place. Indeed, Warren's entire discussion of independent industrialization in the Third World follows this framework.

extend beyond industrialization. Arguing that a substantial extension of capitalist social relations, particularly in agricultural and urban sectors, has taken place, he claims erroneously the " 'stagnation' in the Third World is largely a myth." Clearly, it is absurd to equate stagnation with precapitalist societies, just as it is nonsense to argue that capitalist societies do not stagnate. Furthermore, Warren uses the concept "capitalist social relations of production" so vaguely, without reference to the role of central planning in some countries, as to include (seemingly) incongruous cases—for instance, are *capitalist* social relations spreading to Tanzania, or are *noncapitalist* relations evolving? Similarly, to argue that capitalist social relations of production (which is not necessarily equivalent to commodity production) have extended to agriculture throughout the Third World is an over generalization that neglects an assessment of the considerably varied performance of agriculture by area (generally, Latin American agricultural relations of production are not dynamic), by product (in Latin America the food product is low, and cash crops, subject to world market fluctuations, show great unpredictability), and by its impact upon different classes of producers (for example, the impoverished circumstances of a significant population of agro-laborers and small farmers). In addition, the variability of cash-crop production affects the whole economy; and that observation draws attention to Warren's insufficient sectoral analysis, which ignores economic interrelationships. With respect to the urban sector, Warren argues that another aspect of productive expansion lies in the encouragement of small firms, which "cannot simply be described as second-best occupations for frustrated job-seekers in the modern sector." Again Warren's analysis suffers from an undifferentiated conception of capitalist productive performance. The bulk of industrial productive expansion is not accounted for by "small firms," which characteristically are structurally marginal to the highly monopolized industrial sectors in Third World economies. The phenomenon of urbanization is overwhelmingly accompanied by the proliferation of unproductive "penny capitalists"[8] on the fringes of the modern sector, offering little or no remunerative employment.

In a general overview, Warren argues that the conditions of

independence have promoted an interest among new regimes in restructuring their economies "along lines more suited to a successful indigenous capitalism, less subordinated to the needs of the imperialist countries." This is another example of Warren's failure to specify the conditions and historical experiences associated with economic restructuring. While regimes may be interested in it, economic restructuring has not been successful either in eliciting a massive favorable response from "indigenous" capitalists—whose interests are often tied to those of the land-owning classes and foreign trade/capital—or in being able *over time* to avoid subordination to imperialism. The tendency has been to return to some form of dependence, as we have seen with the regimes of Getulio Vargas, Juan Perón, Paz Estenssorro, and Juan Velasco. Thus, the choice becomes one of establishing state industry or of allowing the influx of foreign capital.

In the context of international relations, Warren suggests that East-West and interimperialist rivalries have had significant positive influences upon the Third World's economic advance. However, if East-West rivalries were conditions for economic advance, then détente should worsen conditions, which hardly squares with Warren's optimistic prognostication. Cold War rivalries did lead in some cases to advantageous circumstances, but not in others—for example, Iran, Guatemala, the Congo, and Indonesia. Clearly, the same may be true of interimperialist rivalries—with the major qualification that, challenged by *social* revolutions, the rivalries tend to diminish. Furthermore, the fact that European and Japanese capital is increasingly being invested in the Third World does not necessarily involve conflict or mean that Europe and Japan are rivals. As the Watson, Perkens, Pearson, and Jackson Reports (1956–1970)[9] foreshadowed, a strong case can be made for joint exploitation—combined investments by consortia are in fact being realized. The interimperialist rivalry is tempered by the interpenetration of capital in large-scale corporations, the formation of consortia, and financial cartels. In any event, there is no evidence that imperial "competition" has led to *national* capital growth: all imperial centers are attempting to expand, not only in competition but also in collaboration, thus limiting the areas of national capital.

The Economic Commission for Latin America (ECLA), which Warren cites to support his argument, is more cautious about the issue. It sees the problem of competition between subsidiaries of firms as a *possibility*—hardly the "new phase of imperialist rivalries" that Warren asserts is upon us. The demiurge of Third World countries rapidly industrializing—*independently* of imperial centers, *because of* imperial centers, or *despite* imperial domination, as Warren variously has it—sets aside the problem of the cyclical pattern of expansion, stagnation, crises, and expansion that characterizes the process. Capitalism in the Third World has expanded over the past twenty-five years through crises and contradictions, extracting an enormous toll because of its irregular growth. What Warren descriptively refers to as "contradictions" (his internal obstacles to "capitalist industrialization") are derivative conditions, which, while politically salient, are not determinants of economic processes, but *products* of them.

The vast differences *between* Third World countries in industrial levels, in terms of the sequences they follow, and contradictions they encounter, in the history of their industrialization, and in the particular imperial circumstances require an analytical ordering of the countries to understand both the conditions for expansion and the limits of it. First, there are the Third World countries which, having begun industrialization early, have advanced the furthest along these lines. Over the past decades they have experienced periods of stagnation, and the least rapid rates of industrial expansion and have encountered problems in going beyond import-substitution industrialization. Then there are the less industrial countries that started industrializing later and have experienced more rapid rates of growth, but which, upon exhausting the possibility of easy import-substitution, enter into stagnation and crisis. Indeed, no country has yet shown the capacity to overcome the phenomena of stagnation and periodic crises, including the most industrially advanced Third World countries. Most evidence is adverse; the Brazilian and Mexican option of substituting industrial exports for a limited internal market has yet to be tested over time. Furthermore, it is not at all clear that the internal conditions and external conjuncture (size, resources, labor market, repression, low living standards) that allowed Brazil to assume its role can be replicated. Certainly, the efforts of Argentina, Bolivia, and Uruguay to follow Brazil were far from smashing successes.

In arguing for the advantages of imperialist rivalries, Warren advances the proposition that foreign capital has favored Third World industrialization, investing so much in heavy and export-oriented industry that the composition of Third World exports has been reversed. Warren even cites Robert McNamara as an advocate of development for counter-revolutionary purposes. Characteristically, Warren provides no data to support this claim. In fact, the great proportion of foreign investment is still in raw materials and industries for internal comsumption; and the quote from McNamara refers to a "minimal degree" of development (not of great leaps in dynamic, export-oriented capital goods industries). Industries that are established for export within the Third World are usually extensions of metropolitan enterprises "exporting" goods back to the home market or are meant to capture regional markets. Precious little is "national" about them: they take advantage of cheap labor and the lower costs of shipping finished products as opposed to raw materials. A great many foreign industries are hardly dynamic movers of the economy—many of their enterprises were nationally owned firms purchased at bargain prices during one of the recurring economic crises. Most foreign industries ship profits out of the country, pay few or no taxes on import duties, pay low rents, low salaries, use domestic savings, capture internal markets, buy up existing national firms—in a word, contribute very little in many cases to "developing" the economy. Similarly, Warren's evaluation of the impact of international financial institutions upon development is superficial and lacks reference to experience. The International Monetary Fund (IMF) has consistently advocated deflationary anti-development projects, while the World Bank has facilitated foreign capital's expansion, the denationalization of capital, agro-development, and little national development. ECLA formulas, while more concerned with national development, have seldom corresponded to the real behavior of ruling classes.

### *The Meaning of Dependence*

Warren's position on the meaning of "dependence" is marked by his refusal to take the concept seriously, choosing instead to extend his thesis of "independent industrialization." This, he concludes, is highly ambiguous. The increase in economic interdependence within the capitalist world and the collaboration of ruling, exploitative, classes throughout the world against socialism and the masses, both mean that the issue would be more accurately posed in terms of equality between previously unequal 'partners' in an increasingly interdependent relationship."

In the course of his argument Warren refers to "*pressures*" that are brought to bear on foreign capital by Third World nations. From this he argues that political independence aids the growth of Third World "industrial power," which in turn enhances "political power," the conclusion being that "conflicts occur within a long-term framework of eventual accommodation mutually acceptable and mutually advantageous to *both* sides." If by "sides" Warren were referring to classes, then this latter comment would have some validity. However, the argument is not conducted at the level of class analysis, and necessarily it considers categories such as "capital investment," "technology," and "nations" as independent/central factors without recognizing that they are subordinated to social relationships.

Lacking clarity over the forms and mechanisms through which dependence can be analyzed, Warren's discussion of "pressures" also lacks specificity. He does not analyze the social forces exerting "pressure," nor their political goals, let alone specify the political direction of sociohistoric forces in relation to the problem of dependence. Warren substitutes an inventory of the aspects of economic processes for a clear understanding of the levels of dependence and attempts to describe (without much success) the control of nationals over discrete aspects of a fragmented process. Never are the social relations between different class forces in the Third World and their foreign counterparts spelled out; the notion of "national" is so mystified as to vitiate any understanding of the bonds and linkages that could lead ruling groups within nations to collaborate with external forces in the process of social and economic exploitation. Capital is mobilized, bargaining takes place, pressures are exerted, nationalization (of sorts) takes place by what are described as the "underdeveloped countries." Warren makes no *critical assessment* of the experiences of the different class-based regimes in the Third World; policies seem to be the product of "underdeveloped conditions." Warren never distinguishes among "bargaining" over the terms of dependence, diversification of dependence, and national development. Nor does he introduce a distinction between ameliorative "bargaining" and revolutionary action. He confuses efforts by a country to alter its exchange relationships with foreign capital (much as a trade union might alter the wages and immediate conditions of labor) with the elimination of imperialist exploitation.

Imperial companies located abroad to exploit cheap labor and resources and to ship profits home are assumed to be acting for the Third World country. No evidence is presented showing the effects of the export of imperialists' manufacturing from the Third World on the development of countries' economies or on the mass of people. Throughout the account, the author assumes what he should be proving. Even his assumptions are mere projections of nascent tendencies occurring in limited contexts (i.e., export manufacturing); for example, the export of manufacturing by foreign subsidiaries of imperial firms to imperial markets is accounted a "remarkable success" for the Third World. When Warren is not assuming that imperial capital is acting for Third World countries, he is arguing that Third World countries have acquired leverage over the operations of imperial capital or "national" control of them. For example, he suggests that "leverage potential for dealing with foreign firms" is gained by funding of foreign subsidiaries from local sources or reinvested earnings or both. The figures he cites to indicate the financial sources of the subsidiaries are submerged in accounting percentages generated for tax purposes, which have little meaning for the financial operations of internationally integrated corporations—which can decide at what point to take out profits. International corporations do not determine their financial dealings by a particular subsidiary's physical location, but by the overall expansion policies for their total operations. Warren's treatment of "national" control lacks a discussion of the mechanisms by which foreign capital uses the appearance of national participation to secure a "low profile," while maintaining the predominance of external decision-making and imperial profit-making. In Mexico, for instance, we have seen the phenomenon of national "front men" who hold stocks only nominally. In Chile, under Eduardo Frei, external control was secured by national stock ownership without management prerogatives. And in Bolivia and the "banana republics," "national ownership" of exploitation: (a) operates as a channel for directing compensation payments to owners, and (b) remains subordinate to processing, refining, or commercial operations that are located or controlled externally. Generally, joint ventures work to integrate national ruling groups into a subordinate position, thus creating political conditions for more effective exploitation. There is no evidence that joint ventures have adversely affected imperial profit margins; there is evidence that coopted groups have identified with the interests of foreign-based companies.[10] The presence of multinationals cannot only lead to cooption, but if efforts are made in the direction of national control, can also spur violent overthrow of governments, military intervention, massacres, subversion, and economic blockades (for example: Chile, Dominican Republic, Bolivia, Brazil, Iran, and the list goes on).

Warren dismisses the issue of technological dependence as something that will wither away in due course with the growth of the industrial base of Third World countries. He tends to regard technology as a mere transferable commodity, without taking cognizance of the structural relationships embodied in it that limit the capacity of a country to break out of the imperial politicoeconomic orbit. Most large and medium-sized firms depend on foreign patents and licensing agreements, *and are content to be dependent*. Warren's thesis of long-term accommodation between imperial firms and Third World nations (noncontradiction between "periphery" and "center") confuse an argument against dependency with the *position* of particular classes in the dependent country. The development of new methods of exploitation (the service and management contracts that Warren regards as independent developments) complements traditional forms and extends the area of external penetration, while opening up the country to new areas of "traditional" (investor) exploitation. The expansion of imperial firms in manufacturing; the Third World's increasing technological dependence; and the financial, planning, and advisory aspects of foreign penetration have transformed the neocolonies by creating a new division of labor—indigenous police and infrastructural controls—and external control of growth and high-profit sectors.

Warren extrapolates aspects of the issue of technological dependence from the larger economic context in which it is embedded (i.e., Western technology is costly and inappropriate to Third World conditions, and along with local bourgeois dependence, it inhibits the development of national technology), and then reinserts his arguments into the context that he has constructed for providing answers in terms of his argument, namely, that "technology is to a large extent embodied in capital goods." Technological dependence is embedded in politicoeconomic *dependence:* without the latter, it is useless to speak of the former. No mere expansion of industry in Argentina, for instance, has led to greater technological independence. Warren's model of industry-research-technology does not apply to the Third World—especially since most dynamic industries are foreign owned and prefer to import technology (as do nationals to avoid long-term investments because of their relatively smaller capital capacity).

Warren's discussion of the "rationality" of foreign technology is contradictory in terms of his own argument. He writes that "the allegedly inappropriate technology of advanced capitalist firms to the needs of underdeveloped countries is, in many cases, actually a rational response to local conditions in these countries, rather than something imposed upon them regardless of local circumstances." Certainly the technology adopted by capital to meet the immediate demands of profit maximization is by nature rational, but from the point of view of the Third World *countries* that Warren is considering—national economies whose production structures do not prefigure those of advanced capitalist economies—foreign technology is inappropriate to the path of "national capitalisms" that he constructs. Technological transfer is blocked, or is expensive, or inappropriate and leads to few secondary effects: the high earnings from modern technology do not spread to the rest of the economy. The issue is one of the sociopolitical nature of a regime's orientation of technology, and the profits resulting from its organization—a dependent regime facilitates the flow of profits outward rather than inward.

In referring to the "integration policy of oil firms operating in the Middle East," Warren describes the expansion of satellite enterprises around imperial enclaves as "the spread of know-how." However, the relationship is one of the national social strata being linked to and dependent on the foreign enclave, which thus benefits from lower costs, the provision of local services, and the creation of political allies for its resource exploitation. The proliferation of dependent services is hardly an example of "spreading know-how" as it is spreading dependence. Permitting local entrepreneurs to extend the areas of exploitation and to act as agents for the transmission of an imperial ethos is hardly promoting *local* technology but is rather allowing the *products of* imperial-controlled technology to penetrate the local level. As a consequence of his empiricism, Warren confuses control with the locus of its application. The circumstances of satellites (or subcontractors) of imperial firms, the technological permeation of national firms, and the lack of national research and development all suggest that no *independent* technological development has taken place. Technological autonomy requires funding for research centers, laboratories, and scientists on the one hand and, on the other, design, application (modeling, pilot projects, etc.), testing, modification, and adaption to specific national uses. Few, if any, of these prerequisites for technological independence occur in the Third World. Indeed, given the small percentage of national firms' earnings going to research, the frequent closing of universities (and their small degree of national support), and the increase in royalties for licenses and patents, it is obvious that technological dependence is growing.

### *Imperialism as a World System*

As has already been pointed out, Warren removes his conception of imperialism from an analysis of capitalism. Capitalism is taken as a constant, while Warren extrapolates the decline of imperialism by discussing certain changing trends in economic processes. He takes a number of economic relationships, such as export growth, balance of payments, debt problems, the question of capital movements, the international division of labor, and the polarization thesis, and seeks to show that each item suggests favorable trends or benefits for the Third World. The logic of his argument is similar to that of constructing a balance sheet, and it gives rise to an assertion of "the disappearance of imperialism as a system of *economic inequality* between nations of the capitalist world system, and that there are no limits, in principle, to this process." Warren characterizes the Left as recognizing changes in economic trends which are "able to modify the imperialist system only within fairly narrow limits," but apparently does not understand that these limits are inherent in the structural-historical relationships through which *capitalism* expands internationally. It was Marx who first systematized the critique of bourgeois political economy, as being adept in its analysis of economic and productive relations, but failing to analyze the sociohistorical origins of its economic categories. Warren himself appears to be unable to address the basic social/class relationships of capitalist production, confining his discussion to economic phenomena. To speak of alterations in economic relationships without attempting an explanation of what they express in terms of the dynamics of international capitalism, gives rise to simplistic conclusions.

Warren speaks of advanced capitalist countries' economic expansion in the 1960s and the resulting increased participation of the Third World countries in trade, particularly as evidenced by "the rapid expansion in their exports of manufactures . . . From the perspective of relative national power balance in the capitalist world [this participation] is relevant." However, if export sectors are largely in the hands of imperial firms, the expansion and growth of trade is hardly an expression of dynamism of

Third World countries. As noted before, the failure to identify the social nature of expanding economic forces is a constant source of mystification in Warren's discussion.

The reference by Warren to the improvement of the underdeveloped countries' balance of payments also requires perspective. The phenomenon of increasing foreign reserves is neither laudable nor an indication of an expanding economy. It suggests instead an incapacity to absorb capital and devise new projects. The Third World countries with the greatest reserves are the most reactionary, i.e., Arab oil regimes. In Brazil, for instance, the accumulation of reserves has been accomplished through increasing foreign debt, which is growing twice as fast as the reserves.

On the issue of debt, Warren remarks, "Conceptually, the existence of debt or even growing debt in absolute or relative terms (e.g., relative to export earnings) is not by itself an indication of a debt problem. Debt is credit and a debt-servicing problem depends as much, if not more, on how the credit is used as on the terms of the borrowing." Warren does not expand on the implications of that comment by mentioning the political and socioeconomic experiences that attend the problem of debt. The salience of the debt-payment problem varies from year to year and from regime to regime—in part changing with the economic conditions in the dominant capitalist countries as well as with political changes in the Third World. Downward shifts in the economies of imperial countries resulting in a decline in imports, declines in the price of export commodities from the Third World, and shifts in the political orientation of a Third World government (from neocolonized to nationalist) have all been instrumental in making Third World countries susceptible to imperial-oriented development projects, such as austerity programs, credit freezes, and devaluations. Such externally induced crises have in turn led to bankruptcies of national firms (frequently purchased at a fraction of their value by imperial firms) and declining standards of living. Debts, debt-servicing, and emergency funding to maintain debt payments have thus been indirectly responsible for denationalizing economies, reducing living standards, and increasing political repression (Chile in the

1950s, Brazil in 1965, Uruguay in 1970, etc.). The imperial countries' use of debt as a political weapon was well illustrated during the Allende government's tenure in Chile.

In describing capital movements, Warren writes: "The theory of imperialism as a system for draining surplus-value from the periphery to the center has, of course, exactly the same defect as the popular equation of debt with a debt problem—that in comparing inward capital flows with the resulting outward flow of interest and profit what exactly is done with the capital 'in between,' so to speak, is ignored." To begin with, imperialism not only "drains" capital but also obtains raw materials whose impact on the imperial economy is multifold: for example, oil allows many industries essential to the imperial economy to function; cotton historically, was the basis of a substantial part of England's industrialization in the nineteenth century. Foreign investment not only creates a profit but also supplies products to the home industries, which in turn increase profits a hundredfold! The loss occasioned by products being integrated into the imperial industrial network is several times any short-term marginal gain that foreign investment provides to Third World countries. Warren's critique of the "capital-drainage" thesis is as follows:

1. Drainage of capital is worth the price paid for the establishment of productive facilities—hardly an argument as it is a "self-evident" truth;
2. Without foreign capital, "the necessary productive facilities would not have been created by indigenous businessmen or state institutions";
3. Despite previous displacement effects, "foreign private capital investment since the Second World War has probably created or encouraged indigenous capitalism." In fact, foreign capital continues to do both—it displaces profitable growth industries by its own dynamic/monopolistic superiority; it creates service satellites; and it encourages the takeover phenomenon, which is well known throughout Latin America (in Argentina, Brazil, Chile, etc.).

In fact, historically private investment in the Third World has extended imperial penetration and accelerated capital accumulation in the imperial centers. This has increasingly forced the imperial countries to rely on force to maintain "open markets" and heightened the interpenetration of imperial economies as nation-states compete for profits and scarce resources; meanwhile the cost of products imported to the Third World has increased. Inequality still persists between imperial centers and the Third World—not at the level of specific products, but at that of the development of the forces of production, whether the inequality be between imperial industrial exporters and Third World agro-mineral exporters, or imperial technico-industrial exporters and Third World agro-mineral exporters with a portion of assembly-part manufactures.

Finally, Warren, along with his image of world capitalism as a collection of distinct national economies rather than as a global system, characterizes world capitalism as "changing hierarchies of uneven development." It would be more precise not only to explain what is meant by the term "uneven development" rather than dissolving it into an empirical configuration of nations or power centers, but also to consider world capitalism as an imperial network that operates from the imperial metropolis through various centers (financial, subimperialist, military, commercial).

## *The Contradictions of Capitalist Industrialization*

Warren's essential argument on the contradictions of capitalist industrialization follows the theme:

> If the extension of capitalism into non-capitalist areas of the world created an international system of inequality and exploitation called imperialism, it simultaneously created the conditions for the destruction of this system by the spread of capitalist social relations and productive forces throughout the non-capitalist world . . . there are now more powerful forces at work than ever before which are spurning capitalist industrialization, and the various elements of imperialist control which exercised a retarding influence have largely disappeared.

As a summary statement of Warren's thesis, that statement reflects an essay full of contradictory statements about so-called basic trends, revealing a profound theoretical and methodological conclusion: all the major Third World countries that have experienced fragmented industrial expansion have done so as extensions of the operation of multinationals; many of the major infrastructural developments, which have been in great part funded by loans from imperial-controlled international financial banks or private imperial financial sources, have largely functioned in their design and execution to widen the scope of foreign capital's operation. The essential political condition that has facilitated industrial growth "from above and outside" has been a series of nonpopular pro-imperial regimes that largely rest on alliances between the military elite and propertied classes whose only recourse, given their inability to mobilize internal resources for development, is to bring in the foreigners. The device for establishing these externally oriented developmental regimes has been the coup by military and civilian officials, who in large part have been socialized and trained by the state apparatus of the imperial metropolis dominant in the region. The function of the property-based political-military regime is to create the political and social conditions that permit externally induced industrial growth without the dangers of "nationalization," wage demands, autonomous trade unions, or other forms of social pressure on profit rates. Thus, the Third World countries with the highest rates of fragmented industrialization are the ones with the highest concentration of foreign capital in modern industrial sectors, the highest rates of exploitation of labor, and the lowest proportion of workers in autonomous class-anchored social movements. Moreover, most are police states; many of their influential officials came to power with aid from the imperial state apparatus. The easy flow of capital that most permit into as well as out of the country is attracted by cheap labor, and it has little or no positive impact on employment or the standard of living.

We are referring to South Korea, Taiwan, Iran, Brazil, Indonesia, and the other examples of rapidly growing "national capitalism" that Warren so absentmindedly cites. Lacking an elementary class analysis of those countries, Warren cannot see that the essential contradiction between imperial-dominated industries/workers and peasants already highly visible in countries like Chile and Argentina (Cordoba especially), and earlier states like Cuba and the Dominican Republic makes nonsense of his statement that "current imperialist-periphery contradictions . . . are basically non-antagonistic." One should read again the memoranda of ITT. What passes for "class analysis" is a pastiche or colorful, if brief and inaccurate, inventory, which purports to describe the origins, orientation, and influence of several social classes. Having decided that the "petty bourgeoisie" and "professional classes" "provide not only much of the compulsion to industrialize, but also very often the social basis and personnel for industrialization of states," Warren neglects to offer any historical examples. The impulse for externally induced industrial growth has not come from the mass of small property holders and clerks but from landowners, export-importers, high military officials, and others of their class. As we have known for 200 years, the small-capital vision of the petty bourgeoisie has never been that of developing industrial societies. A casual observation of social regimes in the Third World shows that at best the petty bourgeois are the shock troops or functionaries of big capital. More important, the petty bourgeoisie has not wielded political power for long (although in particular conjunctures it has some electoral clout, free elections are not the norm, least of all in the rapidly "industrializing" countries cited by Warren), in part because it is such a heterogeneous and internally contradictory class that it lacks any clear notion of class interest and class solidarity except in exceptional circumstances. In the case of Chile, that "class consciousness" (better *Status* consciousness) was used against a regime bent on national industrialization.

In sum, lacking any theoretical anchor in the class structure of the societies which he is discussing, Warren's analysis is comprised of vague conceptions of "national industrialization" induced by mysterious social forces that increasingly pressure for industrialization, state management, and "national capitalism."

## Notes

1. Régis Debray, "Marxism and the Nation," *New Left Review* 105 (September-October 1977): 25–41.

2. Eric Hobsbawm, *The Italian Road to Socialism: An Interview with Giorgio Napolitano of the Italian Communist Party* (Westport, Conn.: Lawrence Hill, 1977).
3. Nicos Poulantzas, "The State and the Transition to Socialism," *Socialist Review* 38 (1978): 9–36.
4. Arghiri Emmanuel, "White-Settler Colonialism and the Myth of Investment Imperialism," *New Left Review* 73 (May-June 1972); also see his "Myths of Development Versus Myths of Underdevelopment," *New Left Review* 85 (August 1974): 61–82.
5. Bill Warren, "Imperialism and Capitalist Industrialization," *New Left Review* 81 (September-October 1973).
6. Ibid.
7. See, for example, the studies on Brazil by M. C. Tavares and José Serra in *Latin America: From Dependence to Revolution*, ed. James Petras (New York: John Wiley & Sons, 1973).
8. See, for example: Clifford Geertz, *Peddlers and Princes* (Chicago: University of Chicago Press, 1963).
9. Some of the more enlightened sectors of the ruling class in the advanced capitalist countries commissioned a series of reports dealing with the basic problems facing underdeveloped countries within the world capitalist system. The reports cited focused in part on the economic and social viability of various growth strategies and on the prospects for stabilization.
10. See in Petras, ed., *Latin America: From Dependence to Revolution* the essays on Argentina.

# 5

# THE LATIN AMERICAN AGRO-TRANSFORMATION FROM ABOVE AND OUTSIDE

Leftists and reformers have criticized Latin American agriculture as anachronistic and inefficient and as being a major brake on development and a source of economic stagnation—in a word, they consider it a semifeudal sector inhibiting the growth of a modern economy. For example, one author notes, "Although there is considerable variation from country to country and from region to region, on the whole the social system in rural Latin America is characterized by the latifundio or the hacienda (*fazenda* in Brazil) system."[1] According to that view, the labor force is organized within this archaic structure along several lines: petty commodity or subsistence production (minifundio) or some form of tenancy or sharecropping or both based on payment in wages and kind. The problems of economic expansion ("modernization") and equity are tied to proposals for "agrarian reform"—the redistribution of land and the reorganization of agriculture into family farms or cooperatives.

The reformists argue that agrarian reform creates the basis for economic development, popular participation, and social justice. Fundamental to this is the view of agrarian reform (in the sense of redistribution of land) as a vehicle for overcoming bottlenecks to capital accumulation. In this scenario, the landlord class is described as failing in its entrepreneurial function: not responding to the needs of the market, engaging in excessive consumption at the expense of investment and indulging in speculative activity.

My sense of the agrarian problem in Latin America is substantially different. One of the major factors affecting the transformation of Latin American rural life is the growing integration of agriculture into the world capitalist system and the concomitant transformation of the social relations of production within the agricultural unit. More specifically, the predominant tendency is the headlong transformation of agriculture into modern capitalist units, which may, however, sustain in a subordinate position precapitalist forms of agricultural activity. For example, the growth of corporate farming and the proliferation of subsistance small holders and marginal day laborers are two sides of the same coin. This capitalist transformation from above and largely from the outside has led to a substantial and sustained displacement of the agricultural labor force, evidenced not only in migrations from the countryside to the city but also in the growth of social movements with a different set of demands from previous agrarianist formations. The following sections explore the essential features of this new type of capitalist transformation, the sources of its dynamic, its relationship to the international economy, and its impact on the class structure and the nature of the state.

Increasingly, agriculture has been transformed into a capital-intensive, mechanized enterprise, with backward (tractors, fertilizers, pesticides, animal feeds, etc.) and forward linkages with industry (food processing plants, paper and pulp enterprises, etc.). The relations of production are increasingly based on wage labor, and a reserve army of unemployed (floating migratory labor) is taking the place of the stable tenant farmer located on the hacienda. These agro-enterprises are high-growth units linked to international markets through the nexus of metropolitan marketing, finance, and shipping firms. The agro-firms linked to the international markets are the dominant units, while farms producing for local markets are the slow-growth ones. "Stagnation" in the former is a function of world demand, not a result of internal relations of production.

The transformation of the peasantry (small holders, tenants, etc.) into a predominantly wage labor force within the nexus of capital growth enterprises has made demands for agrarian reform anachronistic. The new agro-enterprises represent one moment in the industrialization of society, participating as recipients of factory products and suppliers of factory inputs. The new large-scale expansive units have increasingly socialized production while remaining in private hands. The problem today is not to redistribute land but to socialize the agro-industrial sector. To redivide the land is to revert to an earlier form of organization of production, which undermines the development of productive forces (division of labor, technology, etc.).

Moreover, the formulation of an agrarian reform inadequately captures the essence of the labor/capital problem, which today is integrally tied to the industrial-finance-commercial activities that surround agricultural activity. The transformation of land tenure in and of itself fails to deal with a number of specific and general problems: (1) the excess of landed population that is not incorporated into reform units is subject to the exploitation of the new owners (individual or cooperative) or is expelled from productive activity;[2] and (2) the reform beneficiaries depend upon the manufacturers of farm inputs, processors, and commercial exporters that can extract the surplus without the risks of weather or the problems of labor or politics at the point of production.[3] The integration of agriculture within the industrial-commercial network means that agrarian problems can only be seen as part of the larger problems of a capitalist society. The issue is no longer one of the underdevelopment of a backward agrarian sector, but rather the particular forms of exploitation in agriculture that maintain the labor force in a subordinate position within a larger exploitative society. Exploitation of wage labor is the key to the rapid expansion of agricultural exports.

The process of capital accumulation is based on the appropriated surplus from wage labor employed directly or through contract farmers, who are turned into appendages of multinational corporations. The expansion of agro-capitalism has been accompanied by the proliferation of imperial enterprises within the agro-manufacturing sector, the processing industry, in financial and commercial activity, as well as in the direct exploitation of land. Increasingly enveloped in this imperial network, the problem of an agrarian transformation becomes more and more national (part of anti-imperialist movements); to the extent that it remains sectorial or regional, it is doomed. Although in some cases imperial firms have contract relations with local agrarian capitalists (the direct exploiters of labor), *the larger networks are the ultimate recipients of the bulk of the surplus value that is produced by farm labor*. The shift toward nonlandowning forms of economic activity to exploit the agrarian sector is one of the characteristic features accompanying the transformation of agriculture. Within this matrix of linkages imperial capital is playing an ever more important role—defining the conditions of exploitation and capturing a substantial part of the surplus.

Paradoxically, the transformation of agriculture (capitalization and growth) has not increased food production. In fact, there is evidence to show the opposite. The dynamic for transformation has come from the dominant capitalist countries. A new world division of labor within agriculture has emerged in which the Latin American countries specialize in particular commercial crops and increasingly import substantial proportions of their food—or do without it—from the United States. As one U. S. official noted, "AID has cooperated with the government of Colombia in carrying out a development strategy that encourages a switch from wheat production into crops other than wheat, which can be produced more economically. As a result, Colombia now imports over 85% of its wheat requirement."[4] A number of forces converge to set this process in motion, among them: the landowners who respond to profit-maximizing possibilities in the world market; the state, which is interested in obtaining hard currency; the multinationals, which want to sell to the home market; and the international banks, metropolitan state, and others, which finance agricultural development. The net effect is the growth and transformation of agriculture, leading to a decline in the local food supply and the consumption level of the masses.

The existence and growth of capitalist production in and around agricultural units does not mean, however, the transformation of subsistence agriculture. On the contrary, the maximum exploitation of labor encourages the maintenance of subsistence holdings, which lessen the need for enterprises to pay subsistence wages to reproduce labor. Hence, especially with seasonal labor, the existence of subsistence agriculture serves to subsidize labor because the capitalist and its state do not have to assume the costs of reproduction. For example, a study of agricultural labor in northwest Mexico notes: "The majority of these workers are permanent members of the proletariat—which is not to say they are permanently employed, only that they are permanently landless and without recourse to other means of income. But an important percentage of the rural workforce, approximately 40 percent in Sinaloa, is still made up of ejidatorios whose plots of land either produce less than they need for survival or are rented out to large landowners."[5]

The forms of capitalist transformation have varied from place to place. Large-scale plantations, ranches, corporations, converted haciendas, and cooperatives, as well as middle-sized family farms contracted to large-scale commercial enterprises, have all served as mechanisms for expanding production and extracting surplus value.

## Changes in the International Economy: Impact on the Latifundio

A fundamental change has been occurring within the international economy, shifting labor-intensive production in agriculture and industry toward areas having surplus labor.[6] Within agriculture, the new specialization of production is illustrated by the growth of highly mechanized grain crops in the metropole and labor-intensive exports in the periphery.[7] Increasing demands from the metropole, combined with the big capital surpluses of agro-industrial investors, have led to large investments to modernize the forces of production. Parallel to the increasing flow of capital from the metropole has been the growth of a new type of capitalist firm that utilizes modern machinery and is linked to international and multinational banks and tied to international marketing conglomerates. Their development has, in turn, further accentuated the external market orientation of the new agro-bourgeoisie and reduced production for local markets. This shift in scale and emphasis has been underwritten by the development loan programs of the Inter-American Development Bank and the World Bank, which have encouraged investment in this export sector and provided the funds for roads, ports, dams, and other facilities to promote it.[8]

Another result of the growth of agribusiness has been the imperialists' dual concentration in backward and forward linkages with agriculture and the new set of Latin business farmers, who have accumulated wealth, land, and capital.[9] Probably one of the clearest expressions of the growth of imperial linkages is found in this description of the Bajío Valley of northern Mexico: "Three multinational food processing corporations—Del Monte, Campbell's and General Foods—operate canning and packing plants in the Valley. Ford and John Deere tractors till the land, insecticides from Bayer are used to control plant diseases and cattle are fed special formula feeds milled by Ralston Purina and Anderson Clayton."[10] The new monopoly agriculturalists do not conform to the stereotype image of the *hacendado:* the agricultural unit is no longer principally a way of life involving status and family considerations. Basically, it is now an economic unit—an investment and, in many cases, not the only object of an outlay of capital. The pattern in northern Mexico is again illustrative: "These same [Mexican large] growers, partners of U.S. agribusiness companies, also have strong investments in the region's commerce, industry and banking. Families . . . own the distributorships for U.S. farm equipment, automobiles, fertilizer and pesticide products."[11] In place of the older system of obligation and duties, deference and paternalism, there are the impersonal relations of the market in which the principal link between owners and workers is the cash nexus.

## The New Class Context of Agriculture

At the peak of the new agribusiness social structure stand a number of actors who had been omitted from previous descriptions. The functionaries of international and private banks, the agro-manufacturers and the agro-processors and exporters, along with the large landowners, occupy the top position; below them are the contract farmers, who are financed and supplied by the above groups and provide the products for the processors and exporters. Below them are the small-scale usurers, traders, and managers of large and medium-sized enterprises. Then comes the stable labor force of wage workers, skilled operatives, and foremen. At the bottom is the great mass of seasonal workers, migratory laborers, who may combine subsistence farming with wage labor.

In terms of class categories, the first group of occupations represents the monopoly capitalists, whose capital, international or local, may be hegemonic or associated. The second level can be considered a local, competitive bourgeoisie, which has access to national political machinery but is highly dependent for financing, markets, and machinery on the monopoly sector. The local bourgeoisie's degree of autonomy is therefore extremely restricted: it is subject to profit squeezes, and the planting and marketing of products are virtually dictated by monopoly capital.[12] The predominant feature of this class is its dependent status, despite the fact that in some cases it has been able to associate with segments of monopoly capital (especially in the agro-manufacturing and processing sectors) through franchises. The lack of autonomy of the new local bourgeoisie manifests itself in organized efforts to resist most nationalist measures, especially those to which the monopoly sectors object. Thus, in Guatemala when there was an attempt to tax banana exports over the objections of the monopoly exporters, the local banana growers came to the defense of the exporters.[13] The crucial point about the development of the local bourgeoisie in the production sphere is that social relations of production pit *local* capital against labor. The proletarianization of labor and the growth of a reserve army provide the surplus value for local capital accumulation. However, as we have seen, the sphere of agricultural production cannot be separated from industrial production and the sphere of circulation. Moreover, the interrelationship between spheres highlights the error of those who seem to define a mode of production by social relations in the productive sphere.

The whole ensemble of agro-social relations—workers and owners—is, in large part, subordinated to the industrial, financial, and commercial sectors, which appropriate the bulk of the surplus through unequal exchange, interest payments, and monopoly control over marketing. Rather than conceive of agro-production as being dominated by commerce, we should think of the problem as one of the dominion of monopoly capital over competitive capital—the latter in some cases an appendage of the former.

The growth of corporate agro-capitalism has led to a complex process and structure. In one variant large landholdings are leased or sold to local agribusinessmen and farmers, who in turn exploit labor. Del Monte and the banana companies have developed that practice in Central America (Guatemala and Costa Rica), dubbing themselves and the local agribusiness interests "associate producers." Another variant is direct ownership of landholdings by corporate enterprises, which directly exploit labor. This is still the pattern in parts of Central and South America, but less so than in the past. A third variant, which is increasingly used in Latin America, is the transfer of local business capital to agricultural enterprises. A fourth variant is the conversion of extensive hacienda type agriculture into modern corporate farming. That is most pronounced in Argentina, Brazil, and Colombia, as well as Central America. A fifth variant is the state-directed cooperative organized along the lines of a capitalist enterprise, the product of the expropriation of privately owned property. That form is used in Peru, Mexico, and other post-reformist countries. All of the variants have a number of features in common: organization and operation along the lines of a business enterprise, integration into a network of capitalist firms (for inputs and outputs) and almost total dependence on external markets for growth, and the displacement of small producers, who are incorporated into the labor force as a reserve army or as wage labor. The transition from traditional extensive hacienda type agricultural units to modern agribusiness enterprises has achieved its clearest expression in northwestern Mexico and throughout many parts of Central America, Brazil, southern Bolivia, and the coastal areas of Peru.

The growth of agribusiness in the region has produced a wage labor force that is increasingly receptive to appeals from class-anchored organizations and whose demands can only be met through the socialization of agriculture. Agro-mechanization and specialization and the growth of processing industries in the proximate areas has produced large concentrations of wage workers who have become more and more divorced from the land. Citing government data, one study of the situation in Mexico claims that the number of landless farm workers has increased since 1950 from 1.5 million, representing 30 percent of the labor force, to nearly 5 million, over half of the workforce in 1970. The floating labor force ("migratory labor force") doubled between 1940 and 1950 and 1960 and 1970 from 3.5 million to 7.5 million.[14] Nevertheless, it is worth emphasizing that the process of proletarianization often has not been completed for the bulk of the labor force, especially the floating, migratory seasonal work-force, whose members still maintain plots of land to supplement their inadequate income wages. Thus, the social movements that emerge combine the features of trade unions, calling for wage and welfare changes, with demands for the expropriation of land. The form the expropriation would take is conditioned by the movement's ties to the larger society. Lacking a working class ideology, the agrarianist movements drift toward endorsing a cooperative form dependent on market forces. In some cases leaders and segments are coopted and become contract farmers—part of the dependent bourgeoisie.[15] The social orientation of the agrarian wage labor force is thus influenced by past ideologies of agrarianism and the continuing linkage to subsistence landholding, thus preventing the clear emergence of a working-class socialist orientation appropriate to the labor force's objective position.

## Capitalist Agriculture and the State

The growth of corporate capitalist agriculture has received its greatest impetus from the state. The facilities provided, the expanding infrastructure, and the tax and investment programs instrumental to the development of corporate-capitalist agriculture have depended on the existence of a state that is willing to elaborate the prescribed programs. In all cases, a *strong* state has been crucial: either a military dictatorship, as in Central America and Brazil, or a one-party state, as in Mexico, which can contain the inevitable peasant unrest resulting from corporate displacement and exploitation and can guarantee the security of long-term, large-scale investments that are necessary for corporate growth. Due to the need to finance large-scale infrastructural development through foreign loans, the regime must be in a position to open the doors to foreign investment and squelch any and all nationalist outcries. Foreign loans are predicated on an open-door policy to foreign investment. Thus, the regime must serve as a broker between segments of monopoly capitalist interests.

The state possesses dual features: it is a flexible broker in promoting corporate expansion and an inflexible controller in dealing with noncorporate rural classes. The flexibility of the state is evidenced in the ability of the multinationals to shape agro-production to meet their needs and to whittle the autonomy of local growers, harnessing them to the demands of the metropole. The state shares that orientation and intervenes only to further the process, attempting to skim the overflow in the form of added tax revenues—or, in the case of individual functionaries, to join in lucrative associations.

The integration of monopoly capital—imperial and peripheral—marks the coming of age of corporate agriculture, just as the local middle bourgeoisie has emerged as a satellite of the exporters and financiers. The horizontal and vertical ties between economic sectors essentially express the formal dominance of monopoly capital on a national and global scale. Such linkages mean that any agrarian movement will confront the united opposition of the whole bourgeoisie, as was evidenced in Mexico during the employers' boycotts of November 1976 and in Brazil in 1963-1964.[16] Increasingly, the success of any agrarian movement depends on its transcendence of the limits of agricultural production—a distinction that is today largely an artifact of the past.

## The Agro-Imperial Connection: New Dimension to an Old Problem

Since U.S. corporations began to divest themselves of landholdings in the post-World War II period, most discussion of the agrarian problem has avoided tackling its relation to imperialism. There are many problems with such a perspective. First, while U.S. corporations have pulled out of production in some lines of endeavor and in some areas, in other regions they have not. The shifts in Central America and Mexico relate to different product lines: U.S. exploitation of the vegetable and fruit sectors has increased, while that of banana production has declined. While the bulk of landholders are Latin American, key U. S. corporations, such as Cargill, Anderson and Clayton, King Ranch, General Foods, and Ralston Purina, continue to play an important role in the high growth/profit export industries. More important, in the dynamic areas surrounding agricultural production U.S. expansion has been substantial: in sales and production of agromachinery in Mexico, Central America, and many parts of Latin America by Caterpillar Tractor, John Deere and Company; in agro-transport equipment throughout the region by Kaiser and others; in grain marketing in Argentina (Cargill is Argentina's leading exporter of wheat, barley, maize, and other grains); in fertilizer, animal feeds, and pesticide production and sales throughout Latin America by Ralston Purina, Borden, Monsanto, and Dow Chemicals; in banking and finance of agricultural growth throughout the region (Bank of America has 46 branches, a substantial part of their activities being directed toward agribusiness); and in marketing and processing throughout the region.[17] The United States has not moved out of agriculture but has merely shifted from the least profitable and risky sectors to the high-profit and secure areas. The large flow of U.S. capital throughout the economy surrounding agricultural production has been, in some cases, accompanied by political changes—including military regimes—which have undermined oligarchies in favor of corporate capitalist expansion. In that sense, the military coups have been instruments for capital accumulation from above and outside.[18]

The expansion of corporate capitalism has neither reduced imperialist control nor neutralized the class struggle in the countryside. The growth of commercial agriculture and the spread of corporate enterprises have generalized class struggle within an increasingly socialized productive sphere. In other words, the class struggle has been raised to a higher or more general level: from struggles for individual ownership ("land for those who work it") to collective ownership. The intensification of exploitation evidenced in the increasing surplus value extracted from wage labor has already found expression in the growth of mass movements of landless laborers in Mexico and El Salvador and in the revival of the guerrilla movements in Guatemala.[19] The growing integration of agribusiness into the imperial-capital network, the growth of the quasi-totalitarian state, and the comprehensive programs for corporate expansion lay to rest the problem of "development and underdevelopment": the issue is the exploitation of wage labor by corporate capital and the class nature of the state which presides over the exploitation.

## Long-Term, Large-Scale Agrarian Changes from Below

The realities of Latin American rural life are determined in large part by two conflicting social forces: the large landholder and the landless or small-holding peasants. The struggle in the past was largely over the distribution of land. Today the struggle is over how agriculture will be developed: the means and type of agrarian transformation that occurs will have a lasting effect on which social classes pay the cost and which are the beneficiaries. The preceding discussion of the transformation from above outlined one path to development that could define the nature of rural life. Countering that tendency is an alternative form, embodied at least in part in the Mexican, Bolivian, and especially in the Cuban revolutions.

Rural reality is not defined merely by the larger movements of capital, by the decisions of the multinationals, and the dictates of the landlords and their political and military supporters in the state. Historical experience, not only in Latin America but elsewhere as well, has shown that the peasantry and peasant movement can play a decisive role in redefining society. In recent periods, the peasantry has been discovered to be a force for social transformation.[20] The principal point of departure for an analysis of the role of the peasantry as a force for social change begins with a recognition of the internal differentiations within rural society. A number of authors have attempted, in different historical circumstances, to identify segments disposed toward large-scale, long-term change. Eric Wolf has stressed the pivotal role of the middle peasant as the carrier of revolutionary politics,[21] while others have described the importance of the landless peasants and their interaction with centers of working-class political action.[22] Some point to a rising peasant class, aspiring capitalist farmers, as agents of social change against the old order,[23] while at least one writer has suggested that it is a downwardly mobile peasantry, dispossessed of its holdings, which is the force predisposed toward revolutionary action.[24] Whatever the differences between the various theorists, it is clear that there is a common recognition that peasant movements have contributed to redefining the nature of rural society, not infrequently overcoming the obstacles of state and society. If, then, peasants have been protagonists of historical change, what factors have shaped and influenced the direction that change has taken? Basically, land reforms have served both conservative and revolutionary development projects: as ingredients in the consolidation of capitalist social regimes, land reforms prevent more fundamental national social transformations by allying the peasant beneficiaries with political parties and regimes linked to big business. Such has been the case in Taiwan and Japan after World

War II and, more recently, in Mexico. In the conservative cases, agrarian reform served to consolidate existing property relations and to strengthen the power of the urban (and foreign) capitalist class as a counterweight to possible working-class opposition. A variant of conservative land reform experiences could perhaps be found in colonial settler regimes such as occurred in the United States and later in Rhodesia, South Africa, and Israel, where land was appropriated from indigenous subsistence agriculturalists and redistributed among the white settlers, creating bonds between the agrarian beneficiaries and the larger corporate interests. In the post-World War II period, conservative land reforms have occurred within very specific bounds, being externally imposed and executed with tight controls to contain political and social spillovers to other deprived strata of the population. In both cases, the dominant groups executing the reforms were anchored within capitalist production, and the labor movement was unable to link up with peasant demands. The outcome was largely determined by forces outside of agriculture, which ultimately determined the structure and orientation of the land reform beneficiaries.

In the case of revolutionary land reforms, such as in Cuba and in China, radicalized peasants were linked to movements that earlier or later were anchored in working-class political movements. These coalitions advanced demands for land reform as part of a larger transformation of society. The inability of big-property interests to contain rural discontent can be attributed to a variety of reasons, including the linkages that may exist across economic sectors (landowners-urban industrialists) and their inability to isolate and deal with the rural question apart from the nonrural social movements. In this context, agrarian reform movements have been instrumental in transforming the whole of society, furthering the collectivization process, and reordering social values.

These two examples of the political uses of agrarian reform highlight the confrontation in this hemisphere during the early 1960s. The Cuban revolution carried forward the tradition of agrarian reform as an integral part of a social revolution; whereas

President John Kennedy, through the Alliance for Progress, embarked upon a process of agrarian reform to reconsolidate property relations.[25] In that sense, large-scale, long-term change within rural Latin America was substantially affected by global factors: the Cuban revolution and U.S. policy. The competition of those forces for influence in shaping the transformation of agriculture had a profound effect throughout Latin America. There was a proliferation of movements, programs, activities, studies, and organizations—and not a few efforts to formally or informally redistribute land and organize the peasants in many countries. In Peru, Chile, Brazil, and elsewhere, efforts were made to change the nature of land tenure from both a revolutionary and reformist perspective: the former tied to a socialist political economy, the latter to a capitalist. The complex forces involved in this undertaking led, in some cases, to overt expressions of peasant demands; attitudes of passivity and acquiescence often masked hostility and land hunger. Researchers discovered that the problem of studying peasant attitudes toward rural change was complicated first by the centrality of the overall political and social context—the degree and scope of repression and its internalization. Second, peasant attitudes could be studied in several ways: (1) at the level of participation in the social movement or of individual expression; (2) at the level of articulation on a national scale or within the local unit; (3) at the level of viewing the peasantry as an independent actor or as a client of the state, political leader, or whatever. Within each analytical perspective the levels were interrelated; the individual-local-clientelism approach contrasted with the movement-national-autonomous actor approach. Crossing both perspectives were the competing global forces that contributed to creating a set of apparently contradictory notions within rural movements: peasant movements chose radical instruments but embraced conservative views (Peru), and seemingly reformist peasants increasingly turned toward radical national political movements (the shift from Eduardo Frei to Salvador Allende in Chile). The incapacity of U.S. policy-makers and their Latin counterparts to capture the burgeoning agrarian movement and harness it to their industrialization strategy led to a crisis, out of which has evolved the recent emphasis on "development from the outside and above."

## Neofascism and Capitalist Development from Above and Outside

The shift in U.S. development strategy from agrarian reform had a profound effect throughout the continent.[26] Most importantly, the emphasis by the United States on elite modernization contributed to the emergence of a series of military regimes, whose rulership through force and terror bore a striking resemblance to fascism. The Congressional hearings on U.S. intervention in Chile and the detailed accounts of U.S. financial support for the Brazilian, Chilean, and Argentine dictatorships provide ample evidence of the broad basis of collaboration and support between U.S. policy-makers and the neofascist elites.[27] It is not my intention here to examine all the intricacies of that relationship, some of which are explored in the following essay, but rather to point to some of the long-term, large-scale changes that have occurred under the aegis of neofascist militarism. The contrast between rural life in Latin America during the 1960s and today is monumental. In the 1960s, land reform legislation was being debated, peasant unions were being organized, the rights of rural laborers were being recognized, and in some cases land was being expropriated and distributed to peasants. Beyond these institutional changes, there was change in the behavior and attitudes of the peasants; the old patterns of submission were dissolving and being replaced by feelings of competence and self-assertiveness. Interest in national politics, ideologies, and large-scale changes was pervasive: in the fundos, peasants elected delegates and representatives to pressure the reformers in the government, unions, or opposition political parties. For the first time, formal democratic procedures were given substance and life in the countryside.

Today, those democratic aspirations and stirrings have been crushed: independent peasant unions have been destroyed, their leaders imprisoned, harrassed, and assassinated; the parties of reform have been proscribed; the legislative deliberative bodies have been recessed indefinitely; in some countries land reform beneficiaries have been displaced, and landlords have repossessed the land, expelling thousands of peasant families. This process of reversal, accompanied by the destruction of independent organizations, is what defines the demise of national agrarian reform programs. Fear, distrust, and passivity have returned with the re-emergence of an exclusive focus on local, community-based, clientelistic concerns. The free-market rhetoric that accompanies a regime's support of export-oriented, large-scale enterprises is all part of the new reality.

Free-market rhetoric accompanies the reconcentration of land and wealth, while neofascist methods of rule promote the growth of large-scale, export-oriented enterprises and undermine efforts to reorganize independent peasant movements. Just as the Latin countries have been once again reintegrated into the world division of labor, so have the peasants once again been subordinated to the large landowners. The logic of the world capitalist order was temporarily upset by the turn toward the creation of an internal market through agrarian reform and national industrialization. The price of the reinsertion of Latin America into the capitalist world order has been paid by most of the classes outside the export-landed-financial strata—but above all by the peasantry, whose present conditions have yet to evoke any consequential effort to defend their human rights, either in Washington or among the technocrats who advise the military regimes.

## Notes

1. Gerrit Huizer, *Peasant Rebellion in Latin America* (Middlesex, Eng.: Pelican Books, 1973), p. 7. Also Oscar Delgado, "Revolution, Reform, Conservatism" in *Latin America: Reform or Revolution*, ed. James Petras and Maurice Zeitlin (New York: Fawcett Publications, 1968), pp. 381–98, and Rodolfo Stavenhagen, ed., *Agrarian Problems and Peasant Movements* (New York: Doubleday & Co., Anchor Books, 1970).

2. James Petras and Hugo Zemelman, *Peasants in Revolt* (Austin, Tex.: University of Texas Press, 1972) and James Petras and Robert LaPorte, *Cultivating Revolution* (New York: Random House, 1971), chap. 6.
3. In his recent critique of the reformist left's agrarian program in Spain, Aulo Casamayor follows a similar line of reasoning: " . . . The fact that the latifundistas are massively turning toward the employment of machinery, chemical measures and special seeds when it permits them to improve their earnings means that the productionist argument with which the left has traditionally defended its agrarian reform project has lost a great part of its force." "Por una oposicion que se oponga: critica a las interpretaciones del capitalismo español y a las alternativas que ofrece la oposicion politica," *Cuadernos de Ruedo Ibérico*, no. 54 (November–December 1976): 39–40.
4. U.S., Congress, Senate, Committee on Agriculture and Forestry, Subcommittee on Foreign Agricultural Policy Hearings, *U.S. Foreign Agricultural Trade Policy*, March and April 1973, p. 160, as quoted in NACLA, *Latin America and Empire Report* 9, No. 7 (October 1975): 4.
5. NACLA, "Harvest of Anger: Agro-Imperialism in Mexico's Northwest", *Latin America and Empire Report* 10, no. 6 (July–August 1976): 18.
6. U.S., Commission on International Trade and Investment Policy, *United States International Economic Policy in an Interdependent World*, Report to the President (Washington, D.C.: Government Printing Office, July 1971).
7. For further elaboration, see NACLA, "U.S. Grain Arsenal," *Latin America and Empire Report* 9, no. 7 (October 1975): 3–6.
8. Under the influence of the Inter-American Development Bank, Costa Rican export products have increased while food items stagnate or decline.

| *Export (in mil. of colones)* | | | *Local Consumption* | | |
|---|---|---|---|---|---|
| | *1967* | *1972* | | *1967* | *1972* |
| Bananas | 220 | 535 | Beans | 17 | 6 |
| Sugar | 68 | 91 | Corn | 37 | 18 |
| Beef | 163 | 228 | Rice | 69 | 63 |

See Peter DeWitt, "Policy Directions in International Lending" (Ph.D., diss., SUNY/Binghamton, 1975).

9. For a series of case studies see NACLA, "Harvest of Anger." pp. 13–16; NACLA, "Del Monte: Bitter Fruits," *Latin America and Empire Report* 10, no. 7 (September 1976): 12–15 and 24–30; NACLA, "Brazil: Development for Whom?" *Latin America and Empire Report* 7, no. 4 (April 1973): 23–31 especially ("Anderson Clayton Knows No Bounds").
10. NACLA, "Del Monte," p. 12.
11. Ibid., p. 10.
12. According to calculations contained in one study of export tomato farming in Mexico the bulk of profits are taken by the nongrowers:

| | |
|---|---|
| Retailer | .18 |
| Wholesaler | .04 |
| Distributor | .03 |
| Growers' profits | .02 |
| Miscellaneous production costs (seeds, fertilizers, etc.) | .05 |
| Farm workers' wages | .05 |
| | .45 |

See NACLA, "Harvest of Anger," p. 16. Another estimate regarding bananas found that only 11.5% of the earnings remained in the producing countries. See NACLA, "Del Monte," p. 28.

13. NACLA, "Del Monte," p. 30.
14. NACLA, "Harvest of Anger," pp. 18–19.
15. During the land occupation movement in northwest Mexico, the *New York Times* noted "that only the leaders had been given land." One peasant is quoted as saying: "We've been campaigning for land as a group since 1958. We've been paying our leader ten pesos a week to carry on the struggle. Now he has been bought off with a piece of land and has abandoned us." *New York Times*, November 26, 1976, p. A10.
16. *Latin America* 10, no. 43 (November 5, 1976): 341 and 10, no. 26 (November 26, 1976): 362. In addition to the boycott by 28,000 landowners and the $300 million sent abroad, many businesses closed their doors.
17. NACLA, "Bank of America," *Latin America and Empire Report* 4, no. 5 (September 1970): 4–7.
18. In Guatemala, U.S. takeovers have been extensive, with approximately 34 firms bought out between 1960 and 1969. Among the major U.S. firms acquiring agriculturally related enterprises were Beatrice Foods, Cargill Central Soya, Coca Cola, General Mills, Pillsbury, and others. The takeovers included production of cereals,

paper, animal feed, canned foods, instant coffee, flour mill cake mixes, prepared foods, edible oil, etc. See NACLA, "U.S. Strategies for Central America," *Latin America and Empire Report* 7, no. 5 (May–June 1973): 29.

19. *Latin America* 10, no. 49 (December 17, 1976): 388–89 and 11, no. 1 (January 7, 1977): 4. The report states: "The rapid growth of the guerrilla offensive (in Guatemala) over the past year has made them an important factor in the country's agitated political scene for the first time since the late sixties."
20. Eric R. Wolf, *Peasant Wars of the Twentieth Century* (New York: Harper and Row, 1969). See also Jean Chesneaux, *Peasant Revolts in China, 1840–1949* (London: W. W. Norton and Company, 1973); and Douglas Deal, "Peasant Revolts and Resistance in the Modern World: A Comparative View," *Journal of Contemporary Asia* 5, no. 4.
21. Wolf, *Peasant Wars.*
22. Maurice Zeitlin, *Revolutionary Politics and the Cuban Working Class* (New York: Harper and Row, 1970); and James Petras and Maurice Zeitlin, "Agrarian Radicalism in Chile," *British Journal of Sociology* 19, no. 3 (September 1968): 254–70.
23. Wesley Craig, Jr., "Peru: The Peasant Movement in La Convención," in *Latin American Peasant Movements*, ed. Henry Landsberger (Ithaca: Cornell University Press, 1969), pp. 274–96.
24. R. H. Tawney, *Land and Labor in China* (New York: Octagon Books, 1964).
25. James F. Petras and Robert LaPorte, Jr., *Cultivating Revolution* (New York: Random House, 1971).
26. Ibid.
27. Center for International Policy, *Human Rights and the U.S. Foreign Assistance Program: Fiscal Year 1978, Part 1—Latin America* (Washington, D.C., 1978); and James Petras and Morris Morley, *The United States and Chile: Imperialism and the Overthrow of the Allende Government* (New York: Monthly Review Press, 1975).

# 6

# THE RISE AND FALL OF REGIONAL ECONOMIC NATIONALISM IN LATIN AMERICA, 1969–1977

*(with Morris H. Morley)*

## Economic Nationalism in the 1960s

The late 1960s and the early 1970s were a period of rising nationalist movements throughout the hemisphere, especially in the Andean countries. The principal feature of those movements was an effort to extricate the area from its profound dependence on the United States and, at the same time, to discover the means and wherewithal for rapid economic growth. One of the directions policy-makers within the Andean nationalist group took was regional integration. The signing of the Andean Pact and its elaboration was an attempt to create a wider internal market—through the combined populations of the region—and hence a partial substitute for the U.S. market, subsequent to the failure to achieve the reforms heralded in the Alliance for Progress. For the bourgeois nationalists it was easier to aggregate existing markets than to expand internal ones through rapid, radical redistribution of income. The doctrinal highpoint in this struggle for hegemony was the document referred to as the "Consensus of Viña del Mar" in the late 1960s: it raised the issue of the necessity to equalize the terms of hemispheric trade exchange and represented a conscious movement toward national capitalist development in association with (joint ventures) foreign capital, but not dominant over it.

Contributing to the impulse for "regional integration" were the declining possibilities for import-substitution industrialization within the confines of the existing limited markets. This problem was faced by the more "developed countries" in the region, particularly Chile. The pattern of intraregional industrial stratification, however, created tensions and prolonged negotiations as the less industrialized nations sought to ensure themselves a piece of the action. Furthermore, problems ensued when the economic nationalists pointed to the existence of multinational corporations within the confines of the region, which with their greater mobility and external support could more easily capture the new opportunities. The reliance on external funds to finance "national industries" added a note of ambiguity. The financial dependence of the regimes would limit their capacity to grow out of the influence and dominance of the United States. But this was perceived as a "long-run" problem, which would be dealt with when the new productive facilities began to operate; their earnings, it was argued, would pay back old debts.

## The National/Social Underpinnings of Regionalist Strategy

For the regionalist strategy to succeed, national regimes which were willing to develop an adversary relationship with the United States were required. During the late 1960s and early 1970s, the high point of "regionalist" sentiment, a series of regimes whose internal makeup projected the required shift in social composition and policy, did develop. In Peru, the Velasco regime proceeded toward selective nationalization and national industrialization and gave a strong push toward "regionalist projects" based on a strong "statist development philosophy." In Bolivia, the Ovando and Torres regimes followed suit, promoting nationalization and devising plans (hardly definite) for national economic expansion with strong state backing. In Chile, during the later Christian Democratic period, especially at the prodding of Foreign Minister Gabriel Valdés, and subsequently under Salvador Allende, a major effort was made to tighten the conditions for foreign capital's entry while expanding intraregional trade and encouraging the development of complementary industrial complexes. Somewhat further behind were Ecuador and Colombia, the former taking some nationalist initiatives during the ascendency of General Guillermo Rodríguez and seeing in the regionalist strategy a chance to lessen the unevenness of industrial development within the region. Venezuela, a latecomer to the regionalist approach, was initially the foot-dragger. Its bilateral ties with the United States and the insecurity of its "overprotected" industrialists, who were fearful of regionalized competition, created serious obstacles. The nationalist impulse of the period translated a common opposition to overdomination by the United States of the involved economies into a search for a political-economic formula involving a common effort to pool resources and expand markets. Obviously, there were substantial variations in the nature of internal policies and the degree of opposition to the U.S. presence: Bolivia and Chile at first extended state control over vast areas of the economy, while Peru moved more cautiously, and Ecuador's policy was even less clearly defined. Moreover, the disparities between the countries in terms of levels of industrialization and the demands of the "less developed" (Bolivia, Ecuador) vis à vis the more developed (Chile and Peru) were not obviated by their common nationalist purpose. Hard bargaining took place. The most important underlying problem facing the regionalist compact, however, centered on the capacity of each regime to sustain the nationalist posture: to create, in other words, a solid class base rooted in state power.

## Ascending Regionalism Nationalism: The Andean Pact and Decision 24

The Andean Pact, signed by the governments of Chile, Bolivia, Peru, Ecuador, and Colombia in May 1969, was the organizational focal point of this new nationalist challenge to the imperial state policies and foreign capital operations of the United States, and it represented a renewed hemispheric effort at regional economic integration. The agreement delineated three areas of central concern: the elimination of barriers to reciprocal intraregional trade; the establishment of a common external tariff; and the elaboration of strategies for joint economic planning. The centerpiece of this nationalist formation was the foreign investment code (Decision 24), which was intended to limit the influence and impact of the foreign multinationals and to control the overall flow of foreign capital within the national economies. Specific sectors of the economy (public utilities, commercial banking, insurance, transportation, mass media, etc.) were envisioned as being off limits to foreign investment. In other areas, selective constraints would be applied. Restrictions on new and existing foreign investment were to be accompanied by controls on capital repatriation, profit remittances, technology licensing, the utilization of local credit facilities, interest rates payable to foreign lenders, and the licensing of patents and trademarks.

The U.S. investment community was initially hostile when the proposed investment code was released in late 1970. *Business Latin America* interpreted the new regulations as the equivalent of "a near death blow" to foreign capital accumulation and expansion in the region.[1] On closer inspection, however, the obstacles likely to be encountered by foreign investors in the Andean countries appeared to be less formidable than first impressions had suggested. The senior executives of the U.S. multinationals operating in the region exhibited a growing cynicism over the capacity of the different political regimes to enforce Decision 24 in a way that would have a fundamental impact on aggregate capital investments in the region. One U.S. manufacturer observed: "I won't be surprised if it passes, but then I won't be surprised if it stretches like an accordion with all the clauses."[2]

The foreign investment code was formally enacted in July 1971. The most important nationalist features of the code were the following: annual repatriation of profits was limited to 14 percent of an authorized direct foreign investment; annual reinvestment without host government approval was limited to 5 percent of capital; when firms were sold or liquidated, the re-export of capital was limited to the original investment; new foreign investment was restricted to areas not competitive with domestic industry; and local majority control of all enterprises was to take place within fifteen years in Colombia, Chile, and Peru and within twenty years in Bolivia and Ecuador. Other aspects of the investment code, however, reflected how little of a break with foreign capital was projected: companies exporting 80 percent or more of their output to third countries would be untouched by the new controls; up to 49 percent of foreign capital and management participation would be countenanced for an indefinite period in any particular firm; and, above all, governments were given the formal authority through Article 44 of the code to set aside any of the newly devised restrictions on foreign investment whenever they deemed it "necessary": "When, in the opinion of the recipient country, special circumstances exist, that country may apply other regulations than those provided in Articles 40 to 43, inclusive, that explicitly control foreign investment."[3] In practice, Decision 24 represented a compromise between "nationalization" and *laissez faire*. Although specific provisions were interpreted by American investors as hostile to U.S. financial, manufacturing, and mining interests in the region, the code was not viewed in overall terms as an anticapitalist document and did not prefigure any substantial shift in imperial investment flows within Latin America.

The Andean Pact and associated efforts were marked by several crucial ambiguities, which were to plague policy-makers of the new nationalism to the very end. The problem centered on the role of foreign capital within the new scheme of things: its participation was acknowledged, but there was a constant fear of new encroachments, a sense of an inability to "hold the line." National capital was supposed to do the job, but both private and state efforts were largely based on floating big foreign loans from U.S. and European private banks and the "international banks" influenced by the U.S. government. These problems were compounded by the close links between the lending agencies and the multinationals, which meant any move against the latter would result sooner or later in a reaction from the agencies. The crucial unit that tied the private and "international" banks to the multinationals, and coordinated overall policy, was the U.S. imperial state (in particular, the National Security Council and the Departments of State, Commerce, Agriculture, and Treasury), whose appointees, it should be noted, exercised a disproportionate voting power within the "international" banks. The imperial influence of the United States was also consolidated through the activities of the Pentagon, the Central Intelligence Agency, and the various military intelligence organizations. The imperial states' ability to maneuver widened as the debt and trade gaps of the nationalist regimes increased above the projected earnings from the "new investments." The levers of finance were every bit as potent as the overt actions of the CIA's liaisons within the peripheral military and police forces: in fact, the latter's actions were only undertaken in the context set by the former.

Despite the formidable array of problems within the region and beyond, the regionalist project did take hold and did embody the new ethos of economic nationalism. Several progressive steps were taken: trade was liberalized; an agreement was reached on standards for a common external tariff; various restrictions on foreign capital investments were implemented; and a joint policy on trademarks, patents, licenses and royalties was elaborated.[4] In addition, there was a small but indentifiable growth in intraregional trade.[5] The success—at least initially—of this venture depended, first, on the political composition of the member states. Regionalist "nationalism" could only succeed to the degree that the policies of the regimes of the member nations were compatible with the larger project. The specific conception of a common market to promote national industrialization was based on a fortuitous conjunctural occurrence: the emergence of nationalist regimes with a common purpose and, in some cases, with similar social bases.

The nationalist regionalist strategy was bourgeois in conception but originated within the state apparatus and was elaborated from there. Those new forces within the governing military planning bureaucracies sought a shift in relations with the United States (not a break) and worked toward a greater degree of autonomy. The strategy was to maximize intraregional expansion while maintaining ties to U.S. markets, goods, and technology. A gradual or relative decline in the connection with the United

States could mitigate against any precipitous actions on the part of that country and could lead, ultimately, to more equal and prosperous regional units over the long run. Thus thought the state capitalists and their advisors, and thus followed their practice—to a disastrous end. For whatever else might be thought of them, the U.S. state, the banking system and the multinational corporations (MNCs) were not passive and impotent spectators, their rhetoric of "low profile" notwithstanding.

## The U.S. Imperial State, the Multinationals, and Their Differing Perceptions of a "Regionalist Strategy": An Overview

From the vantage point of the functionaries of the imperial state, modifications in trade and industrialization within the overall hemispheric ensemble of U.S. hegemony was compatible with Washington's policy. But the *internal* changes in the regimes that underwrote the regionalist strategy also implied, in some cases, a shift toward greater autonomy vis-à-vis the U.S. in hemispheric relations. That is to say, they reflected a relative decline in the hegemonic position of the United States and thus were not acceptable to U.S. policy-makers. Insofar as some regimes seemed to combine a regionalist strategy with internal changes of a structural sort and with shifts in the international sphere, the U.S. imperial state began to move forces to undermine those regimes. The downfall of the governments of J. J. Torres in Bolivia, Salvador Allende in Chile, Juan Velasco in Peru, and Guillermo Rodríguez in Ecuador was the immediate result, and, as a by-product and further gain, the regionalist pact was severely undermined.

The response of the MNCs was at first substantially different from that of the imperial state. Overall, the multinationals condemned changes in the *laissez faire* free flow of capital within the region. They attacked restrictions, such as those on profits, investments, and ownership, that infringed on the historically rooted free hand of U.S. business in the hemisphere. On the other hand, their opposition to regional economic arrangements designed to encumber and control foreign investment abated somewhat as the MNCs minimized the impact of the agreements at the operational level. The policy responses of the MNCs were quite varied, running the gamut from improvisation to adaption to outright opposition: efforts were made to evade a strict application of rules; shifts from direct to indirect investments occurred; new ties and associations were announced; disinvestments took place; and selective investments with maximum short-term advantages were undertaken. The discrepancy between the responses of the imperial state and the MNCs persisted until the global shifts and structural reforms within the Andean Pact nations propelled the imperial state to seek to overthrow the nationalist regimes, joining in the cause with the MNCs, which for different reasons ("opposition to limitations") ultimately sought the same outcome. The result was the end of détente between the imperial state and the regional forces, the reestablishment of bilateral ties and the reintegration of the MNCs within the area on their own terms.

## The Trajectory of Nationalist Accommodation and the Impact of the Chilean Coup

The nationalist peak of the Andean Pact, from 1969 to 1971, coincided with, and largely grew out of, the emergence of statist political regimes in Peru, Bolivia, and Chile. Beginning in mid-1971, however, internal conflicts within the "weak" member states over the role of foreign capital in the national economy set the stage for a downgrading of the more nationalistic aspects of the regional economic alliance. The private business community in Colombia forced the government to vacillate on the issue of implementing the foreign investment code.[6] In Ecuador, the MNCs operating in the banking, public service, insurance, transportation, and basic products sectors of the economy were exempted from the 51 percent local investment requirement.[7] In

Peru, an almost identical exemption was granted to those sections of foreign capital.[8] The overthrow of the Torres government in Bolivia in August 1971 was followed by a new government policy of "foot-dragging" on the application of Decision 24.[9] During 1972 and 1973, the overall process of denationalization gathered momentum. In the area of patents, the original provision of the foreign investment code prohibiting the use of foreign trademarks on all products manufactured in the Andean region from January 1977 onward was eliminated.[10] The general narrowing of the scope of Decision 24 was most marked in Ecuador and Colombia, but even the Peruvian government had begun to move more and more in the direction of granting new concessions to foreign capital and applying the Article 44 exemption clause. In Bolivia, not surprisingly, the new military dictatorship of Hugo Banzer immediately moved to elaborate a development strategy based on large infusions of capital "from the outside," which represented a qualitative weakening of the nationalistic character of the Pact. But the overthrow of the socialist government in Chile in August 1973 by procapitalist internal class forces in alliance with the U.S. imperial state was the most decisive setback for the Andean Pact in particular and regional economic nationalism in general.

In Chile, the attempt to develop a democratic socialist society with strong regionalist ties was undermined, despite strong popular support, because of the opposition of internal classes acting in concert with external forces. Its lack of firm control over the state prevented the Allende government from eliminating or limiting the extremist activity of the opposition. Hence, the nationalist option was foreclosed in that class-divided society with the state apparatus, particularly the military and police, on the opposition's side. The overthrow of Allende led to the reversal of his nationalist policies: beginning with the devolution of state property, it continued to an open-door policy toward foreign investment, rupturing the basis of the regionalist pact, undermining its reason for being.

The new Chilean approach to foreign investment was incorporated in the military junta's promulgation of Decree Law 600. This legislation was designed to weaken, and ultimately undermine, the Andean investment code, principally through the elimination of restrictions on the "fade-out" of MNCs' activities within a specified period of time and the abolition of any limits on profit remittances by imperial investors.[11] Following a roundtable discussion with leaders of the military dictatorship in Santiago in June 1974, Business International Corporation concluded:

> Chile's leaders, without exception, are eager for private foreign investment and anxious to create conditions to encourage its entrance. They indicate that they will make the most liberal interpretation possible of the foreign investment rules of the Andean Common Market. They would also support changes to lessen or eliminate any negative effect of the Ancom rules on investors.[12]

The effort by the Chilean junta to secure foreign investment and its dependence on foreign financing were to define the new *de facto* bilateral relations which now increasingly characterized the region.

The "foot-dragging," which had now taken hold among the member governments of the Andean Pact undercut any sustained opposition to the Chilean position. On the contrary, in Colombia, for example, the government accelerated the loosening of restrictions on foreign investment in the country. In January 1974, specific measures regarding Decision 24 were instituted, which rebounded to the benefit of foreign financial institutions, firms engaged in domestic marketing, and those engaged in basic product exploitation. Those actions elicited a favorable response from *Business Latin America:* "This move, limited as it is, suggests that the government is ready to be more flexible in its treatment of foreign capital. . . ."[13] In fact, foreign investment in Colombia rose from $16.8 million in 1972 to $62 million in 1973, and during the first seven months of 1974 investment projects totaling $76 million (of which approximately $25 million was for the establishment of new companies) were approved.[14]

In April 1976, the secretariat of the Andean Common Market (ANCOM) signaled its willingness to substantially capitulate to the Chilean interpretation of Decision 24 when it countermanded the prohibition on foreign investors acquiring locally owned enterprises. At issue was the Chilean government's decision to dismantle the state sector and sell enterprises formerly within the "social area" to external investors. Those enterprises were redefined by the junta as existing investment and, hence, were exempted from the equity "fade-out" timetable for majority foreign control of national industries.[15] Furthermore, by then all member countries had waived the 14 percent ceiling on dividend remittances in favor of various alternatives, ranging from the complete elimination of any upper limit to a specified and agreed-upon maximum and minimum rate.[16] Although the Andrés Pérez government in Venezuela continued to publicly support a more rigorous adherence to the letter of Decision 24, in practice it proved "tardy" in implementing the investment restrictions: "A recent *BLA* [*Business Latin America*] survey of international companies with firms in Venezuela (undertaken in mid-1976) reveals that few of them have encountered any specific requests or pressure to divest."[17] In effect, all Andean Pact countries were now in practical agreement with the "elimination of controls" stance adopted by the Chilean junta:

> ANCOM is encountering a number of problems with mechanisms adopted to meet the region's development objectives. Investment incentives through industrial allocations, internal import reductions, and important protection have not materialized. Moreover, a uniform foreign investment code has not been realized . . . .[18]

The evolution of the Pact's sectorial development programs, especially after 1974, reflected in a striking fashion the degree to which foreign capital was looked upon as an important participant in the overall regional development project. In March 1974, for example, the sectorial program for the edible oil industry was eliminated from the larger project in line with recommendations drawn up at a March 1972 meeting between the Andean Common Market secretariat and the private oil industry. The decision was described by representatives of the U.S. multinational corporations operating in Latin America as "a welcome example of the expanding role and voice of the private sector in policy formulation."[19] ANCOM draft proposals for other sectorial development programs during the same period accelerated the profit-making opportunities for foreign investors. The chemical fertilizer industry's proposal was designed to accord only minimal tariff protection from third-country imports to member countries: "For international companies, this approach means that the 1.5 million ton annual market for chemical fertilizers projected for 1980 will not be closed off to them through high tariff barriers or allocated production sites."[20] The petrochemical industry's sectorial development program envisioned an even more lucrative windfall for U.S. and European capital. Of the estimated $2.5 billion required for the production of products allocated under the program, foreign capital was expected to account for $1 billion of the total amount: "In addition, the local share of investment will also require financing imported machine tools, components and know-how, all of which provide opportunities for international companies."[21] In 1976, ANCOM concluded that for the steel industry's sectorial program to reach its goal of 12 million tons by 1985, approximately $9 billion in total investment would be necessary, a substantial proportion of which would be elicited from external private capital sources.[22] The recent agreement on an automotive sectorial program is expected to allow foreign capitalists in the region "an expanded market through duty-free access to the entire Andean region."[23] The increasingly central role of foreign capital within the regional development scheme between 1974 and 1977 was also facilitated by the concurrent decisions of the member governments to extend the initial deadlines for both agreement on the products to be included in the industrial development programs and implementation of the common internal/external tariff.[24]

At the same time that the Chilean military junta was playing a major role in undermining the larger regional effort to redefine the nature of relations with multinational capital, it was also engaged in obstructionist tactics to prevent the emergence of a common external tariff that would allow for industrial and trade expansion within the area. Efforts to accommodate the Chilean position by other Pact countries were to no avail. In September 1976, junta officials rejected two proposals offered by the other five governments to reduce the common external tariff, first to 70 percent (they wanted it fixed at 30 percent to 35 percent) and then to 26 percent (they insisted on a 12 percent maximum level).[25] *Business Week* observed of the military dictatorship's overall development orientation: "Chile is the model, in purest form, of the new strategy of economic development based on market competition, free enterprise, and an 'opening to the exterior' among countries of the 'Southern Cone.' "[26]

Following the withdrawal of Chile from the Andean Pact in late 1976, the remaining member countries moved, paradoxically, further in the direction of an "opening" to foreign capital. The foreign remittance ceiling was increased from 14 percent to 20 percent and, in practice, became open-ended because each government had the option of raising the upper limit at its own discretion. In addition, the 5 percent ceiling for automatic reinvestment of registered capital was increased to 7 percent, thus raising the capital base on which future profit remittances and reinvestment allowances would be calculated. Finally, MNCs were accorded access to local short- and medium-term credits, were allowed to purchase shares in existing locally owned companies, and were granted a new extension for complying with the "fade-out" rules. "The foreign capital rules as they now stand do no more than maintain the fiction of common controls on investments, as there is little practical difference between the Group's position and that of Chile."[27] In the wake of these changes, *Business Latin America* re-evaluated the medium-term investment possibilities for foreign MNCs in the Andean region: "For executives, the developments surrounding Chile's withdrawal mean that the common market warrants a fresh look for possible benefits for their firms."[28] For their part, a U.S. corporate community more or less unresponsive to "the recent measures by Ancom to liberalize some of its rules,"[29] welcomed the disruptive influence of the Chilean withdrawal on the regional organization. At the same time, its favorable response to the lifting of specific restrictions on foreign capital accumulation and expansion was tempered in the short term by a desire for greater clarity and consistency in the application of the "rules of the [investment] game" throughout the region.[30]

## Financial Dependence and the Demise of Peruvian Nationalism

A number of nationalist regimes in the Andean area were products of military coups, largely directed by "technocrats" with a state-capitalist orientation. Tied to a vision of national capital accumulation which antagonized foreign capital while continuing to marginalize the population, these regimes reflected the interests of a limited stratum of the population. The process of formulating policy and designing development strategy was the province of a small core around the central governments. The regimes were buttressed by their influence within the armed forces and their ability to secure external funding for widespread state-promoted activities. When the foreign banks began to squeeze, the "liaison" or strategically placed forces within the military were able to overthrow or transform the regime with virtually no resistance, and could then reverse the nationalist project. Subsequent to the coups, there was a turn toward private interests, an increase in the influence of external banking institutions in collaboration with the U.S. government, and efforts to facilitate new flows of capital. All this loosened the bonds at the regional level and served to undermine the whole nationalist effort. The most striking single example of this chain of events took place in Peru.

The erosion of the nationalist project in Peru began during the late Velasco period and picked up momentum following the ouster of Velasco and the remaining national-developmentalist cabinet ministers in August 1975 by sectors of the governing military junta under the leadership of General Francisco Morales Bermúdez. The overthrow of Velasco augured a substantially changed climate for foreign investment in Peru: "The administration [of General Bermúdez] will go easier in its application of

ANCOM Decision 24 'in search of conciliatory and constructive formulas.' This is another first for Peru—acknowledging the new international realities that weaken the Andean group's resolve to maintain its stance on foreign capital and technology."[31] A U.S. government study noted that during its first six months in office, the new military regime "has taken a very conservative approach" in implementing Decision 24.[32] The turn toward foreign capital was accompanied by a downgrading and contraction of the social property sector within the overall development project. Formerly the priority sector of Velasco's "economic pluralism" program, it now assumed a subsidiary position to the interests of the private property sector.[33]

When the Bermúdez government took office, Peru's international debts were estimated to total approximately $3.5 billion, of which around $1.9 billion represented borrowings from foreign (primarily U.S.) private commercial banks. Much of that borrowing had been undertaken during 1974–1975, and the due date for substantial repayments of principal and interest was fast approaching. In early 1975, the Velasco regime had initiated discussions with its major private banking creditors in the United States (Manufacturers Hanover, Bank of America, First National City Bank, Chase Manhattan, Morgan Guaranty, and Wells Fargo Bank) for additional loans amounting to $400 million. The banking consortium informed regime officials that the issue of Peru's "creditworthiness" was at stake and that short of decisive economic measures new loans would not be forthcoming. In essence, that translated into the Peruvian government's acceptance of an International Monetary Fund (IMF) "stabilization" program. The complicating factor in the debt discussions with public and private creditors in the United States was Velasco's decision to nationalize, without compensation, the U.S.-owned Marcona Mining Company in July 1975. The New York bankers "let Peru know how they felt," while the U.S. government applied considerable pressure to gain a settlement favorable to the nationalized U.S. company, including temporarily withholding government-assisted food shipments to Peru pending an agreement in principle to compensate the U.S. investors. According to a Treasury Department official, credits to Peru from the

U.S. Commodity Credit Corporation were held up pending "good movement" on the compensation issue.[34]

Despite the rhetoric of "creditworthiness" espoused by U.S. banking and government officials, in August 1975, immediately following Bermúdez' ascension to power, but prior to a settlement of the Marcona compensation issue, the U.S. banking consortium decided in principle to approve a $240 million loan to the new political regime. Meanwhile, the U.S. government "leaned heavily" on the Bermúdez government to speedily resolve the Marcona case. These combined public and private pressures achieved the imperial state's overriding objective in October, when Peru agreed to satisfactorily compensate the U.S. owners of the nationalized iron ore facility.[35]

By the end of 1976, Peru's estimated external medium- and long-term debt was put at $5 billion, which included about $1.7 billion (as of June 30, 1976) owed to private banking organizations in the United States. The decision of the Bermúdez government to accept an IMF mission to the country in November-December and the expectation of the foreign banking community that austerity economic stabilization measures would be imposed were instrumental factors in the agreement by U.S., European, Canadian, and Japanese private banks to refinance Peru's debt by up to $400 million in new loans.[36] An added ingredient in this decision was the elimination of all outstanding compensation issues between the Peruvian government and nationalized foreign-owned property holders. Last, the foreign banking community was accorded an important supervisory role in putting the new economic policies into operation. Their role was reinforced by the unique arrangement between the U.S. private banking consortium and the IMF, whereby private bankers, not officials of the Fund, would be primarily responsible for overseeing the application of the "stabilization" program.

## The Venezuelan Anomaly and the Devolution of Regional Political Statism

The nationalist restructuring in Venezuela carried out by the Pérez government was initiated at a late date (1973), in comparison with the timing of the experiences of the other Andean Pact countries, and it was implemented in a regional context where statist and development projects were no longer on the immediate agenda. The delayed appearance of Venezuelan nationalism reflected the impact of global forces, in particular the regime's extracontinental alliance with the oil nationalists in the OPEC cartel; the government's accumulated capital resources; and the existence of a favorable regional and global conjuncture that allowed for the nationalization of U.S.-owned iron ore and oil properties in 1975 and 1976. State capitalists in the regime, with the benefit of an independent base, sought to promote Latin American MNCs by gaining outlets for capital.

U.S. corporations were apprehensive over the government's outspoken verbal support for Decision 24 of the Andean foreign investment code, especially those clauses that provided for equity ownership of all new foreign investment within a fifteen-year time period and a 14 percent limitation on profit remittances abroad: ". . . no matter how liberal their implementation, these regulations change the foreign investment climate in Venezuela. They mean completely new operating procedures for companies already located in Venezuela and new ground rules for companies considering the oil-rich Venezuelan market."[37] However, as the nature and scope of the regime's nationalist capitalist program unfolded, it became clear that it was to be elaborated in a fashion that did not establish long-term structural barriers to the reassertion of foreign capital. That partly explains the ease with which the obstructions to capitalist expansion were dismantled in a relatively piecemeal fashion beginning in late 1974. By the end of 1977, the nationalist dismemberment had come almost full circle. The Pérez government introduced a proposal to Congress to fundamentally revise and undermine Venezuela's adherence to Decision 24. The new legislation called for increasing the dividend remittance ceiling, raising the reinvestment limits, and allowing national companies (more than 80 percent locally owned) to convert to mixed status (51 percent to 80 percent locally owned). An influential source within the U.S. business community pinpointed the larger ramifications of the proposed legislation: ". . . it would clarify and liberalize the treatment awarded foreign investment, thus whetting investors' waning interest in Venezuelan opportunities."[38] The high point of the Pérez government's efforts to accelerate growth (1973–1974) reflected Venezuela's relative strength in Latin America but, unfortunately, it did not reflect the internal shifts within the continent. The collapse of statism and the re-emergence of pro-foreign investment regimes prevented the effort from taking root. At best, what remains in the region are bilateral state-to-state agreements, which, however, are rooted within a matrix of private-capital-dominated political-economic regimes and are essentially agreements in which state corporations provide large-scale capital (which the private sector could not or would not invest) to obtain scarce raw materials, energy sources, and other resources for the private sector and to provide these resources at lower prices.

In summary, the convergence of a series of nationalist regimes in the late 1960s and early 1970s accelerated the move toward nationalist-regionalist development. This occurrence, however, was a conjunctural event, reflecting similar economic and political purposes but based on rather fragile state structures. The demise of those structures, either through the working out of their conflicts and contradictions or through outside pressure, has paved the way for a revival of bilateralism in which the links between the periphery and core have been strengthened at the expense of regional ties.

The creation of durable regional ties, then, does not depend on the "economic rationality" of the project—the scale of the market or operations, the "need for complementarity," etc.—but rather responds to the coming together of regimes with similar or related class bases, common national purposes, and adversaries. There is a need for a political class to bring it all together. Moreover, this class can only sustain the regionalist strategy if it has developed a state structure compatible with its new orientation: the social basis of the regime must be congruent with the organization and orientation of the state.

## Confrontation and the Consequences: From Regionalism to Bilateralism

The common impulse and converging perspectives around a common nationalist economic project facilitated the negotiations leading to increased economic exchanges and growing complementarity of economies. The very class forces which served to unify countries within the region, however, created cleavages within the nations and in the hemisphere, which led to confrontations. The overpowering presence of the United States within those societies (through liaison groups) and the resurgence of U.S.-backed military forces ultimately led to the dismantling of the regional nationalist coalition. The result is that the reemergence of bilateral ties provides major benefits for the multinational corporations and their counterparts within the national society. The key units facilitating bilateralism today are the international and private banks, whose policy prescriptions and strategies are devised to maximize the flow of capital from the metropolitan centers. The demise of the technocrats in the state-capitalist and democratic-socialist regimes has allowed the functionaries in the international and private banks to serve as the economic arbiters of investment decisions. The general direction of their policy dictates is toward the dissolution of barriers to foreign penetration and the denationalization of state enterprises. The Chilean military junta serves as the model for what can be expected within the rest of the regional bloc. The recent events in Ecuador and Peru are indicative of this general trend. The most important outcome of the replacement of the nationalist oil minister, Colonel René Vargas Pazzos, in Ecuador in early 1977 has been a decisive move toward providing "attractive incentives" and concessions to increase foreign multinational investment in the nation's oil industry. In Peru, the oil sector was similarly "opened up" to foreign capital via new concessions (exploration and production contracts) and incentives. In addition, the *Comunidad Industrial* of the Velasco period has been modified in order to marginalize the earlier worker participation schemes and restore decision-making and ownership prerogatives to management and, indirectly, to private shareholders.[39] The predominance of imperial over "regional" linkages is closely associated with the new receptivity to foreign capital and the privatization and denationalization of the economy.

From the mid-1960s until 1974, there was a small but steady overall decline (relative stagnation) in U.S. direct investment in the Andean Pact countries, although such investments continued to account for approximately 70 percent of foreign investment in the area.[40] Yet from around 1973 onward an uneven pattern of accommodation with foreign capital began to take hold and spread throughout the region, encompassing not only the free-market capitalists in Chile but also the bureaucratic state-capitalists in Venezuela. With the exception of Chile, the Andean Common Market's controls and restrictions on foreign capital's operations were neither directly challenged nor forcibly and quickly dismantled. Instead, as the various political regimes began to move away from their original nationalist aims, they adopted the tactic of an incremental dissolution of the central investment controls that defined Decision 24 and other constraints on capital accumulation "from the outside." The utilization of those loopholes and qualifications had rendered the foreign investment code increasingly obsolete and irrelevant in the new context. Obviously, different methods, styles, and measures were employed by the different regimes to achieve similar ends—from structural changes (Chile) to a combination of structural and incremental changes (Peru) to primarily incremental changes (Venezuela, Bolivia, Ecuador, Colombia). But while the procedures employed to disintegrate the nationalist structures that defined the essence of the Andean Pact were not correlated, what was common to all the regimes was the growth and expansion of foreign politicoeconomic ties and external MNC investment throughout the region.

Through the end of the decade, we project a continued break down of the nationalist constraints and a renewed expansion of foreign capital flows. In retrospect, the Venezuelan oil nationalizations are likely to be seen as the last gasp of the nationalist interregnum. Nonetheless, the results of the new regional policy toward foreign capital, and the latter's impact on capital growth and expansion, will not be clearly reflected in the short run. The changes in political regimes or in the political-economic policies of existing regimes will not result in a massive immediate change in the levels of foreign investment. What is immediately observable, however, as in the case of Chile, whose economy has absorbed only $40 million in new direct foreign investment during the two-year period from 1974 to 1976,[41] is the appearance of a "lag period" between the partial or fundamental dismantling of controls on foreign investment in the member countries and the response of the MNCs in increasing capital flows. By the end of the 1970s, we foresee a significant expansion in foreign capital activity throughout the Andean region and the hemisphere as a whole.

In conclusion, we note the emergence of a seeming paradox in the area of intraregional trade. Although representing under 6 percent of the Andean countries' total imports and exports, such trade did not fall in concert with the decline of the nationalist component of the regional pact. On the contrary, it rose by 13 percent in 1976, compared with a 1.6 percent rise in 1975.[42] A number of factors may account for this phenomenon, including the particular time period involved during which many of the industrial development programs were just getting under way; the slow organization of marketing arrangements; and the increasing role of the foreign MNCs in taking advantage of the large existing regional market to expand their operations. What appears to have occurred is not an increase in intraregional trade growing out of the nationalist programs of the area, but the phenomenon of *foreign capital inheriting the market advantages established by the nationalist forces*. At the moment that a viable market begins to manifest itself, foreign capital is in the best position to decide on the levels and types of exchanges that will define its future trajectory.

The reformulation of the regional schemes that may emerge will have a rationality based on the predominance of the multinationals. The purpose will be to facilitate the flows of capital and broaden markets for the multinational rather than to increase the weight and size of national state and private industrial enterprises. Rather than serve as a defensive weapon to strengthen and concentrate local capital, the regionalist project will now be part of the division of labor elaborated within the metropole. Efforts will be made to specialize the countries in the production of goods and resources oriented by the profit and strategic needs of the imperial center. "Inefficient," "duplicating" activities that compete with those of the multinationals will be allowed to disappear. Capital will be concentrated in strategic areas, especially in raw materials or in particular lines of production. The region's reinsertion into the new division of labor brings with it an open door for foreign investment, accompanied by the tutelage of international functionaries and the rise of fragmented and depressed economies linked to the imperial world.

## Notes

1. "Foreign Firms Get Cold Shoulder from Proposed Ancom Investment Regulations," *Business Latin America*, November 5, 1970, p. 353.
2. Quoted in "How Will Multinational Firms React to the Andean Pact's Decision 24?" *Inter-American Economic Affairs* 25, no. 2 (Autumn 1971): 57.
3. See "Andean Foreign Investment Code," in U.S., Congress, House, Committee on Foreign Affairs, *Inter-American Relations*, 93rd Congress, 1st sess., Committee Print, November 1973, p. 394.
4. See, for example, International Bank for Reconstruction and Development/International Development Association, "Tariffs and Trade Policy in the Andean Common Market," prepared by Bela Balassa, Development Research Center (Staff Working Paper, no. 150, April 30, 1973).
5. See Inter-American Development Bank, *Economic and Social Progress in Latin America/Annual Report 1974* (Washington, D.C., 1975), p. 134.
6. "Ancom Investment Rules Bring Protest From Business Sectors in Colombia," *Business Latin America*, February 25, 1971, p. 61.
7. "Ecuador Exempts From Ancom Code Oil, Banking and Certain Other Sectors," *Business Latin America*, August 12, 1971, pp. 254–56.
8. See Edward S. Milensky, "Development Nationalism in Practice: The Problems and Progress of the Andean Group," *Inter-American Economic Affairs* 26, no. 4 (Spring 1973): 56–57.
9. "Report Card on Progress of Ancom: Most Key Decisions Put Into Effect," *Business Latin America*, November 9, 1972, p. 358.
10. See "Ancom Eases Proposal on Patents, Trademarks," *Business Latin America*, June 15, 1972, p. 187.
11. See Business International Corporation, *Follow-up Roundtable with the Government of Chile*, February 27, 1975. Confidential Document (New York: Business International Corp.), March 17, 1975, pp. 6–7.
12. Business International Corporation, *Business International Round-*

*table with the Government of Chile*, Santiago, Chile, June 25–28, 1974. Confidential Document (New York: Business International Corp.), July 25, 1974, p. 3.

13. "Colombia Exempts Some Sectors From Stiff Ancom Regulations," *Business Latin America*, January 23, 1974, p. 31.
14. "Investment Is Up in Colombia Despite Ancom Strictures," *Business Latin America*, September 25, 1974, p. 310.
15. "Ancom's Sweeping Changes May Result in More Viable Market," *Business Latin America*, April 28, 1976, p. 129.
16. "Ancom Is Pressured to Focus Attention on Decision 24 Issue," *Business Latin America*, July 14, 1976, p. 218.
17. "Firms in Venezuela Continue to Wait for Greater Clarity," *Business Latin America*, August 18, 1976, p. 263.
18. U.S., General Accounting Office, *U.S. Direct Investment in South America's Andean Common Market*, Report to the Congress (ID-76-88), June 7, 1977, pp. 34–35.
19. "Ancom's Junta Displays Pragmatism and Strength," *Business Latin America*, March 20, 1974, p. 95.
20. "Ancom Fertilizer Sectorial Pact Seeks Low Prices, Not Protection," *Business Latin America*, April 24, 1974, p. 134.
21. See "New Ancom Programs Hold Some Opportunities for Foreign Investors," *Business Latin America*, November 7, 1975, p. 360. Also see "Ancom Petrochemical Proposal Provides Investor Opportunities," *Business Latin America*, March 27, 1974, p. 102.
22. "Ancom Junta Releases Sectorial Proposal for Steel Industry," *Business Latin America*, March 10, 1976, p. 79.
23. "Ancom Automotive Program Is Ready for Signing with Something for All," *Business Latin America*, September 7, 1977, p. 286.
24. "Eleventh hour rescue for Andean Group," *Latin American Economic Report*, April 16, 1976, p. 61. On the limited regional industrial development, see Jonathan Kandell, "The Latin Andean Pact is Not Working Out," *New York Times*, November 21, 1976, p. E3.
25. "Andean Group meeting postponed," *Latin America Economic Report*, September 10, 1976, p. 140.
26. "Latin America Opens the Door to Foreign Investment Again," *Business Week*, August 9, 1976, p. 36.
27. "Andean Group survivors favor foreign capital," *Latin America Economic Report*, November 19, 1976, p. 180.
28. See "Ancom Appears Undaunted by Chilean Withdrawal from the Pact," *Business Latin America*, November 10, 1976, pp. 353–55;

"Ancom Modification of Decision 24 Turns Out Quite Extensive," *Business Latin America*, September 15, 1976, pp. 292–93.
29. "Survey of MNCs in Chile Reveals Few are Put out by Pullout from Ancom," *Business Latin America*, December 8, 1976, pp. 387, 389–90.
30. See Alejandro Koffman O'Reilly, "Andean Pact Crisis Underlines Differences," *Journal of Commerce*, September 10, 1976, p. 21.
31. "Malleability on Decision 24," *Business Latin America*, August 11, 1976, p. 250.
32. U.S., General Accounting Office, *U.S. Direct Investment*, pp. 99–100.
33. See International Bank for Reconstruction and Development, *Peru's Social Property Sector: Development Through December 1975 and Prospects for Expansion, With a Postscript Covering Development in 1976*, Development Finance Companies Div., Projects Dept., Latin America and Caribbean Regional Office, December 30, 1976, pp. 46–56; "Peru Soft-Pedals Revolution: Hard Times, Deepening Foreign Debt Bring Move to Right," *Washington Post*, August 29, 1976, p. A10; "Social property eclipsed by Peru's new priorities," *Latin America Economic Report*, January 7, 1977, p. 4.
34. Don Oberdorfer, "U.S. Banks Impose Conditions, Set $240 Million Loan for Peru," *Washington Post*, August 29, 1976, p. A10.
35. "Peru claims 'profit' from Marcona compensation," *Latin America Economic Report*, October 22, 1976, p. 163; "Marcona Settlement Opens Door to Foreign Loans for Peruvian Government," *Business Latin America*, October 27, 1976, pp. 342–44.
36. See Ann Crittenden, "Loans to Developing Lands By U.S. Banks on Increase," *New York Times*, November 10, 1976, pp. D1, D7; "Peru's debt casts cloud over economic future, *Latin America Economic Report*, January 28, 1977, p. 14.
37. Business International Corporation, *Background Paper/Roundtable with Government of Venezuela*, Caracas, Venezuela, November 10–14, 1974 (New York: Business International Corp.), p. 30. Also see "Decision 24 in Venezuela: Harsher Than Anticipated," *Business Latin America*, May 29, 1974, pp. 175–76.
38. "Important Changes Coming in Venezuela's Foreign Investment Law," *Business Latin America*, October 19, 1977, p. 329.
39. See "Ecuador: oil change," *Latin America Political Report*, February 18, 1977, p. 54; "New oil minister announces policy changes in Ecuador," *Latin America Economic Report*, February 18, 1977, p. 25; "Peru reduces participation to attract more investment," *Latin*

*America Economic Report*, February 11, 1977, p. 21; "Peru announces new rules for foreign oil companies," *Latin America Economic Report*, March 11, 1977, p. 37.

40. See U.S., General Accounting Office, *U. S. Direct Investment*, pp. 20–22. "Investments within the region and within each country appear to be distributed based upon two primary criteria: (1) the presence of an exploitable natural resource and (2) the availability of an internal consumer market. Colombia, Venezuela, and, to a lesser extent, Chile, the three more developed Andean countries, have been able to attract U.S. investment in the manufacturing, trade, finance, and petroleum sectors. The other three Andean countries, with lesser developed internal markets, have traditionally attracted the majority of U.S. investment to the extractive sectors." Ibid., p. 23.
41. Investment total quoted from *El Mercurio*, in "Chile opens door wide to new foreign investment," *Latin America Economic Report*, March 25, 1977, p. 45.
42. "Growing importance of trade within Pact Countries," *Latin America Economic Report*, November 11, 1977, p. 206.

# 7

# THE DIVERGENCE BETWEEN SCIENTIFIC WORK AND POLITICAL ACTION

## Introduction: The Problem and Its Historical Antecedents

One of the central issues facing the Left is the divergence of theory from practice. The gap exists on many levels and in innumerable contexts: academics unconnected to a mass movement formulate new problems and theories, but their work has little influence on the tactics and strategies of activists. Practice and "theory" (meaning both theoretical and empirical/historical analysis) have been separated at the cost of both. Activists, increasingly oriented by practical experiences at a time of accelerating change both in the objects and instruments of history, have been left adrift—reacting to past situations, incapable of seizing initiatives or of creating the circumstances for action. Theorists and researchers, on the other hand, stand passively by as prophets of doom or oracles of success, or as commentators on philosophical texts or current events, or as theorists and analysts of historical processes dissociated from contemporary influences.

The break between academic Marxists and revolutionary socialists is, of course, situationally determined. But in most cases it is a circumstance which finds its expression in one form or another, in varying degrees, in many countries. Academic leftists see themselves as "objective" observers of the laws and processes of capitalism that lead to socialist revolution, whereas revolutionary activists claim their position in the class struggle as a basis for resolving the contradictions of capitalism. The loss of "faith" between the two is a by-product of the Left's incapacity to overcome three historical forces that have shaped the context of intellectual work and political struggle: (1) the rise of Stalinism and its aftermath in the international movement, (2) the circulation and diffusion of the ideology of "modernism" and "developmentalism" by the U.S. agencies of intellectual propaganda (academic outlets as well as mass media) and international research, and (3) the sociopolitical circumstances surrounding past and present theoretical work and political practice.

The first phenomenon, Stalinism, is of long-standing importance, although in recent years profound fissures have weakened its ideological hold.[1] Paradoxically, however, some of the cracks (such as the Sino-Soviet conflict) have not led to a critical and basic reappraisal of theory, but, especially in the Third World, to the reappearance of the same dogmatic formulas, with the same contentless forms serving the apparent foreign policy needs of one or the other of the contending parties. Categories divorced of historical meaning, ripped from their societal contexts, have been transformed by bureaucratic edict into defining characteristics of all societies. Hence, a whole series of characters emerge on the stage depending on political expediency. For example, the same bourgeoisie is, at one time or another, "compradore," "national," "progressive-democratic," "proimperalist," "fascist," and so on. The subordination of analysis to the exigencies of a bureaucratic collectivist "center" has been a prime factor in debasing theory and emptying analytical categories of their utility.

Much more pervasive in Latin America has been the spread of "modernist-developmental" ideology.[2] The process of capital accumulation and exploitation, which is at the center of economic activity has been obscured by the discussion of growth; and the process of "expansion," which derives from exploitative social relations, has become the focus of debate. The inundation of all intellectual effort by this U.S.-sponsored approach is apparent even within the leftist opposition, where intellectuals seek to refute the "facts" with other facts, reconstructing theory to fill the gap left by the lack of "critical" thought in the modernist-developmental school. The "New Left" merely substitutes "dependence" and "development" for "modernization" and "development." In a fashion similar to the Stalinized Marxism of the Russian and Chinese schools, the "modernist-developmental" school and its radical counterparts define economic and political processes economistically, without including the determinant of the social relations of production, which leads to efforts to locate the "correlates" of underdevelopment and the "mechanisms of decapitalization." Today it is called "goulash socialism," in the past "pig iron" socialism. Their critique focuses on quantitative output, not on the quality of the social relations of production, i.e., the issue of exploitation, and does not embody the classes-in-action, just as the classes-in-action do not embody the revolutionary theory. Their mechanical analysis anchors the problem in various associations between isolated factors without spelling out the theory that unites the parts into a whole.

One historical explanation for the separation between revolutionaries and social scientists must be the failure of revolutionary working-class movements to take root and to successfully wage political and social struggles. Outside of Chile and Cuba, the Communist parties have not become mass parties in Latin America but, at best, have led fractions of the labor force in the relatively small urban industrial proletariat. The major vehicle of mass mobilization has been "populist" movements, usually characterized by a "manipulative" leader using a hodgepodge of welfare and nationalist rhetoric. Thus, the political base for sustaining intellectual radicalism that combines action and research has been quite limited. Insofar as the Communist Party itself (especially during the Stalinist period) did not encourage research, the possibility of the intellectual developing new lines of inquiry that might have overcome the Left's isolation from the "populist" masses was sharply circumscribed.[3] The efforts by the intellectuals to attach themselves to the mass populist movements as a method of combining theory and practice were hardly more successful: they either became publicists and ideologists for the leadership or directors and technocrats in short-lived and ill-fated development and planning institutes.

The political and intellectual vacuum of the 1950s and 1960s left by the crises of populism and the failures of the Latin American Communist parties led directly to efforts to substitute action for theory. Armed by the ultravoluntaristic doctrines of Régis Debray, the revolutionary Left turned from theory as a guide to action, to action as a way of constructing theory.[4] The nature of the guerrilla effort—divorced from the masses and the intellectuals and anchored in militaristic conceptions of social transformation—undercut any formal basis for unifying action and research.

Present circumstances in Latin America have done little to facilitate the union of theory and practice. Under the aegis of a series of quasi-totalitarian U.S.-supported military dictatorships, the major research and teaching centers in Latin America have been dismantled and their personnel ejected, jailed, exiled, and assassinated. Intellectuals who conduct research that has implications for political action have no place in today's Latin America. In Uruguay, Argentina, Chile, Brazil, Bolivia, Paraguay, and, increasingly in Peru, the social sciences have been purged and, in some cases, whole departments abolished. The social scientist must function as a guerrilla, carrying on a clandestine existence that does not permit the freedom of research. There is, in other words, no objective basis for social scientific work oriented toward social transformation in most of contemporary Latin America. Social researchers in Latin America have been reduced mainly to data collecting and, occasionally, providing documentation and oblique criticism. Their survival depends on the use of Aesopian language. Hence, the defeat of the mass popular movements and the destruction of democratic freedoms are now the major obstacles to the reunification of research and political action.

However, to conceive the problem as one of a symmetrical weakness between theorists and activists is to overlook the tremendous upheavals that remade world history in the second half of the twentieth century. The process of transformation in China, Cuba, Vietnam, and now in Africa suggests that a social revolution involving the destruction of the old capitalist order is possible without an elaborated theory. The intuitive insights of

Fidel Castro, Mao Tse-tung, and Ho Chi Minh, combined with their great tactical and strategic skills and sense for political power, fashioned successful mass revolutions. But it does not deprecate their enormous political achievements to point out that their followers' incapacity to replicate their accomplishments testifies to the lack of a guiding body of writing that could provide the "tools" for repeating their successes. The example of successful empirical examples has been the gravedigger of subsequent efforts by followers. The attempts to codify *operational techniques* (by Debray and scores of Maoists) have been as much amiss as the efforts of the CIA's counterinsurgency experts.

Moreover, it is not altogether clear that a collectivization process, unfolding without the benefit of a theory tied to a class-conscious labor force, is capable of transcending capitalist social relations. The material base of the revolutionary society is distorted by the theoretical weakness. The same successes that precipitate a seizure of power can become the source of painful distortions in the content of the collectivist form.

## The Intellectuals and the Activists

What factors have divorced intellectuals from the revolutionary struggle? At the ideological level (which is primary for them) is the fascination with an intellectual tradition, which has recourse to a specialized language outside the sphere of political struggle. By fastening on the intellectual traditions and the problems fashioned by "leading thinkers" of the western world, intellectuals, with their concentration on "universalistic" themes, have little time for a systematic consideration of the specific structures, histories, and issues facing the mass movement. Inside the "grand tradition," the intellectual work is evaluated and pronouncements and rankings are accorded. Prestige, recognition, and institutional mobility are accorded. Within the intellectual sphere the norms that govern the intellectual are dictated by the chief mandarins of the profession. Seldom overtly ideological, the key determinant is frequently the capacity to encompass "universalistic" categories that transcend social systems—and leave the contemporary mass movements in the cold.

The pressures on the intellectual—the problems and approaches—are largely a product of the intellectual milieu, where notions of excellence and relevance, the style of work and language all flow from the direct contact between intellectuals. Insulated from the larger society, finding a university audience most compatible with their views and efforts, intellectuals-in-their-milieu retain esteem and stature as long as they approximate the norms of their academic colleagues. Their work is removed from experience by the abstraction with which they work: drawing from reality, they aggregate and generalize, formulating rich theoretical propositions.

Of prime importance then in limiting the capacity of the intellectuals to become involved in the mass movement is their intellectual call, their concern with status ("sense of importance"), and the conditions for their recognition. Whether social mobility is their *primary* concern is irrelevant, but it, nevertheless, accompanies recognition of excellence as defined within the intellectual milieu and dictates the nature of their work.

The style of intellectual work is also shaped by the conditions of academic employment. What is permitted varies, but generally the major distinction is between writing "for" a movement and writing "within" a movement. Within the academic world, certain members uphold the norms of professional behavior, which they selectively apply: castigating academic activists within mass movements while quietly engaging in consultantships at the top. Lacking the anonymity of the mass movement or the solidarity of the factory, the academic activist is vulnerable from all sides: among colleagues and authorities they are easily identifiable targets and ready-made rules of professional behavior are available for application. The recognition by the academics of their vulnerability inhibits them from acting, from stepping outside the given boundaries and falling victim to repression. This internalized sense of limitation establishes the intellectual's separation of the theoretical from the practical work of political struggle.

Apart from the stick, there is also the carrot—the ease of bourgeois society. The power of seduction is none other than the seduction of power: the opportunity to realize ambitions, to demonstrate to one's colleagues the capacity to "do," to act upon the world, to move people—even if it be through a bureaucratic apparatus within narrowly defined and predetermined boundaries. The divorce from the mass movement (as a condition for employment) and the sense of impotence induces their opposite—a gravitation toward the existing centers of power. That is why so many "academic Marxists" resolve the contradiction of their situation by paradoxically serving their enemies: "theory in action" becomes translated into serving as "Marxists" for the ruling class. Both the social costs and the political favors turn the intellectual into a self-nurtured world of academic exercises—and practical consultant. "Academic" Marxism becomes the price of survival. The world of reason becomes an end-in-itself: the practice of theory becomes defined as the theory of practice, largely in limbo, remote from the actual struggles, at best, working through proxies.

On the other hand, political activists have also contributed to the split between scientific work and political action, often by adopting a "vulgar empiricism" which claims involvement in a particular struggle as the sole and sufficient source of knowledge and which is often combined with a veneer of "theory," essentially citations from familiar political texts.

Among certain activists, a tendency toward anti-intellectualism deprives all intellectuals and their work of political significance. But when activists carry over this animosity to all systematic research—empirical, historical, and theoretical—and to all attempts to formulate and refine instruments of analysis to better account for social complexity, they are undermining one of their potential sources of support. Instead the anti-intellectual animus glorifies oversimplification and the use of formulas and homely refrains culled from this or that "red book." This overreaction to "academic Marxism" is no corrective but is merely the other side of the coin that divorces research from practice.

Another tendency among activists is to substitute the "wisdom" of a revolutionary "center" for their own efforts to elaborate and systematize their understanding of society and social relations in a way that applies to struggle. Instead of historical and empirical research, there is an oracular figure embodied in the leadership cult and a fetishistic belief in the organizational apparatus and the political liturgy. The leadership, organization, and political formulas then are substituted for analysis: processes and structures are squeezed into categories and prescriptions ordained by the center. The minds of the militants are reduced to elaborating tactical nuances.

Despite the frequent claims of dialectical reasoning, the actual process of movement is eminently pragmatic: trial and error and the process of "muddling through" dominate the practice of most activists. Political practice has had a terribly difficult time shedding time-worn approaches to political action. Adaptation to new situations, new types of adversaries, new scales of repression, and new conditions for struggle has only slowly and painfully been learned—and in many cases unlearned.

## Four Case Studies: Divorce of Theory and Practice

As noted above, serious shortcomings on the parts of both academics and activists have contributed to the divorce of theory from action. It is perhaps worthwhile to discuss some attempts to do research-for-action and to note some of the problems that face the Left in reintegrating theory and practice.

Four cases, in which I was personally involved, include (1) a study of peasant land seizure in Chile in 1965;[5] (2) a national voting study (at the municipal level) in Chile for 1958 and 1964 utilizing over eighty variables;[6] (3) a study of the linkages between the bureaucracy, the legal system, the class structure, and the agrarian sector in Chile in the mid-1960s;[7] and (4) a study of the linkages and attitudes of the Argentine industrial elite toward foreign capital.[8]

### *Case Study I: Peasant Land Seizure*

Focused on the first major peasant land seizure during the Eduardo Frei presidency in Chile in 1965, this was an empirical study of peasants undertaken to identify the determinants of class consciousness, the degree to which peasant invasions can be generalized, and the conditions which detonate direct political action on the part of peasants.

The study was designed to contribute to Leftist action among peasants in order that they increase their support among peasants, as well as build peasant organizations. The researchers encountered many problems with various segments of the Left, including:

1. *Suspicion*. Leftist leaders at the regional and national level were concerned about the purposes of the study (information for what?) and the ultimate beneficiary (whom will it serve?).
2. *Charges of irrelevance*. The Leftist leaders counterposed what they conceived as the only reliable source of data, "practical information," to what they considered the "academic study." The political people accepted certain sources of information as adequate and sufficient: day-to-day experience, personal contact, political relationships, party activity and programmatic study, and ideology and leadership.
3. *Grudging permission to carry out the study*. The decision to permit the study was largely a personal favor to one of the coauthors (who happened to be on the central committee of the party involved).
4. A *questioning of research techniques*. Efforts to study the biographies of rank-and-file peasant activists were challenged by party leaders, who thought they could better inform us of events and circumstances. In conceptualizing the problem, especially of identifying the various types of peasant responses, the political leaders sought to substitute political formulas for political realities.
5. *Research findings*. The Left did not understand the techniques and was skeptical about the use of "academic" research in policy-making, seeing little, if any, application to practice.

In contrast, the following characterized the reaction of the Right, that is, the Frei government.

1. *Differential receptivity*. The Right manifested great interest, including offers of subsidy, an invitation to La Moneda to see the minister of agriculture, and so forth. The government demanded access to the preliminary report and perceived that research on the land seizure might have general applicability. The Right could see that by "learning" the "language" of the peasants, it might gain information that could be used for manipulation.
2. *Differential capacity to utilize research*. Given the different backgrounds, Frei's government was more attuned to a "modern" outlook—the use of new research techniques, the application of social science research to politics, the manipulation of findings (extrapolating aspects of the study for integration into alternative perspectives)—and was in a much better position to benefit from our research.

The growing peasant radicalism based on interaction with cities, previous contact with Left/PDC parties, a linkage between short-term economic demands and large-scale structural changes, and the internal stratification of farming society led to polarization between skilled and unskilled labor on the one hand and "favored employees" on the other. The shift to commercial agriculture had undercut old ties without offering substantial improvements; the capacity to expand the commercial activity of tenant farmers conflicted within the latifundio with the monopoly control of the landlord. The political outlook of the peasantry was contradictory—that is, it was radical within the context of the old land system but conservative in terms of post-reform activity.

Some of our findings had direct relevance for policy-making on the Left.

1. Our research confirmed the existence of peasant radicalism after 1965. Frei's Christian Democratic Party (PDC) had initially won the majority of peasant unions. Only its shift to the right, the defection of left PDCers, and left-wing control of the state apparatus allowed the Left to gain a hegemonic position.

2. The PDC's distribution of individual holdings played on the "conservative" side of the peasants' contradictory consciousness, creating a stratum of land-reform beneficiaries that sided with the PDC throughout the period.
3. The connection between peasants' dependence on national political and economic complexes and their political attitudes was never fully grasped by the Unidad Popular (UP) government; hence efforts to reorganize rural areas into cooperatives, collectives, and state property floundered because no matter what the property form, as long as the capitalist market and the privately owned distribution networks were operating, the peasants' political orientations were dictated by segmental self-interest. The over-riding importance of firming state control over the market and distribution, as well as credit facilities, is key to forging a worker-peasant alliance. Our research clearly illustrated how tenuous peasants' allegiance to the Left could become if the urban nexus was broken. However, our attempt to uncover the deeply contradictory attitudes among the peasants and the ambivalences within "peasant socialism" had little or no impact on the Left's policy-making machinery, given the skepticism about academic research and the notion of politics based on first-hand knowledge.

The Left's initial resistance to the study was warranted: the information we collected on peasants could have been used by the ruling class to reassert its control over the movement. One of the researchers was relatively unknown, and his political and social purposes for conducting the research were not clear to the leaders. Nevertheless, the other member of the research team was an intellectual, a member of a leading body in a major leftist organization, and hence in a position to safeguard the organizational interest of his party and its constituents. Although publication was blocked by the Christian Democratic officials in the training institute (ICIRA) for several years, the study was eventually published during the Allende presidency by the government printing house. That suggests that while not originally perceived as useful by the party leaders, the research was released as some of the problems discussed in it became increasingly evident. As the Left shifted from being in opposition to forming a government, it became increasingly open to policy suggestions and research that was directed to concrete analysis.

What is most striking in this case was the failure by the political activists to see the relevance of our work to their activities. They questioned how "biographies" of peasants would help in the development and formulation of policy. Reliance on "practical experience," party directives, and perhaps traditional political texts was seen as a sufficient basis for political action. No doubt, the fact that the researchers were "outsiders," one from the capital and the other a foreigner, may have contributed to their disinterest. The active participation of the peasants and their leaders after the initial meeting and following clearance at the national level was based on the expectation that favorable results would be forthcoming. This is a crucial factor. Peasant cooperation with researchers is premised on their receiving some benefits from the study. Hence the study's successful completion was based on the participants' assessment of how well the researchers succeeded in making their research part of the struggle.

A final point: the study of the peasantry occurred at a time of a rising leftist movement in a climate of relative freedom where the Left was in a position to capitalize on the information. Such conditions no longer exist in Latin America; thus, this kind of research subject and method are politically inappropriate.

### *Case Study II: National Voting Study*

Maurice Zeitlin and I designed a national voting study, examining eighty variables in every municipality in Chile to identify the sources of political support and weakness for the Left. The study sought to identify crucial variables that could allow the Left to increase its support, to refute the Right's arguments that the Left was weak among "modern" workers, and hence to argue that the Left grew with the *expansion of capitalism*, in opposition to the view that support for the Left was a product of backwardness or declining industries and could be obliterated through "modernization."

Data was collected through government offices. There was no

need to obtain cooperation from the Left and no opposition from the Right. The data were processed by a commercial enterprise, with no financial or other support from the Left. The project received neither great encouragement nor discouragement. At best, there was a kind of benign indifference.

Our voting study found a strong base of support for the Left among workers employed in "modern" and "traditional" industries and mining areas. We hypothesized that radicalism was not a product of backwardness, traditionalism, or declining industries but rather of expanding capitalist social relations within an essentially class-organized political system. Contrary to the discursive works of some Latin American Marxists and U.S. social scientists, we found that "populism," or nonclass politics, was on the decline and that there was a growing polarization between basically propertied and propertyless groups, in the countryside and in the city. Specifically, we found a higher receptivity to leftism among landless laborers, tenant farmers, and sharecroppers than among small holders: equally important, through an examination of the positive political impact that centers of organized leftism in mining areas had had on surrounding peasant municipalities, we pointed to the possibility of the Left creating linkages between labor and the peasantry. The conclusions of our study pointed to the possibilities of the Chilean Left capturing political power by capitalizing on trends evident in the mid-1960s.

Data cards had never been used by the Left to the best of our knowledge. We suspect that the use of punched cards, computers, and quantitative data was regarded as impersonal and foreign, and therefore that no effort had been made to apply new modes of aggregating information to practical activity.

Paradoxically, the demise of the Camelot Project, which had been actively led and publicized by the Left, did not stir radicals to learn from the scientific study of society, but rather their opposition to the project encouraged an anti-intellectual attitude. "Research" was identified with the CIA, "surveying" with spying; and the Left somehow justified its refusal to develop a scientific team to collect and process data for its own political ends.

Our cross-sectional, intraclass, and interclass analyses would have been useful in projecting political alignments and formulating policies that took realistic account of allies and enemies. But the Left missed the opportunity because it would not appropriate the modern techniques of analysis from the bourgeois schools for its socialist project.

The growing polarization between basically propertied and propertyless groups was obscured by left-wing political formulas borrowed from "revolutionary centers" that promoted the idea of a "progressive" bourgeoisie. The predominance of a popular front ideology, apart from being ungrounded in reality, led the Left to underestimate its own capacity to win elections. While by 1967 we were predicting the probability of the Left's victory in 1970, on the eve of that election the Left had no site for a victory celebration and had to improvise at the downtown headquarters of the Student Federation (FECH).

Few, if any, detailed economic plans had been prepared in advance, and improvisation became the order of the day. Immersed in the day-to-day, short-term, direct contacts, the Left relegated middle range, or strategic, conflict with "capital" to an abstract slogan. Events dictated the course of action. The period of greatest social conflict between labor and capital over the control of industry became something to be "managed," not led, to successful fruition.

## *Cast Study III: Agrarian Reform in Chile, 1965–1970*

Robert LaPorte and I conducted a study of the linkages between the administrative agencies of the state and the agrarian class structure and their impact on the implementation of agrarian reform legislation during the Frei period (1965–1970).

No interest and not much cooperation was manifested in the initiation of the study. We proceeded with data collection, analysis, and publication without attracting attention. The Christian Democratic government cooperated in interviews with officials and peasants. As in other cases, the Right showed a greater willingness to appropriate the findings, even those of a study designed to serve other class interests.

The study was of great pertinence insofar as it indicated:

1. It was impossible to carry out large-scale redistributive changes through existing parliamentary and administrative institutions whose key personnel continued to be tied to the ruling classes.
2. The legal and juridical systems hindered effective application of the law.
3. The social orientation of the government was a necessary but insufficient instrument for change without an organized mass base and a court and coercive system congruent with its demands.
4. The only effective mode for realizing radical redistributive changes was through their forcible imposition upon the ruling classes, as the case of Cuba indicated.
5. Incremental changes in competitive political circumstances led to increasing radicalism and polarization; the outcome is the disintegration of the center.

The difficulty of consummating change through existing administrative, political, and judicial channels was acknowledged by most political activists (before, during, and immediately after the study). The Left's efforts to overcome these problems once it entered the government were ingenious and, in some cases, relatively successful in the short run. Allende's legal advisors discovered laws that empowered expropriation; new administrative agencies were established to circumvent bottlenecks in the existing administrative agencies; the peasants and activists themselves took direct action to counteract sabotage by hostile political, social, and administrative forces. All this, it could be argued, suggests that successful change does not require previous in-depth knowledge, that political action creates it and provides solutions. Nevertheless, the piecemeal successes of the early years of the Allende period were short lived. The structural constraints imposed by a civilian-military apparatus, captive to the Right, blocked the consummation of the process and eventually reversed most of the basic changes. Even within the process of transformation, the lack of a common appreciation of social reality led to different approaches and policies: those who viewed the bureaucracy as "professional" favored an in-system approach, while those who saw it as a class instrument advocated a restructuring of the state. Such conflicts undermined efforts at formulating a coherent policy. Strategy based on ideological position replaced systematic understanding. Thus, while piecemeal changes were successfully undertaken without the benefit of an overall analysis, long-term, large-scale changes suffered immensely from this "pragmatism."

The "outcomes" discussed in this study were largely accurate. In Chile, the PDC did lose control over the peasant movement; its administrative agencies were incapable of proceeding to a thorough reform because of their durable linkages to the elite. The Allende government that followed was able to extend and deepen the agrarian reform, but found its effective follow-up hindered by administrative sabotages from within and political constraints from without, eventually leading to the coup. Thus, both cases illustrate the impossibility of thoroughgoing reform within an essentially capitalist state framework.

In neither case, however, did the study have any direct impact on political activists who had been socialized by forty years of parliamentary institutions and were incapable of transcending them. In addition, the then-popular concept of "peaceful transition" blinded many to the political constraints and violent opposition inherent within the state. On the other hand, we lacked any firm political ties to the organized political movement, and therefore our findings could not influence policy.

The Left's relatively successful record in winning elections and displacing the Christian Democrats through reliance on "practical knowledge" reinforced the Leftists' commitment to the traditional methods of "information-collection"—so-called impressionistic empiricism and discursive Marxism—and neglect of the empirical and historical foundations of Marx's own work. But while these methods served to win elections, they could not sustain the effort to transform society. The dogma of the peaceful route required that the crucial agencies of the state remain abstract entities, either denounced on ceremonial occasions and at crucial moments of conflict or praised as professional, apolitical entities when the situation so dictated.

## *Case Study IV: Argentine Industrialists and Foreign Capital*

This study of Argentine industrial executives occurred in the midst of a broad political debate within the Left over whether the revolution would be "socialist" or one of "national liberation." The notion of national liberation implied an *alliance of classes* (including important sectors of the bourgeoisie), a program of national industrialization and capital expansion combined with populist redistributive measures, the expropriation of landed property and foreign firms, and a *political organization* and leadership (the Justice Party led by Juan Perón) that could do all that.

The socialist position identified the conflict as being primarily between labor and capital and the principal alliance between labor and its subordinate partners within the petty bourgeoisie and related strata. The program was one based on class struggle directed to the complete nationalization of the economy within which the bourgeoisie, essentially tied to foreign capital, would be a major enemy. The position called for an independent organization of the working class outside the Peronist framework.

The research was directed toward that debate by trying, through a survey of 110 executives of foreign subsidiaries and national enterprises, to investigate the degree of realism in each position. We wanted to examine whether significant differences existed between "national" capital and foreign subsidiaries in regard to dependency, as well as to analyze whether, dependency influenced the behavior of "national" capitalists.

The study found both foreign and national capitalists favorable toward foreign participation in the national economy, with the executives of foreign subsidiaries wanting unrestrained entrée and the executives of national firms favoring some form of market-sharing. Politically, the executives emphasized pragmatism: they countenanced parliamentary politics as long as it could control the growth of radicalism. More significant in terms of ideal projections, they leaned toward the most authoritarian rightist regimes, i.e., the Brazilian model.

The findings generally confirmed the non-nationalist nature of the bourgeoisie, though certain conflicts over the "terms of dependency" were identified. The bourgeoisie's lack of internal commitment, its instrumental view of democracy, and its strong support for Argentine's President Onganía and the Brazilian dictatorship suggested that the Peronist "alliance" was indeed a very fragile reed on which to rest hopes for "national liberation." Thus, the policy of the Peronist Left was indirectly challenged by this study, since the Left's political orientation was to work through the "radicalization" of the Peronist coalition. Perón's early definition of a nonradical, non-nationalist economic policy was clearly in line with the attitudes of the executives interviewed. If Perón's return coincided with the reassertion of bourgeois hegemony, the Left had no place within the Peronist coalition—as it eventually discovered after numerous and costly losses. The deepening repression and massive violence against the trade unions, unleashed before and after the fall of Isabel Perón, and the open door to foreign capital, coincided with the articulated orientations of the big business group. The resurgence of outright dictatorial rule had indeed been anticipated by the guerrilla Left (Peronist and non-Peronist).

## Conclusions

The differential receptivity of the Left and the Right to scientific research and the Left's reliance on old-fashioned "rules of thumb" severely handicap efforts by Leftist intellectuals to bridge the gap between their isolation in academia and the active world of mass politics. Clearly the Right is more attuned to social research and has a greater capacity to secure and apply its results. This circumstance is especially serious in a period of rapid shifts of power and of the introduction of new techniques and policies—many of them directed from metropolitan centers—whose purpose is to alter drastically the conditions for political action. The *past*, as it is known to the Left, is of little value in evaluating the evolving situation. Hence, the knowledge intellectuals have of the new programs emanating from the "center"—the communications networks, counterinsurgency programs, corporate "associations," and so forth—affords them a special tool for dealing with the new realities. The efforts by the political leaders to *substitute* political experience or political formulas borrowed from other historical experiences was and continues to be a serious shortcoming. There is a need to complement first-hand experience with a systematic appraisal of social forces and to integrate the two into any comprehensive diagnosis that serves as the basis for political action. Sweeping historical rhetoric, matched by impressionistic close-up observations, overlooks the crucial middle-range research which examines in a systematic way the aggregate of social forces that forge the links between past political experiences, "historical lessons," and programmatic realities.

No doubt, successful movements may continue to emerge without benefit of the scientific insight of committed intellectuals. Moreover, accurate diagnosis does not always produce political victories. Yet with greater foresight and a more intelligent handling of circumstances, the Left would not always be in the positon of "waiting" for changes to occur and reacting to adversity, but could begin to shape its own future. The problems within the hemisphere are enormous, and political conditions have never been worse. The failure of both peaceful and armed efforts at revolution has been matched by the equally disastrous results of externally induced reforms, e.g., the Alliance for Progress. Clearly, U.S. imperialism has refashioned a system of client regimes with a new intensity and repressive vigor. The military and the entrepreneurs have demolished all hopes of peaceful democratic change and have abandoned all pretext of upholding democracy, autonomy and civil freedoms. Whatever the problems and obstacles of the past, Leftist intellectuals must establish their credibility and break down the barriers to effective communication (first by discarding their exotic and bizarre jargon) with the mass movement.

The world has seen a whole generation of Latin America's most courageous and consequential political activists and intellectuals fighting and dying to liberate their countries and people. Ernesto Guevara, Luis de la Puente, Yon Sosa, Luis Turcios, Camilo Torres, Fabricio Ojeda, Miguel Enríquez, Inti Peredo, Mario Santucho, Carlos Marighela, Francisco Caamaño, Lucio

Cabañas, and tens of thousands of others have made history through their moral force and political commitment—and the struggle continues, intensifies, and increasingly involves everyone; there is literally no place for the "apolitical intellectual." The difficulties of carrying on scientific research under the present quasi-totalitarian controls are enormous, as are the risks of relating research to political action directed at fundamental social transformation. Despite all dangers, the effort is being made in whatever form possible. The alternative for intellectuals is to become the brain trusts and technocrats of the dictatorships, the accomplices of political assassins.

Intellectuals in Latin America have not developed, in most cases, organic ties with the labor movement. For example, intellectuals did not play an important role in making the Cuban revolution but, rather, offered their support after it succeeded, many of them returning from abroad. Their subsequent writings did not reflect the shared experiences of the revolutionaries but the expatriate view of what the revolution was about. This did not prevent many of them from securing a privileged niche in the revolutionary society. As self-identified revolutionaries without a revolutionary theory, they artificially filled the gap within the revolutionary movement. Their writings attempted to define the content of the revolution without any grounding in revolutionary theory or practice. The conflict that later emerged, epitomized by the Padilla affair, pitted a revolutionary government without a revolutionary theory against a nonrevolutionary intelligentsia that defined the cultural content of the society. The lack of a revolutionary cultural perspective (because of the regime's past reliance on the intellectuals) forced the government to resort to bureaucratic methods to confront its "nonrevolutionary" opponents. The regime faced a choice: admit that its cultural policy in the past had been inadequate, that it lacked a revolutionary cultural past rooted in an intelligentsia organically tied to the struggle—in other words, critically analyze past policies to begin the process of formulating a new policy and fostering a "cadre" of revolutionary writers—or deny the past and suppress its logical products—the Padillas. The latter course was doubly counterproductive: it obscured the historical and political basis out of which the writers had emerged and prevented rectification. The bureaucratic measures, in a sense, papered over more fundamental problems in the relations between the revolutionary process and the role of the intelligentsia.

We must insist on the importance of the organic linkage of intellectuals to the social and economic process—but obviously no "mechanical identity" of method or of expression—because of the pervasiveness of the doctrine of the "relative autonomy" of culture, politics, and the state, which is a mode of rationalizing intellectuals' evasion of commitment. For within the cultural and political realm, those who claim "autonomy," that is, demand freedom from the constraints of class and party, include the intellectuals. The concept is both a description and prescription embodying the ambivalent role of intellectuals within a revolutionary movement: the wish to be "of" the struggle but not in it. Hence, this seeming conceptual "flexibility" inserted into the praxis of the intellectual captures the dual allegiances to the collectivity and to their individual aspirations. The notion of "relative autonomy" is, above all, an opportunistic formula.

Having said that, however, we must consider the historical circumstances within which the notion of "autonomy" has emerged. The concept is a direct response to the decades of Stalinist hegemony on the Left and to the bureaucratic-authoritarian control of the party. It served to legitimize the freeing of the intellectuals in the cultural realm without challenging the bureaucratic conception of the relationship between class and party. The "autonomy of the political" served the party bureaucracy's identification of party and class, prompting the intellectuals to attempt to establish political space (free expression) through the notion of "relative autonomy" (of the political and cultural).

Thus, both Western Marxists and Third World revolutionaries tend to separate intellectual work from revolutionary struggle. In the West the divorce of Marxism from class struggle is codified in the notion of "relative autonomy," whereas the newly revolutionary societies lack a clear notion of the relationship between revolutionary practice and cultural work. Instead, they tend to alternate between subordinating cultural workers to administrative routines—such as promoting party directives about production goals and a *laissez faire* approach that tolerates "alienated" forms of individual expression. The problem of the intellectual's role in the revolutionary process is thus linked to defining with precision what is meant by the adage, "Everything within the revolution, nothing outside."

## Notes

1. See Perry Anderson, *Considerations on Western Marxism* (New York: Humanities Press, 1976) for an informed and succinct discussion of the impact of Stalinism in the European context.
2. For a critical discussion, see James Petras, "Sociologie du développement ou sociologie de l'exploitation," *Tiers Monde* 17, no. 67 (July–September 1976): 587–613.
3. Fernando Claudín, *The Communist Movement from Comintern to Cominform* (New York: Monthly Review Press, 1976).
4. Régis Debray, *Revolution in the Revolution* (New York: Monthly Review Press, 1967). Various critiques are collected in Paul Sweezy and Leo Huberman, *Régis Debray and the Latin American Revolution* (New York: Monthly Review Press, 1968).
5. James Petras and Hugo Zemelman, *Peasants in Revolt* (Austin, Tex.: University of Texas Press, 1972); in Spanish, *Proyección de la Reforma Agaria* (Santiago, Chile: Quimantú, 1972).
6. James Petras and Maurice Zeitlin, *El radicalismo político de la clase trabajadora chilena* (Buenos Aires: Centro Editorial de América Latina, 1969).
7. James Petras and Robert LaPorte, *Cultivating Revolution* (New York: Random House, 1971).
8. James Petras, ed., *Latin America: From Dependence to Revolution* (New York: John Wiley & Sons, 1973). Major essay appears in *Política de Poder en América Latina* (Buenos Aires: Pleamar, 1974).

# 8

# REFLECTIONS ON THE CHILEAN EXPERIENCE: THE PETTY BOURGEOISIE AND THE WORKING CLASS

## Introduction

The United States and the Chilean military did not and could not have acted independently of the class struggle in Chile between the working class and the bourgeoisie. The assertion that the coup was merely the result of the activities of the CIA and a handful of puppet generals leaves unexplained the fact that those same forces were unable to carry off a successful coup between September 1970 and July 1973, although several aborted efforts were attempted. United States and Chilean military efforts could only succeed when the polarization of class forces within Chile had created conditions propitious for a counter-revolution. U.S. and Chilean *golpista** efforts were mediated through the Chilean class structure, which is dominated by a local ruling class with its own specific interests, strategy, and political organization. There is no doubt that United States and Chilean military efforts played

* *Golpe* means coup in Spanish; a *golpista* is thus one who participates in or supports a coup.

a decisive role in the making of the coup; but those maneuvers and their ultimate success rested on the capacity of the Chilean bourgeoisie to organize and direct the political struggle against the Allende government. If the overthrow of the Popular Unity (UP) government was within the sole power of Washington, Allende would never have been allowed to take office; and the Pinochet mafia would have overthrown him in April 1972, when they began plotting the coup. What was missing in both instances were the political and social conditions that would have enabled a coup to succeed: a mobilized and organized petty bourgeoisie linked to the bourgeoisie; together they would be able to castigate the government and paralyze the economy as well as to influence and win over the necessary cadres in the military and federal police that were not yet committed. The inability of the UP government to use its early success to rapidly dispose of the leadership of the bourgeoisie and to capitalize on the growing socialist consciousness of the working class enabled the bourgeoisie to preempt the leadership of the petty bourgeoisie and to direct its growing discontent toward the government. Such a loss of government initiative cannot be laid to lack of a "program": the major effort of the last two years of the UP government was directed toward appeasing the petty bourgeoisie. Loans, credits, special representation on government bodies, and other inducements were proffered—and yet the opposition increased, precisely because those concessions (derived from the UP program) were channeled through the leadership and organizations of the Right. The issue is not whether sufficient concessions were made to "win over" the petty bourgeoisie—but the way in which those concessions were granted, the organizational channels through which they proceeded, the political context in which they were granted, and the consequences they had on the central struggle between the workers and the bourgeoisie. In its treatment of both the ambiguity of the petty bourgeoisie and the radicalization of the working class, the UP government failed to consider the factors influencing the formation of class consciousness, the fluidity of class consciousness, and the centrality of political organization not only in devising programs but in directing their outcome, as well.

## Petty Bourgeoisie: Structural Position and Political Orientation

By all indices, the petty bourgeoisie in Chile, as in the rest of Latin America and perhaps throughout the Third World, is a very numerous stratum. Concentrated in the large metropolitan areas, where the nerves of government and power are usually located, the petty bourgeoisie when organized and mobilized by the bourgeoisie can be a significant impediment to social revolution. For example, in greater Santiago almost 60 percent of the labor force is in services compared with 32 percent in productive activities (agriculture, mining, industry, and construction). Furthermore, of the 26 percent of the labor force in industry, almost one-half is employed in small machine shops and artisan establishments—where the owner usually is also a worker. The number of workers in the large and medium-sized industries of Santiago is roughly 150,000, slightly less than the 178,000* employed in commerce. In the transport sector, owner-operator truck owners greatly outnumber salaried truck drivers by a substantial margin. Only about one-third of the trucks are owned by large firms, while the rest are owner-operated. The "incomplete" and uneven character of capitalist development in Chile is the product of an incremental-additive style of change initiated under several petty-bourgeois regimes; monopoly capitalist penetration is encrusted upon a larger preindustrial constellation of small enterprises, which the monopolies have retained as service subsidiaries, maintenance satellites, and distributive dependencies. The enclave nature of the mining and industrial sectors, one serving foreign firms, the other a limited internal clientele, precluded a thoroughgoing industrial transformation, the full development of capitalist social relations, and the proletarianization of significant sectors of the urban population. As a result of urbanization and the industrial underdevelopment of most Third

---

* The pattern of uneven development is clearly evidenced in Chile's industrial sector, where 114 firms control the bulk of production, while 35,000 firms (which, however, employ the bulk of labor) vegetate on the margins of the industrial system. Nationwide, the retail owners' associations comprised about 160,000 members, small shopkeepers predominantly, supermarket owners excepted.

World countries, commercial and administrative strata continue to proliferate, providing the mass base for nationalist and populist, as well as rightist, movements. The least organized and capitalized area of economic activity is commerce. Historically, commercial activity was the link between the colonial metropolis and the agro-mineral centers in the interior of the country, which were under the control of large foreign and domestic trading companies. Later, however, retail trade serving the internal market (as well as government employment) mushroomed into a sector by default: ambitious individuals were confined to small-scale commerce because the other areas of capital accumulation (mining, agriculture, banking, and industry to a lesser degree) were taken up by the oligarchy. Operating in the interstices of dependent but monopoly capitalist society, the petty bourgeoisie, not withstanding its meager resources and short political reach, was not altogether insignificant as a political force, since it was especially susceptible to clientele politics. Numerous, relatively more active and organized than the lower class, concentrated in the big cities, it was available to whatever political power was capable of organizing and directing its grievances. While the petty bourgeoisie may have been mildly attracted to the "antimonopoly" aspect of the UP program, it also abhorred its collectivist vision. During the early phase of the UP government, it was attracted by the easily available credits and loans from the government, the increases in sales (because of the lower class's increased consumer power and the high spending of the frightened upper class), and the large-scale importation of consumer goods. Later, however, it grew increasingly hostile to the government because of price freezes, shortages of goods, and labor militancy. As exploiters of labor enforcing the most brutal conditions (lowest pay, longest hours, least social benefits, closest personal "supervision") small employers were forever fearful that their businesses, containing their life savings, would be taken over by their workers (which in fact occurred with some frequency in the latter stages of the government), despite the UP's protests to the contrary. The issues that became salient to the petty bourgeoisie (shortages of consumer goods, raw materials, replacement parts, fears of labor militancy, etc.) were determined by the bourgeois political organizations which seized the leadership of the petty-bourgeois *gremios*, or employers' associations.

Included among the petty bourgeoisie are owners of small businesses, owners of small factories (under twenty workers), truck owner-operators, as well as self-employed professionals (doctors, lawyers, etc.). Several structural features of this stratum make it at one and the same time a significant and yet unstable group in times of political mobilization.

Consider, for example, the position of the small shopkeeper and retailer or owner of a workshop or a truck. Throughout Latin America (Chile being no exception) the lower middle class is probably the most numerous stratum in society outside of the working class and peasantry. Whether in commerce or production it is involved in a highly competitive world: side-by-side, hundreds of like-minded shop owners and small business owners compete with scarce resources for a shrinking market encroached upon by large-scale enterprises. What separates the petty bourgeoisie from the big bourgeoisie is not only a disadvantageous competitive position but the lack of capital and, more important, easy credit. Subject to price changes, fluctuations in the flow of goods and services, and exorbitant interest rates for short-term credit, the petty bourgeoisie is quite vulnerable: day-to-day, they are always on the verge of bankruptcy, their meager holdings a precarious guard against the abyss of propertylessness. Closely related to their generally vulnerable condition, the petty bourgeoisie is dependent on monopoly capitalists in daily transactions. Suppliers or wholesalers provide goods on whatever terms the mass of petty bourgeoisie can bear; truckowners charge whatever the freight will bring in—leaving the shopkeeper with a constant sense of being squeezed on all sides by large and small competitors, creditors, shippers, wholesalers, and so on. In such a world of hostile forces the petty bourgeoisie depends on its clientele for survival, and in many cases must conform to their politics. Petty-bourgeois businesses operating in bourgeois areas conform to the dominant political orientation. In the same vein, petty-bourgeois establishments tend to be concentrated in downtown urban areas in close proximity to the business, professional, and white collar employees of major corporations, subject to the pressures, values, and political orientation emanating from these groups. The petty bourgeoisie is exploited by and depends upon the bourgeoisie. In the calculating world of small business the problems of daily life are reduced to questions of prices and profits: political resentments and hostilities grow out of the cash register. The petty bourgeoisie is equally hostile to the government, which controls prices, and the wholesaler, whose higher prices lower profits. They resent competition from big corporations and tremble before the threat of nationalization.

The political rhetoric of the petty bourgeoisie combines an opposition to collectivism and monopolies with an idealized projection of the small business ethos of individualism, hard work, and public order. Unable to restructure the modern world in its own image, incapable of climbing out of small-scale production by the rapid accumulation of capital, the petty bourgeoisie is nevertheless, because of its size and location, a critical political force in Chilean politics. Between the two major contending forces in society, the workers and the bourgeoisie, this large amorphous stratum vacillated in the Allende years—until the choice was decided, and then it committed itself with a vengeance.

What explains the political orientation of the petty bourgeoisie is not its structural position per se (which was ambiguous) nor is it purely its social relationship to other classes; instead, this grew out of (1) the political ties and organization that determined which of the conflicting orientations it would act on; and (2) the organizational and political dynamics of the two contending social classes and the relationship of power between the proletariat and the bourgeoisie. While the parties of the proletariat dominated the political scene, the bulk of the petty bourgeoisie was quiescent; once the bourgeoisie gained enough momentum to create a pole with the power to influence and shape the direction of social development, the petty bourgeoisie increasingly flocked to its banners. Without the bourgeoisie's initiatives challenging the proletariat's dominance, the petty bourgeoisie would not have become the mobilized counter-revolutionary force it became. Finally, the political orientation of this class is determined by the general economic situation: during periods of economic upswing and expansion the petty bourgeoisie "goes along with Left"; during hard times it grows discontented; in periods of dislocation it looks for order and authority, which, if lacking from the Left, it seeks from the Right.

The petty bourgeoisie was one of the principal social strata supporting the overthrow of Allende. Although the reasons for its support of and participation in right-wing politics are numerous and complex, they can be analyzed in three ways: structurally, organizationally, and ideologically. At each level there existed a "possibility" that the petty bourgeoisie could have been prevented from being mobilized en masse as a force for the Right. The structural position of the petty bourgeoisie was sufficiently contradictory, its ideology sufficiently diffuse and ambiguous, and its organization sufficiently autonomous to have allowed for the development of alternative political trends within it that could have at least defused the political energy of the petty bourgeoisie as a spearhead of right-wing politics.

## Right-Wing Strategy: Blueprint for a Coup

While the Left was concentrating almost exclusively on the organization of industrial workers and landless peasants, the Right began to encourage the organization of small business people, farmers, and segments of other small property owners. The Right combined its initiative with efforts to join petty-bourgeois associations with those of large property holders in a common organization or confederation that brought the petty bourgeoisie directly under the leadership and direction of the bourgeoisie. The process of subordination of the petty bourgeoisie to the big bourgeoisie was enhanced by the ideological emphasis on their "common" ownership of property—against the propertyless proletariat. Within that common organizational and ideological framework the differences and conflicts between big and small property were blunted, and the resentments and hostilities of the small property holder were directed at the government and the working class.

Four types of right-wing political formations can be distinguished. The Christian Democratic Party represents a fraction of the construction, service, industrial, and commercial bourgeoisie, foreign capital, a substantial part of the petty bourgeoisie (shopkeepers, professionals), a large proportion of the white-collar employees, and a small proportion of industrial workers, especially those still influenced by Catholicism. The party tended to favor a capitalist social order in which the state intervenes to protect and promote a national bourgeoisie in association with foreign capital. While only a minority of the liberals in the party were initially opposed to the military coup (though contributing heavily to its eventual success), with the militarization of the regime after the coup, a substantial number of the conservative leaders, having been excluded from the government, expressed some mild criticism. The Christian Democrats represented that wing of the Right that sought to use the coup to restore a parliamentary capitalist regime purged of the Left and capable of organizing a social order in which the national bourgeois state and foreign capital would have a free hand in exploiting the country.

Somewhat further to the right is the National Party, which represents the bulk of the landowning, commercial, banking, and industrial bourgeoisie, foreign capital, and a substantial segment of the petty bourgeoisie (lawyers, doctors, and small-business owners). The National Party, with its narrow sector of the electorate, had few illusions about the possibilities of ever returning to government through the ballot box—even without the Left's presence. In close collaboration with the employers' associations (the *gremios*), it sought to use the coup to eliminate the whole bourgeois-democratic political machinery and has with few exceptions endorsed the military regime. It probably favors a corporate political system in which the elite position of its members (who lack popular support) would determine its political influence.

Somewhat to the right of the National Party but with overlapping interests, personnel, and orientation is the extra-parliamentary paramilitary organization, Fatherland and Liberty. Pro-capitalist, it was generally supported by those sections of the national and foreign bourgeoisie that had been expropriated (ex-landowners, ex-bankers, etc.). Its direct-action approach attracted the bourgeois youth of the National Party; its extensive financial resources were useful in recruiting lumpenproletariat. The most aggressive and influential political force on the Chilean Right is the army and the federal police (*carabiñeros*). Described before the coup by the Communist Party as a "national-patriotic and constitutionalist force," the military leadership is largely antiparliamentarian, procapitalist (especially pro-foreign capital), and intent on imposing a corporate or militarized form of rule. While many of the officers are drawn from the "petty bourgeoisie," their class origins have been less influential in their choice of development strategies than the political and social alliances they developed before, during, and after the coup. The bourgeoisie, the U.S. government, and through it foreign financial capital have in the main determined socioeconomic policy. The rule of military terror has been in part a product of the effort to secure a development policy designed to suit the interests of the regime's principal social base in the face of overwhelming real and potential opposition.

Concomitant with the vertical ties between big and small property, links were formed between the leaders of the big property associations and the right-wing political parties. Individual leaders within the association had dual membership—being at the same time in the association leadership and members of one of the right-wing parties or groups (National, Christian-Democratic, Fatherland and Liberty, and so on). These ties were sufficiently flexible to allow the association leaders to organize actions on their own initiative, while at the same time the political allies began to attract large numbers of small-business owners, "apolitical" associations. It should be noted, however, that while the right-wing parties were able to utilize and influence the associations through the dual membership of individuals, the associations contained "nonparty" (and "antiparty") elements who, while accepting the support of the parties, jealously guarded the associations' independence in acting.*

The ties and linkages among associations and between associa-

* These antiparty association leaders have been the staunchest supporters of the militarized police state in Chile and, in some cases, have received influential positions in the government.

tions and political parties and paramilitary organizations laid the basis for combining their activities. The overlap of membership facilitated communication and allowed for coordination among the varied sectors and subgroups within the business and professional associations. During the first year of the Allende presidency, the isolated protests of individual groups and associations were neither effective nor "cumulative" (did not add new forces). During the second year, the impact of the combined organizational force of several propertied and professional sectors was sufficient to begin to paralyze the spheres of economic activity and public life. More important, the increased power resulting from the combined resources of the associations and their political allies began to attract large numbers of small-business owners, property holders, and professionals who previously had been politically inactive or undecided. The creation of a "property-based" political pole with seemingly unlimited resources, efficient organization, visible leadership, and a capacity to carry out successful actions led to a rapid accumulation and activation of social forces. Petty-bourgeois individuals and associations subscribed money, time, and energy as they came to believe that the tide was turning against the government and that the big property groups were increasingly in control of the situation.

At the tactical level, and partly at the insistence of the "nonparty" leaders, the associations initiated the struggle against the government over economic demands: seemingly specific grievances bound to immediate circumstances began to serve as pretexts for boycotts, lockouts, and protests. The immediate effects were disruption of economic activity and pressure on the government to divert time and resources from other areas toward negotiation. As discussions proceeded and a settlement appeared in sight, new demands would be added. When negotiations broke down, the leaders could raise their underlying political platform before the membership, thus setting the stage for political confrontation with the government. In cases of temporary settlements, the leaders of the associations could enhance their authority and tighten the discipline of the organization through their control of the distribution of government benefits. Successful struggles over issues thus served to reinforce the leadership of the most irreconcilable right-wingers within the associations, to attract new forces, and to undermine any attempts by pro-government forces to appeal to the rank-and-file small-business owners.

Political confrontation thus initially appeared to rank-and-file business owners as stemming from the "intransigence" of the government and from the "determination" of their "apolitical" leaders to improve their economic position. Later, as this pattern was repeated, substantial sectors of the small-business community no longer required economic priming and responded directly to the political appeals of their leaders.

In the midst of a situation which saw a rapidly politicized lower-middle class mobilized by the domestic property groups against the working class and subsidized by external funds, all the latent resentments and hostilities toward the underprivileged came to the force. The government's tolerance and promotion of working-class activities that enhanced its political and social power were viewed as challenges to the existing social order. The cooperative efforts at food distribution and price and speculation control became the target of rightist-led small-business owners who had come to believe that their illusory world of profit and expansion would soon come to an end under socialism. Their ties to the big bourgeoisie and right-wing parties and the ideological apparatus through which they viewed the world precluded them from observing that many of the shortages, losses of sales, and profit squeezes were engineered by the U.S. corporations from the outside and by the wholesalers, distributors, and transport owners from the inside. This "misperception," with its attendant political orientation, was the product of the petty bourgeoisie's organizational allegiances and the ideological direction supplied by the bourgeoisie.

The reordering of society was seen as "disorder"; the increasing influence and organization of workers were viewed as threats to "property"; the equalization of services and the decline in the lower class's deference, as well as the relative rise in the prestige of the working class, were described as a "loss of respect." The increase of lower-class mobility, freedom, and activity was viewed as "abnormal." The latent (and not so latent) authoritarian tendencies of the lower-middle class fused with the economic interests of the big property owners: the parliamentary system came into disrepute, and a military dictatorship increasingly was looked to as embodying the values of hierarchy, property, order, and normality. To absolve themselves of any misdoings and to avoid any reconsideration of the circumstances that might have suggested the need for thoroughgoing changes, the bourgeoisie popularized the myth that foreigners and Jews were responsible for arousing the passions of the lower class. Among the lower-middle class and the affluent classes, xenophobia, and to a lesser degree anti-Semitism, was, and is, nurtured to obfuscate the re-emergence of Chile's economic dependence on U.S. corporate and banking capital.

Militant associational and party pressure was directed toward securing a military regime. Initially the goal was to place military officials in the government—thus maintaining a constitutional "form" while radically changing the substance and direction of government policy. For a brief period the divisions among the top military officers prevented any decisive shift in policy. Nevertheless, the Right gained sufficient leverage at the executive level to prevent the government from defending itself from the political, administrative, and economic (sabotage) that the associations and parties were about to launch. The military-association-party coalition provided the political base for the massive campaign of disruption and urban-rural terror organized by the right-wing paramilitary formations. The operational procedures of the anti-governmental coalition followed a predictable pattern: during terrorist attacks the coalition declared the government "illegal," thus legitimizing terror; the coalition charged its prosocialist victims with the crimes committed against them by the terrorists; it emphasized the damaging *consequences* of the terror but blamed it on the government; finally, it both exploited the disorders caused by the terrorists and denied the government the legal and administrative instruments to eliminate the source of the agitation. While the coalition provided an indispensible "cover" for terrorist activities, the hooligans reciprocated by purging the coalition organizations of dissidents: physical attacks, psychological intimidation, and assassination were the most common techniques for homogenizing the membership and facilitating the smooth implementation of the leadership's policies. Hence, as the right-wing movement gained momentum, legal and illegal measures and group activities were increasingly complementary in reinforcing the overall effort to destroy the authority of the government in order to create the pretext for a military takeover.

The final and critical link in the chain of organizations and activities that formed the anti-Allende coalition was the U.S. corporate-CIA-military-governmental complex and Brazilian military-corporate groups. Acting on their own, as well as with the support and encouragement of the opposition coalition, U.S. public credit agencies and private banks shut off short-term credits, and U.S. firms delayed deliveries—thus creating acute shortages of everyday necessities. The shortages adversely affected lower-middle-class consumers, truckers, small-business owners, and professionals—all of whom depended on U.S.-made products. Organized, informed, and directed by the right-wing leadership of the associations, the mass of the petty bourgeoisie turned its hostility toward the government. And since the government had chosen to maintain a facade of amicable relations with the U.S., it was unable to mobilize its forces in any serious fashion against the real source of the supply disruption. The government gained nothing economically in not rupturing relations and lost enormously on the political side. The opposition coalition, on the other hand, maximized its external support without being visibly identified with it: substantial financial and military supplies and tactical and logistical support flowed in from the U.S. and Brazil. Along with the promise of a new "golden age" and the threat of physical attacks, the coalition offered immediate tangible payoffs to individual and associational affiliates willing to hinder the flow of goods and services. In such circumstances, surrounded by a formidable array of forces, which were simultaneously hostile and enticing, even the more apolitical, routinized truckowner, shopowner, busdriver, or doctor was highly likely to heed the calls for "unity" against the government. In such a milieu the individual petty bourgeois (even one who was a democrat or even a socialist) had little choice; the opposition coalition allowed none, and the government did not challenge its control.

The middle and lower-middle classes, faced with the choice of a parliamentary socialist order or a dictatorial military regime, chose the latter. In so doing, they supported activity that was prejudicial to political stability, openly defied legal norms, encouraged terror, and created disorders; moreover, they fashioned legal and illegal organizations to engage in subversive activities against the constitution and openly embraced values that denigrated the democratic basis of politics. Their values and behavior reflected the structural dislocations resulting from a society undergoing rapid change; nevertheless, the ambiguities built into the position of the lower-middle class prevent easy generalizations from its structural position to its political practice: the organizational intervention of large property owners and right-wing political cadres occupying strategic positions in the associational structures fostered and directed the seething discontent of the petty bourgeoisie. A different outcome perhaps would have occurred if the Left had actively intervened in the associations with force and vigor, contested the leadership with the Right, applied the force of the state apparatus against illegal action and terrorist activists, channeled resources to the petty bourgeoisie through its own leadership, rewarded collaboration with governmental policy, and withdrawn support for noncompliance.

Because of the contradictory structural position of the petty bourgeoisie and the gradual manner in which it was incorporated into the right-wing coalition it was not at first a reliable source of sustained opposition to the UP. It became so only after it had tasted a series of victories and had won concessions from the government under the leadership of the Right. Its commitment to the Right was strengthened by the disintegration of the legal/political order and the inability of the government to control events impinging on its day-to-day activities. An alliance of the petty bourgeoisie with the bourgeoisie is *conjunctural and unstable*: in the postcoup period, the petty bourgeois who had contributed to the coup have not been its beneficiaries. High prices, scarcities of goods, declining purchasing power, and the lack of credits and loans have cut heavily into the standard of living of the petty bourgeoisie. Hundreds of small truck owners—those who spearheaded the downfall of Allende—are out of business because of the high price of petroleum and the lack of transport goods. The bourgeois-military dictatorship, which came to power on the back of the petty bourgeoisie's revolt against the proletariat, has now turned against its erstwhile ally. It is not surprising that the petty-bourgeois wing of the Christian Democrats led by Bernardo Leighton has declared its willingness to join the Anti-Fascist Front proclaimed by the Communist Party. If the Left succeeds in overthrowing the dictatorship, it remains to be seen whether the stage theory of revolution—now firmly ensconced in the Anti-Fascist alliance—will be replayed. From the muse of history, the Chilean workers deserve better than tragedy and farce.

For the Left to have acted with "force and vigor," it would have had to work toward creating an alternative politico-administrative base of power: parliament was the graveyard of all government initiatives and ministers. To have been able to intervene successfully in the struggle to win or neutralize the petty bourgeoisie, the UP would have had first to base its activities and develop its policies on the expansion and deepening of working-class organizations. In the latter stages of the Allende government, under the pressure of violent head-on confrontations, local working-class militants did create fighting organizations—but to no avail.

## The Development of Working-Class Consciousness

The discussion of working-class consciousness has been blighted by the static and predictable stereotypes that emanate periodically from the Left. Thus, for assorted Maoists and Trotskyists, the Chilean working class was a revolutionary force throughout the 1970–73 period, striving for socialism but led by "traitorous" bureaucratic reformist leaders who misled and misdirected it from its "natural course." On the other hand, communist and social-democratic accounts describe the workers as essentially "economistic" and capable of developing socialist consciousness only after a prolonged period of socialist education and gradual economic change under the party's tutelage. Both perspectives fail to comprehend the notion that socialist consciousness is a *process* that develops out of the class struggle, in which the working class develops its own instruments for controlling and directing the economy.* The Chilean experience illustrates that observation and reveals the inadequacy of a "static" analysis of working-class consciousness. The "ultra-leftist" account fails to explain the pervasive and intense support among workers for the electoral and welfare politics of the first year of Allende's government. The "reformist" account fails to explain the emergence of confrontation politics and autonomous centers of working-class power during the last year of the Allende government. In a word, the problem is one of failing to understand the circumstances under which a reformist working class supportive of a reformist** political leadership (including its strategy and program) developed into a revolutionary class, albeit without a revolutionary leadership. Without having passed through the period of reformist politics, the working class would not have been in a position to develop a revolutionary perspective that went beyond the framework which guided their "formal" leadership. In that sense, the reformist period was a necessary condition for the mobilization of the class, creating the conditions for revolutionary struggle. But unable to transcend its original political premises and adopt a new strategy more in keeping with the

---

* The role of the party is to organize and deepen this "spontaneous" process, preparing the way (through military and political measures) for the struggle for power. The party is neither identical with the class or "outside" of it; through its working-class cadres it inserts itself in the struggle of the class.

** The following are characteristic reformist political tendencies: (1) a stage theory of socialist transformation in which the focus is on structural changes not incompatible with nationalist-capitalist development; (2) the lack of an effort to link nationalist democratic changes to the struggle for socialism: that is, to create military and political organization for taking power; (3) the adoption of the following as a method: to "permeate" existing institutions, to influence bourgeois sectors (army), to accept legitimacy of bourgeois institutional order—even when bourgeoisie no longer accepts it or its rules; (4) the identification of the electoral struggle as the central focus of political activity, subordinating all other activities and organizations to that arena: social struggles are directed to serve the outcome of elections.

changing political circumstances, the reformist leadership became a serious obstacle to the struggle for socialism.

Initially (September 1970), the majority of the Chilean working class supported an electoral approach to government and social policy based on welfare state measures. Six months later, over three-fourths of the working class endorsed electoral politics and social welfare measures (municipal elections, April 1971). In two years and five months, over three-fourths of the working class favored confronting the increasingly extra-parliamentary enemy with an extra-parliamentary approach (occupying factories, preparing for direct action, criticizing the weakness of the elected government toward the Right) in order to socialize the economy, augment production, and institutionalize new forms of worker power.

The quantitative increase in those supporting electoral methods in the first six months can be attributed to several factors: (1) a check on the use of coercive measures by the state and employers, (2) the social welfare measures of the government, (3) the declining effectiveness of the demonological propaganda of the Right, and (4) a bandwagon effect (join the winning side).

The government, which "led" the workers toward broad political and social changes, including agrarian reform and the nationalization of U.S. copper mines, was later pressured by the workers toward extending nationalization to domestic privately owned industries; extending government control of transportation, commerce, and construction; and recognizing the legislative power of worker-controlled councils—measures that the government resisted to the end.

Initially, it was the UP leadership that increased the number of workers supporting the socialist government and organizations through its highly visible "populist" measures (wage increases, price freezes, health facilities, and so on), which clearly favored the interests of the working class. A community of interests between workers and government was created. The attacks directed at government policies by the right-wing political opposition and property-owning groups served to reinforce the workers' allegiances, to heighten class cleavages, and to crystalize a sense of class solidarity or class consciousness among workers. The numerical size of the working-class base of support for the UP government remained constant from about the middle of 1971 to the overthrow of the government. The government and its component parties can be credited with increasing the size of support for the Left. However, fundamental changes took place within the working class regarding the political basis of their support for the Allende government and their adherence to the political methods used by the government, as well as over questions of tactics, strategies, and organization. *From simply being an active supporter of a welfare program initiated and administered by the executive branch, the working class became an increasingly active participant in the process of transforming property relations.* From being a mere spectator at mass rallies, the disinterested subject of parliamentary debates and trade union congresses, an occasional participant during election campaigns, the working class began to develop its own continuing organizations of participation. During the three years of the Allende government, the working class moved from a largely "economistic" position toward a socialist perspective. This *qualitative* change was largely the product of the social struggles that occurred during the last year of the Allende government. The structure, direction, intensity, and breadth of these social struggles served to heighten class consciousness.

Curiously, the initiative for provoking the social struggles that led to greater class consciousness among workers was taken by the property-owning classes and their allies in the professional associations. The Allende government had initiated far-reaching changes but had stopped short of nationalizing most industrial, transport, and commercial firms. The owners of these firms, organized in private associations and linked with rightist political parties, military officials, and paramilitary formations, attempted to force the collapse of the government through a lockout; by closing factories and businesses and paralyzing transport and professional services, they sought to facilitate a coup. The united action of the property-owning groups in defense of their economic interests forced workers to act in concert: they responded to the lock-out by occupying and operating the factories.

Production was organized without employers. Despite the difficulties throughout the economy, *the practical discovery that industry could function without the capitalist class was a major element in radicalizing the working class*. Out of the necessity to organize production, transportation, and distribution, networks emerged that brought together workers from different sectors who previously had been isolated. The repeated and violent efforts by the employers and their political allies to paralyze production led to the formation of paramilitary working class formations whose purpose was to protect productive installations.

The transformation of working-class consciousness began through a series of defensive actions against the employers' efforts to undermine a redistributive government. The qualitative changes were the products of the experience of workers' self-management; once having taken over an industry "in defense of the welfare state," the exercise of managerial powers and prerogatives became part of the workers' outlook. The confrontation between the government and the employers led to a massive mobilization of forces, increasing working-class solidarity and organization around the issues of the control and administration of the means of production. There the divergence between workers' consciousness and the political orientation of government officials manifested itself in a practical way. For the officials, the problem was one of maintaining the government; they saw the workers' activities as a means—positive, but temporary—to force the bourgeoisie to respect the political norms of the parliamentary system and to return to producing "normally" for the country. The workers, on the other hand (who up to that point had been critical of particular aspects of government policy but who, in fact, probably shared the government's perspectives on the political-economic process), began to develop an altogether different and more radical perspective. Completion of the socialization of industries (worker-occupied and -operated factories) was seen by the industrial workers as an end in itself, around which the government should orient its policies. The intensity of the class struggle had moved the workers beyond the schematic and abstract process of socialization which was being projected by the government officials.

"Abstract socialism" refers to several related phenomena, including the separation of the institutional practices of the regime from the practices of the masses. For example, the UP spoke of a workers' government but continued to depend on a bourgeois-controlled parliament while marginalizing the role and activities of the workers' organizations (Workers' Belts, municipal councils, peasant councils). The day-to-day activities of the Left and the organizational structures through which it operated within the nationalized mines were essentially the same as those established by the previous owners. In addition to its practice, the Left constantly exhorted the workers to participate, to produce, to become socialists—without providing the organizational channels or even, in some cases, the personal examples to orient the class. "Socialist education" was conducted through lectures and pamphlets, while the day-to-day work experience and the society at large were still structured according to bourgeois norms. That is what defines "abstract socialism." This approach included a socialist strategy that was essentially concerned with the electoral victories of parliamentarians and their representatives in the executive branch, who then negotiated changes with the leaders of the principal bourgeois party, the Christian Democrats, with the tacit consent of the "patriotic professional army officers." The process of change only incidentally involved the masses, who were brought into the picture as negotiating counters to pressure the opposition into making concessions. The changes themselves were conceived of as taking place over a prolonged period of time—that is to say, after the "national-democratic revolution" was completed (which essentially involved hastening and expanding capitalist social relations and increasing the productive capacity of the national economy, free of imperialist control and the latifundio). It is not altogether strange then that the Communist Party was the staunchest advocate of those collectivist forms of social organization that most closely resembled those of capitalist production: boards of directors, autonomous managers, bureaucratic principles. Given this conception of the process of transformation, it is clear why the Communists focused most of their attention on "normalizing" society, providing incentives, subsidies, credits, and loans to Chilean capital ("invested" in the counter-revolution), why they approved the law for the control of arms (used to disarm workers and arm the Right) and, above all, why they focused on the problem of "increasing production." The expansion-of-production slogan (as absurd and idiotic as it was in the midst of a pre-civil war/coup period) was a logical outgrowth of their vision of socialism in stages. The Communists were only fulfilling the role that the bourgeoisie refused to play. In playing out that role, their socialist declarations were increasingly remote or abstract from the daily experiences, events, and conditions of workers in Chile.

Up to that time, the officials of the Left had perceived the workers as lacking in socialist consciousness: as essentially "economistic." They had made some efforts to broaden the workers' political concerns by combining educational and redistributive programs. Nevertheless, while some workers were perhaps made aware of the larger implications of socialist politics through these methods, the workers' practical experiences in administering the factories fostered a socialist consciousness among the mass of ordinary workers. The official Left's separation of socialism (the didactic approach to abstract socialism) from the practical experience of working-class struggle at the point of production was itself an important factor in hindering and delaying the qualitative transformation of working-class consciousness. It is not surprising then that the mainsprings of the radicalization of the working class came from external sources in opposition to the government. The opposition posed the essential issue as one of conflict at the point of production: it was not, as the opposition pointedly stated, a question of production (as the officials of the Left argued) but of who controls the means of production. By locking up the factories the employers were refuting all the "productionist" arguments of the official Left: the fundamental issue of class hegemony was being asserted and tested. The growth of working-class consciousness followed in the wake (and obviously in the opposite direction) of ruling-class consciousness. If indeed the problem of production was subordinated to the control of the forces of production, the workers had a choice of joining the lockout under the leadership of the capitalist class and against the government or of taking over industry from the capitalist class for the government. The workers chose the latter; the official Left refused to choose.

The triangular relationship that developed (between workers, official Left, and employers) did not lead, however, to an organizational schism between the Left and the working class because no viable alternative organizational option was available to the radicalized workers.

The Left changed and did not change: in the heat of struggle it accepted the transformations resulting from the working class's actions and pressure in piecemeal, ad hoc fashion (expropriation of factory, land) or accepted the organized initiatives of the working class and turned them to serve their own conventional political ends. For example, the Workers' Belts were not opposed, but were used in an attempt to pressure the bourgeoisie to respect bourgeois legality. Cordons were not opposed, but either were subordinated to the United Confederation of Workers (CUT), which was controlled by reformists, or were isolated without resources or tasks after confrontation.

On the local level, the leadership of the working class did change. Workers began to shift their support to Left socialists, the Movement of United Popular Action (MAPU–Garreton), Left Christians (IC), and the Movement of the Revolutionary Left (MIR); but the fragmentation of the Left and the fact that the Left socialists stayed in the Socialist Party (SP)—fearful that their departure would hasten Allende's downfall and "divide the class," and hopeful that with time they could gain the support of a majority of the class through militant struggle within the party—short-circuited the mass exodus of the working class and trade unionists out of the party. In one sense, the left SP was the bridge between the extra-parliamentary Left and the UP; but it was also an available outlet for revolutionary workers, allowing them to act on the local level in all sorts of direct action but without providing any national leadership or direction. The fact that the left SP had a program that resembled that of the extra-parliamentary Left obscured a fundamental issue: it provided no organizational means or strategy (and could not) to its mass of followers for realizing that program. Organizationally tied to the UP, which in turn was obsessed with reaching a pact with the Christian Democratic minority, which in turn was tied to the Frei leadership (which was preparing the coup), the left SP with its rhetoric and local action drew away the mass of radicalized workers who could have formed the basis of a revitalized revolutionary pole. The MIR by itself did not have the working-class cadres in the key industries, nor the day-to-day contacts and networks, to significantly influence the major revolutionary force in Chilean society—the industrial working class. Largely outside of the factories, the MIR, despite its correct strategy and disciplined organization, was helpless in shaping the direction of the coming confrontation. The social and political bonds between workers and the traditional Left parties, shaped over decades of common struggles and experiences, were not easily broken. Workers found it easier to shift from one wing of the party to another, from one tactic to another, than to break with the party in search of an organization with few, if any, roots in the factories.

There are several other, secondary, reasons why an alternative Left organization did not emerge, despite the growth of socialist consciousness among the mass of the workers. Among those is the fragmentation of the revolutionary Left over essentially secondary issues: MIR, MAPU (Garreton), IC (Left Christians), and other groups competed for the same social base, wasting resources, confusing workers, and dissipating energies. That fragmentation, in turn, was in part induced by the excessively "personalistic" character of the leadership of these groups.

The last major electoral campaign in Chile, the March 1973 congressional election, witnessed a massive working class vote for the Left, but no longer on the basis of "economist appeals" (food shortages and the end of redistributive measures precluded that kind of campaign). The workers voted for the Left on the basis of their positive experiences of class struggle, class solidarity, and of sharing power. A prerevolutionary historical moment presented itself, but the Left leadership failed to realize it.

The autonomous organizations of the workers (the Workers' Belts, the municipal councils) established in the course of the struggle were both instruments in the struggle for state power and organizations directed toward the defense of their socio-economic gains and the Allende government. The October

1972 confrontation and the June 1973 military coup were the setting for a massive mobilization of the working class and peasantry that created a prerevolutionary situation: the massive factory occupations, the takeover of whole areas of the city, the establishment of self-defense units, the clear identification of the bourgeoisie as the principal enemy to be fought to the bitter end, the divisions within the army, all of these objective and subjective factors were conducive to a revolutionary struggle—if there had been a mass revolutionary party ready and willing to organize the insurrection. Lacking that party, the workers' organizations served, in part, to bolster the Allende government and to extend the social sector of the economy within the existing political framework. Workers' organizations became, in effect, expressions of revolutionary syndicalism because the Left political parties confined their activities to precisely that position. But revolutionary syndicalism was neither the product of conscious choice by the workers nor of an ideological tendency within the class so much as it was the product of the deliberate policy of the parliamentary Left to confine the working-class organizations to an essentially defensive role vis-à-vis the existing organization of political and administrative power, i.e., to defend their factories. The final outcome of that policy was that when the coup occurred, the factories to which the workers had been confined became their death traps.

Having placed themselves in government to advance the working class toward socialism, the Left officials failed to incorporate the experience, organization, and developing socialist consciousness of the workers into a strategy for the revolutionary struggle for power. They were captives of their own version of abstracted Marxism: socialism continued to be a theoretical project distant from the day-to-day political realities—even as the political realities closed the gap between day-to-day politics and the fundamental question of political hegemony.

# 9

# THE VENEZUELAN DEVELOPMENT "MODEL" AND U.S. POLICY

*(with Morris H. Morley)*

After Acción Democrática (AD) won the 1973 Venzuelan elections by a substantial margin, the Carlos Andrés Pérez government's failure to implement most of the reformist measures proposed in the postelection period was followed by a turn toward an "entrepreneurial" capitalist development strategy. Among the "reforms" actually carried out was the nationalization of the iron ore and oil industries, which was hailed by some leftists (including Fidel Castro) as a major step toward breaking with imperialism.

The U.S.-owned iron ore mines accounted for 96 percent of total Venezuelan production, and company officials assessed their combined net book value at approximately $200 million. However, the companies (Bethlehem and U.S. Steel) accepted the Pérez government's offer of $104.4 million in compensation without significant resistance because what interested them as much as the level of compensation, if not more, was the nature of the ongoing ties offered by the regime: "In both cases a one-year contract has been signed for a managerial team to remain at work in all the main installations. In addition there is a two-year 'technical assistance' contract and . . . both Bethlehem and U.S. Steel will continue to receive the same quantities of ore as at present. . . ."[1] Likewise, the foreign-owned oil companies, which estimated the combined value of their assets at $5 billion, agreed (with the exception of El Paso) to accept as "satisfactory" an offer of approximately $1 billion in compensation payments[2] because it was part of a "package settlement" that also provided for continued technological contributions to the nationalized industry, as well as marketing agreements for the international trans-shipment of the country's petroleum exports. According to Venezuelan Minister for Mines and Hydro-carbons Valentín Hernández, the oil companies would be offered between eight and fifteen cents per barrel for technical aid in discovering and extracting oil and a similar fee for refining technology. Transport costs were also expected to add another seven to fifteen cents to Venezuela's cost for each new barrel of oil.[3] As a result, some informed analysts maintained that "Exxon will make more money on Venezuelan oil than before nationalization. . . ."[4]

Whether Exxon's case is typical of other oil companies or not, the fact remains that their profits approximate those prior to nationalization—without the risks, labor, or political problems of the past. The oil companies' decision to accept the Venezuelan compensation offer was not only conditioned by the accompanying offer of multiple short- and long-term "payoffs" (principally new areas of exploitation in oil-related activities) but also by their inability—individually, collectively, or in collaboration with the U.S. government—to force an upward revision of the total compensation payments and a more favorable arrangement regarding the form of payments.

Our thesis is that nationalization strengthened capitalist development in Venezuela and led to forms of "association" with imperialism, leading toward accommodation, rather than confrontation, with it. Our purpose is to analyze what the iron ore/oil nationalization meant in terms of its impact on the Venezuelan class structure and Venezuela's relations with imperialism, including how the nationalization and its relationship to capitalist development was viewed by crucial executive agencies of the U.S. imperial state.

## Nationalization and Capitalist Development

Both the form and content of nationalization vary from one regime to another. Thus, a distinction must be drawn between a nationalization that contributes to the growth of capitalism—state-capitalism—and one that provides the instrumentality for collective planning of the national economy. Clive Jenkins, in describing the nationalization process and the structure of the nationalized forms in England, posed the essential question—nationalization *for whom?*[5] Although some knee-jerk conservatives (in the U.S. they include most business and political leaders) continue to flail away at any notion of government ownership, in most countries both conservatives and businessmen assume that some forms of government ownership in certain areas of the economy are necessary for the development and expansion of private enterprise. Hence outside of the extreme "privatism" of the U.S., public ownership in itself is neither novel nor innovative. The crucial determinations are the roles the public firms play in relationship to the private sector and who controls and benefits from the nationalized property.

State-capitalism is a social system in which the principal sources of surplus production are owned and directed by the state and in which the state becomes the principal source of capital accumulation within a market economy. The mere "intervention" of the state in economic activity is characteristic of other systems in addition to the state-capitalist.

In Venezuela, state-capitalist nationalization, which captures the surplus from foreign capital, invests only a part of it in state-directed and -controlled firms. The rest is channeled through banking institutions to the private sector and, in some cases, new foreign investors.

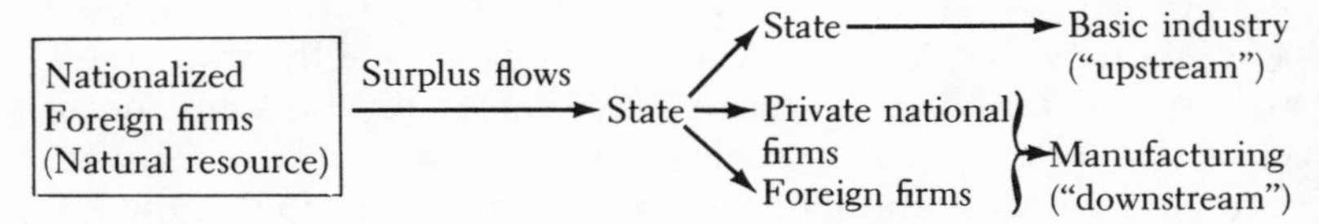


In the short and medium run, state-capitalist nationalization is a vital instrument for strengthening national capital. In addition to providing a rich source of new capital funds, the state's control over allocations promotes a whole series of related industries and their offspring. According to The Central Planning Office (CORDIPLAN), the investment strategy involves "selective foreign investment participation" and, more important, "promoting national investment, encouraging public and private savings as a means of offsetting the effects of the restrictions on foreign capital, [and] channeling it especially toward the dynamic and strategic sectors of the economy."[6] In the 1975 report of the Organization of American States (OAS), "Recent Developments in the Venezuelan Economy," the linkages between the state and the private sector were made more explicit: "Intervention by the state as an entrepreneur in the petroleum, gas and iron and steel industries and in certain special services provides for a broad field for action by private enterprise. . . . In large measure, public activity has been, and will in the future, be directed toward the promotion of priority activities by the private sector. This governmental activity includes the creation of basic infrastructure (as well as monetary, credit, fiscal or institutional measures) . . ."[7]

The nationalization of oil provides the basis for the development of a series of petrochemical plants, followed by plastics, fertilizers, and derivatives. The concentration of wealth in the national state gives rise to the proliferation and diversification of industry, opening opportunities for state and private capital. The political and economic function of state-capitalist development in the case of Venezuela has been to strengthen the national private, as well as the bureaucratic, capitalist classes. The funding and elaboration of industrial expansion has been accompanied by a "package" of regulations, decrees, and laws whose fundamental intent is to allow industrialization in order to gain an "equal" association with foreign capital. The new rules of the game for foreign participation can be summarized as follows: (1) "Foreign investment will be welcome, mainly as part of technology packages in which minority equity holding by the foreign investor would be encouraged";[8] (2) local content requirements are being pressed to promote national industrialization; (3) sectors reserved for national companies have been specified—

including domestic marketing, public service, and communications; (4) a 5 percent reinvestment limitation has been imposed on foreign-owned firms (except if the investment occurs outside the Caracas area as part of a decentralization scheme); (5) royalty payments between subsidiaries more than 49 percent foreign-held and parent companies must be restructured;[9] (6) a fifteen-year fadeout period is required of wholly foreign-owned firms; (7) annual net dividends have been limited to 14 percent of authorized and registered capital; and (8) equity holdings of foreign banks in financial houses have been limited to 20 percent, minimum capital requirements have been increased.

While these measures enhance the position of national capital, foreign capital has other, equally good, reasons to participate in Venezuela's development. Corporate taxes, among the lowest in Latin America, are in fact the lowest among the larger Latin states. Financial operations are far easier than in any other Latin American country because of the well-developed financial system, the ample funds, and the minimal controls on local or foreign financing. Despite some minor limitations on the cost of borrowing, foreign subsidiaries have access to local credit. Furthermore, under U.S. business pressure, Venezuelan officials have modified ("clarified") the limitations on foreign capital. The superintendent of foreign investment has ruled that a firm can be considered a local manufacturing firm as opposed to a domestic marketing outfit, even if it locally produces less than 51 percent of what it sells—only 35 percent of local value added qualifies a product as Venezuelan.[10] Legislation on equity transfers and the limitation on profit remittances and reinvestment has also been modified.

The new rules on the role of foreign investment provide for collaboration between foreign capital and its new allies among the private/bureaucratic bourgeoisie. Foreign investors must share the exploitation, not displace the local bourgeoisie. In summary, the new rules are not very restrictive and compare favorably with those of Mexico and Brazil—long considered lucrative areas of profit-making activity. Key to Venezuelan state-capitalist economic development is the provision of more opportunities for Venezuelan investors through state regulation of foreign capital. Thus regulation of foreign capital and promotion of growth and expansion of national bureaucratic and private capital lead to a new historical bloc of classes in which national and foreign industrial capital collaborate. Within that process the financial sector has a dominant influence on the economy. Through its access to state funds and its linkages to private/foreign capital, the banking financial system is the pivot, allocating resources and directing industrialization.

Ties are opening for state and foreign capital in large-scale petrochemical enterprises, and for national-private and foreign capital in industrialization that extends beyond assembly plants (with both having access to local funds through the private banks); agro-bourgeois and foreign capital are linked in the marketing and processing of agricultural goods and the production of equipment.

To best understand the positive relationship that exists between the Venezuelan business community and the Pérez government, it is important to analyze the government's investment institutions and the manner in which they distribute funds. The three primary sources for investment financing are the Venezuelan Investment Fund, the Industrial Investment Fund, and the Agricultural Investment Fund. The vast bulk of investment funds in industry and agriculture has been directed toward large and "middle"-sized private firms. Forty times as much investment funding has been allocated to middle-sized and large enterprises as has been directed toward funding small firms.[11] Almost all funding is through private banks whose links are with big business and which justify loans on the basis of their "risk" and of the collateral they require. Obviously, large and middle-sized capitalists have far superior access to the state apparatus than do small business owners, President Pérez's rhetoric to the contrary notwithstanding. In 1974–1975 the Fondo de Inversiones (Investment Fund) provided 13 billion bolivars for state and big private firms in basic industry; the Industrial Credit Fund provided funds (two billion bolivars) for middle-sized and large firms (enterprises capitalized at 6 million to 50 million bolivars), while the funding organization for small and middle-sized firms, CORPO, provided only 400 million bolivars.[12] If the allocation of investment funding is used as an indicator of the nature of the government, the Pérez administration must be considered a representative of the interests of national monopoly capital, with a satellite sector of small and medium-sized firms tailing along.

The allocation of investment resources in agriculture during 1974–1975 substantiates the notion that the entrepreneurial class forms the principal base of the current government: 86 percent of loans, amounting to 860 million bolivars, went to cattle ranchers, and only 14 percent was distributed among farmers, the bulk of whom are large and middle-sized commercial farmers.[13] The enormous disparities led to protests from the commercial farmers and in 1975–1976 the agricultural fund increased loans to non-cattle sectors—apparently the commercial farmers outmuscling the ranchers for the moment. These allocations in agriculture suggest a decided shift from the half-hearted peasant-oriented agrarian reform strategy of the 1960s to a full commitment to large-scale mechanized agriculture. The emphasis in governmental policy is on enhancing the position of the entrepreneurial sector and abandoning the small producers to a marginal position.

The personnel and investment criteria within the investment fund agencies reflect the current priorities of the Democratic Action (AD) government: almost all their directors are corporate executives and act upon business criteria in distributing funds. Obviously, the choice of personnel is ideal for facilitating the smooth flow of resources to the large private landowners. The existence of elaborate ties between the investment fund agencies and the large private-sector firms, however, does not lend itself to a populist interpretation of the regime. Rather, it denotes a very elitist strategy, which has taken "efficiency" and "productivity" as its bywords and relegated redistribution of income and rewards to the lowest level of priorities.

The response of the business community to the Pérez government's "entrepreneurial" orientation has generally been favorable, with few overt and strident critics. Hans Neumann, a major corporate executive, president of Corporación Industrial Montana, a holding company for fourteen firms, expressed the general sentiment when he stated, "I have full confidence in the present government."[14] The leading business association,

Fedecámaras, reiterated its general support of the Pérez administration soon after the establishment of PETROVEN, the state petroleum holding company, as an "autonomous" enterprise—declaring its "great confidence" in the country.[15] Fedecámaras' enthusiasm was also manifested in its decision to collaborate in the formulation of the National Plan within the framework of "joint planning" between the state and the private sector. Having a probusiness regime in power, it is logical that its business supporters should call for "unity" and "consensus" around its leadership and program; the nationalist rhetoric becomes an ideological weapon to elicit political support for its social program—benefiting big business. Eloy Anzola Montauban, president of a major insurance company, talks of giving a "free hand to the government in the management of industry."[16] In the same vein, Humberto Peñaloza, a corporate executive in the petroleum business, called for confidence and unity around the present government.[17] While supporting the government's initiatives in the area of nationalization because they are the prime beneficiaries, Venezuelan big business (despite its newly adopted nationalist posture) is concerned with any eventuality which might adversely affect its other relations with capitalist countries. The same Peñaloza who is so ardently defending the nationalization of petroleum and OPEC-proposed commercial agreements with the multinationals (MNCs) to market the oil, partnerships with the MNCs to build a shipping fleet and other forms of "association" with foreign capital, is qualifying his support of foreign capital by asserting that the ties should only take place on the "international plane" and not the national territory.[18]

## Capitalism and the Class Structure

It's too early to give a thorough account of the social impact of the entrepreneurial strategy of the Pérez regime. Nevertheless, there is a logic to the process and there are indicators that foreshadow the future configuration of social forces.

The drive to promote heavy industry and to provide competitive exports has yielded a development plan which banks heavily on up-to-date technology. As a result, we can expect that industrialization will have only a minimal effect on the unemployment problem. In this regard, the proposals by Merhav promoting a "parallel economy" and Decree 21 of the Pérez government providing make-work (encumbering automatic elevators with operators) are merely increasing forms of disguised unemployment.[19] This type of employment provides neither skills nor adequate remuneration. More important, it does not substantially reduce the unemployment rate over the long run.

The second element in the entrepreneurial formula is the loosening of price controls, restricting wage increases, and decreasing social welfare benefits—thus increasing profits and other incentives to private investors, while depressing the standard of living of wage laborers. The conservative daily, *El Universal*, noted at the end of the first year of the Pérez government that "in general terms the quality of life has not improved substantially, owing to the inflationary impact on the real purchasing power of the economically weakest levels of the population (70% of 12 million inhabitants). . . . Notwithstanding the general increase in salaries and wages of 15%, the rate of [price] increase was equal."[20] During 1975 there was a deterioration of the standard of living of the working class. The Jesuit economist, Manuel Pernaud, pointed out that the price increases of basic necessities *exceeded* wage increases. He cited as an example sugar which "costs 1.5 bolivars today [March 31, 1975] when it was valued at one bolivar [a year earlier],"[21] though he could have gone on to consider increases of 25 percent in food prices as well as substantial rises in clothing and shoes which exceed wage increases.[22] As with the industrialization strategy, the price policy is designed to promote capital accumulation of the industrial-commercial classes at the expense of the working class. This policy is promoted by the regime, even though it is a well-known fact within the various government agencies that higher profits do not necessarily lead to increasing investments in productive activity.

In the areas of housing, the Pérez regime built less than half the number of houses in 1974 (31,405) as were constructed in 1973 (70,000).[23] What is more significant from a class point of view, the public sector Banco Obrero, which builds for low income families, constructed less than the private sector. In education the budget was substantially increased to five billion bolivars (over $1 billion) and yet its impact on the quality of education was minimal, in large part, because no serious effort was made at designing and implementing an overall plan. The lack of commitment to a social policy oriented toward improving the conditions of the working class is the other side of the coin of an economic policy that provides a profusion of resources for the entrepreneurial class.

The third element of the entrepreneurial approach involves lowering the labor costs of production. The intensification of exploitation can be seen, for example, in the systematic nonenforcement in factories of the health and safety codes. According to a study by the official Office of Inspection and Evaluation of Professional Risks and Occupational Medicine, 38 percent of the workers employed in a sample of twenty-eight firms (792 workers) were afflicted with occupational diseases.[24] The industrialists' single-minded obsession with profits has resulted in frequent warnings from the Ministry of Health, but rarely have the threats been enforced. Both the regime and entrepreneurs have no intention of reducing the rate of exploitation, since both have the unhindered expansion of capital as their primary goal.

The fourth element in the entrepreneurial formula is popular repression. To contain the protests of the working class and peasantry, the government has initiated a series of repressive measures, and selectively applied them, which confine politics and social struggle to the parliamentary-electoral arena where the government party predominates. In Miranda, the repression of peasant organizations prompted the moderate Partido Social Cristiano (COPEI) parliamentary representative, Pedro Humberto Calderón, to protest the government's harassment and jailing of 300 peasants, whereas landowners occupied public lands without the National Guard intervening.[25] There is little doubt that the current level of government repression could increase substantially if the opposition were to effectively mobilize the increasingly discontented electorate which is abandoning the AD. The growing level of discontent was clearly evident at a meeting of middle-level AD activists who almost uniformly attacked the government's failure to implement its minimum promises to the lower-class barrio dwellers. Luis Molina, an AD barrio leader, pointed to the contrast between the electoral promises and the party's performance in government: "Here is the party, here are the Carlos Andrés Pérez kids who went to the barrios making promises . . . and now every time we go to a barrio or to a hollow we are asked where are the results. The governing class must realize that if it's true that we believe in President Carlos Andrés Pérez, the people are waiting for the works that were promised."[26]

The growth of arbitrariness, arrogance and repression—mixed with anticommunist demagogy—is directly related to the regime's failure to comply with its electoral promises. COPEI parliamentary leader, Eduardo Fernández, cited a survey in which over half of those who voted for Pérez expressed discontent and frustration with his regime.[27] He went on to argue that the unfulfilled program and the arrogant style of rule were "a grave danger for democratic stability."[28] President Pérez apparently is aware of how fragile the social basis of his new entrepreneurial development program is, pointing out that his regime is the last opportunity for democracy. That leads to the fifth and final element in the entrepreneurial formula: a loyal, reliable military and police force. With Pérez's commitment to nationalist-capitalist development and the resulting erosion of the AD's electoral base, a tough-minded civilian or military regime may be necessary to sustain his effort and contain popular discontent through authoritarian, nondemocratic methods, similar to those of the Betancourt-Leoni regimes of the 1960s. There is little doubt that Betancourt's preoccupation with Movement for Socialism (MAS) influence in the armed forces was premised on his understanding of the military's role in the AD's policy of repressing popular discontent and harassing opposition trade union and party activity. The National Guard and the police forces will become important levers in later stages of the development experience; hence, the AD seeks to monopolize their ideological training and political manipulation. Any sharp downturn in oil prices or production that resulted in severe cutbacks could lead to a breakdown of the coalition of bankers, businessmen, military, public sector employees, and the trade union apparatus. Under those circumstances, the military would step in—with either a "Brazilian" or "Peruvian" style of development.[29]

## Nationalization and U.S. Policy

Since World War II the position of the United States as a dominant imperial power in a competitive world capitalist system has been largely rooted in the continually growing opportunities for capital expansion and accumulation through the exploitation of social classes in the peripheral and semiperipheral areas of the world economy. When he was secretary of state, Henry Kissinger succinctly summed up the issues: "The international economic system has been built on these central elements: open and expanding trade; free movements of investment capital and technology; readily available supplies of raw materials; and institutions and practices of international cooperation."[30]

Any fundamental challenge to the arrangements that comprise the "present economic system" is regarded by U.S. policy-makers as inimical to basic U.S. interests. "America's prosperity," according to Kissinger, "requires international economic stability."[31] Such stability is equated with the maintenance of the basic features of the "present economic system."

Beginning in mid-1973, Kissinger and the National Security Council assumed the primary responsibility within the U.S. imperial state structure for defining the contours of Washington's international economic policy. The fundamental importance of economic issues in foreign policy was clearly recognized by Kissinger: "It became clear that almost every economic policy had profound foreign policy implications."[32] The involvement of the United States in the world economy has reached the point at which a substantial part of "internal" development is tied to an external dynamic: economic expansion on a world scale has become a necessity for the growth of most major U.S. corporations. Inextricably, foreign policy and the international economy have fused to become central concerns of U.S. decision-makers. Foreign policy-makers' concerns range from providing loans for new investment areas to providing arms and supplies to pro-capitalist forces intent on overthrowing nationalist regimes. The growth in the scope and depth of commitment of U.S. economic involvement on a world scale has been paralleled and promoted by the activities of the imperial state. The purpose of its foreign policy has been to facilitate the most favorable terms for U.S. economic expansion, not infrequently to the disadvantage of capitalist competitor nations and Third World countries.

The Third World's efforts to equalize the terms of exchange with the industrialized capitalist countries—principally through OPEC—has generated a hostile response from U.S. policy-makers. Basing their policies on the ideology and imperial structure of the status quo, U.S. spokesmen have sought to maintain their privileged position in the world economy. The oil challenge in Latin America was concentrated in Venezuela. In confronting it and in the subsequent evolution of Washington's policy toward the economic nationalism of the Pérez government, policy-makers situated this major U.S. petroleum supplier within a global, as well as a hemispheric and bilateral, context.

Although the imperial state was not prepared or interested in a full-scale confrontation over limited losses sustained by particular firms in Venezuela, it certainly did not view even the losses of individual firms as totally acceptable, expecially those of the oil corporations. Initially, it exerted limited pressure to secure a favorable outcome. Although the policy-makers seriously considered proposals which would have avoided the picking off of individual firms, massive retaliation by the imperial state was not an appropriate response to piecemeal nationalization, but neither was tacit acceptance. The debate over the appropriate ways to relate larger issues of systemic importance to the particular interests of individual firms continues, some officials adopting a position supporting closer scrutiny and more direct involvement by the state in each conflict and others proposing the more "flexible" position of seeking new economic ties rather than defending old ones.

The selective nationalization of foreign-owned properties by the Pérez government did, however, "complicate" relations between the United States and Venezuela. From the point of view of U.S. policy-makers, these actions exposed the need for "a more coherent policy [on nationalization], particularly vis-à-vis oil companies, than we have now." Within the imperial state concern was increasingly expressed "that the oil companies are no longer a match for the producer governments."[33] This issue was debated in the National Security Council (NSC) in May 1975 during its annual country assessment and strategy paper on Venezuela. The then-U.S. Ambassador to Venezuela, Robert McClintock, proposed that the U.S. government "take a leading role in direct negotiations with Venezuela concerning oil."[34] However, the NSC rejected his suggestion and decided, on the basis of an appreciation of the class nature of the expropriation, that a policy of nonconfrontation would be followed.

The political context of nationalization—the social nature of the regime pursuing it, the area(s) of the economy subject to it, the extent of it—determines the U.S. response to Third World governments' efforts to implement national development projects. In Venezuela, the nationalization of U.S. properties occurred as part of a national-capitalist (nonsocialist) development strategy and in a way not antagonistic to basic U.S. interests in industry, trade, banking, and even oil and iron ore. The Venezuelan experience under Pérez is, in the words of one Treasury official, "unradical enough to be within the bounds of tolerance."[35] In Chile under Allende, nationalization of U.S. properties in the context of an anticapitalist (socialist) development strategy generated a hostile response on the part of U.S. policy-makers. The difference in the U.S. responses to Venezuela and Chile is rooted in internal political-economic differences that explain why in the one instance the conflict was negotiable but in the other it was not.

The key to U.S. policy-making is the relationship between internal developments in Venezuela and U.S. economic and political interests. The existence of a capitalist regime which provides key raw materials and markets for U.S. industry and investment opportunities for foreign investors is a decisive consideration in Washington.

The limited populist measures of the Pérez regime were a transitory phenomenon of the immediate postelection period (April–October 1974), as were the declarations restricting foreign capital. Subsequently, it became increasingly clear that the incentives—profit-making opportunities—that remained for foreign investors in Venezuela more than canceled out the constraints. An official of the U.S. Chamber of Commerce put it quite succinctly:

> U.S. businessmen are pragmatic. . . . What's being done with nationalization is being done with compensation. There is no question that the rules are changing, and the country has money to make the rules work. Secondly, everybody realizes that Venezuela is going to have a lot of money coming in, and the sensible thing to do is be constructive.[36]

In a situation where the U.S. government lacked the capacity to pressure Pérez "from the outside," where the development strategy was characterized by sectoral, not structural, change, and where petroleum revenues had generated new opportunities for profitable activities, the U.S. business community decided to adopt a pragmatic approach and adjust to the new "rules." "Constructive" behavior superseded a conflictive posture and became the basis for the continuing relationship. As the process of "clarification" and "nonimplementation" of the regime's policies unfolded, the U.S. multinationals began to move into nonextractive areas of the economy and to elaborate the basis of new ties and associations through collaboration with the local private-bureaucratic bourgeoisie—to "share" in the benefits of capitalist exploitation.

## U.S. Economic Interests in Venezuela: The Basis of Accommodation

The total value of U.S. exports to Venezuela grew from $753.7 million in 1970 to $1.85 billion in 1975 (January–October), an increase of over $1.1 billion for this 1970–October 1975 period.

What is even more striking, however, is that during the period 1973 to 1975—under the impact of oil price increases and an expanded Venezuelan market—the value of U.S. exports increased by $823 million, accounting for approximately 82 percent of the total increase between 1970 and 1975. Put another way, of the total $7.08 billion of U.S. exports to Venezuela between 1970 and 1975, some $4.63 billion was accounted for during the 1973 to October 1975 period. The rate of expansion during 1974 and 1975 has slowed in comparison with the staggering 70 percent increase in the value of U.S. exports to Venezuela between 1973 and 1974, but the growth pattern continues and compares more than favorably with the 1970 to 1973 period. Among the fastest growing sectors for U.S. exports within the Venezuelan market during 1973-1975, and especially since 1973, are those of machine industries, manufactured goods, transport equipment, and automobiles. Nevertheless, a variety of U.S. capitalist interests have clearly benefited substantially from the impact of Venezuela's oil price increases—as the significant increases in the value of their trade with Venezuela indicates.[37]

U.S. manufacturing investment, as compared with oil investment in Venezuela, has increased significantly since 1966. The ratio of petroleum to manufacturing investment has declined from 5.5:1 (1966) to 3.9:1 (1969) to 2.5:1 (1972) to approximately 1:1 (1974). Between 1966 and 1974 oil investment declined from 72 percent to 37 percent of total U.S. investments in Venezuela, while manufacturing investment increased from 13 percent to 34 percent. Since 1966, U.S. investments in chemical and food products and machinery and transportation equipment have increased by over 100 percent and in the area of metals the increase is in the vicinity of 300 percent. In other words, U.S. capitalists have diversified their investments in Venezuela and the relative weight of new industrial-manufacturing investment is growing over time. It has surpassed oil investment and has become the major element in overall U.S. investments.[38]

Thus, the area of trade, rather than investment, is now presenting U.S. capitalists with greater opportunities for maximizing profits; the total nonoil stake is central to any explanation of the countervailing tendencies (e.g., opposing confrontation over nationalization) at work in the making of United States policy toward Venezuela. In 1974, the combined value of U.S. exports to Venezuela and U.S. manufacturing investment there amounted to approximately $2.9 billion, compared with U.S. petroleum investments totaling $659 million. The magnitude of the U.S. nonoil economic stake in Venezuela, especially its growth since 1973, has been largely responsible for the evolution of a U.S. policy of accommodation and negotiation rather than hostility and conflict; U.S. capital has reassumed a dominant position in the Venezuelan economy by working "from within."

Washington has not strongly resisted Venezuela's sectoral nationalization of particular resource areas because it was accompanied by the opening-up of other "downstream" areas for foreign capital investment. The Departments of State and Treasury recognize that nationalization, rather than making inroads into profits, provided an environment for capital expansion and accumulation. Once the iron ore and petroleum nationalizations appeared inevitable, Washington moved swiftly to ensure that the terms of expropriation were acceptable to a coalition of bourgeois elites (U.S. and Venezuelan). The expropriated companies were offered satisfactory "package settlements"—compensation and future profit-making opportunities in areas related to oil and iron ore. U.S. businessmen recognized that foreign capital was to be regulated, not eliminated, to provide space and opportunities for national capital to develop and flourish. Both private and public U.S. officials have come to recognize that Pérez's foreign policy, while occasionally critical, is accommodating and that his domestic policy promotes national private capital expansion and the diversification of foreign investment into the nonenclave areas of the Venezuelan economy.

In this context, U.S. strategy, which was less flexible and more "hardline" during the "populist" phase of the Pérez government (April–October 1974), soon became one of "negotiated conflict." The Venezuelan decision to compensate expropriated U.S. investors, to encourage foreign capital expansion into nonenclave economic sectors and exploitation of them, and to ignore the 1973 Arab oil embargo contributed to a definitive shift in U.S. policy: support for the development of new ties rather than efforts to restore old ones.

Other factors also contributed to the changing U.S. position: Venezuela's emergence as "an important player in the world of the new international economy as a consequence of its oil wealth";[39] the increasing U.S. dependence on Venezuelan oil in a period of increasing global demand (oil imports rose by almost one-third between 1972 and 1973);[40] Pérez's decision to recycle oil revenues via bilateral and multilateral agreements ($2.5 billion committed by December 1974) that helped to buttress and stabilize pro-U.S. regimes and to expand the possibilities for trade and investment in semiperipheral arenas of the world economy (Latin America) where the United States is hegemonic; and Venezuela's limited anti-imperialism, which is primarily confined (in practice rather than rhetoric) to developing national capitalism and changing the terms of exchange. Finally, U.S. policy-makers had, and continue to have, little access within the Venezuelan state and society from which to pressure Pérez to reverse specific policies, such as nationalization. On that issue, the United States lacked a significant internal political base among right-wing elements once the AD government decided to take the initiative. Unlike Allende's Chile, Venezuela was not vulnerable to an external economic "squeeze" by the U.S. government in collaboration with the so-called international banks. Venezuela's petrodollars eliminated the medium-term possibility of financial dependence. Therefore, given its minimal area for maneuvering and Venezuela's decision to maintain ongoing ties and create new areas for capitalist expansion, the U.S. government devised a policy of accommodation and negotiation over areas of limited conflict.

## U.S.–Venezuelan Relations: The Basis of Limited Conflict

The limited areas of conflict between the U.S. and Venezuela revolve primarily around the issues of oil prices and trade preferences. United States policy-makers continue to criticize, explicitly and implicitly, Venezuela's leading role in pushing for oil price increases within OPEC. In July 1975, Treasury Secretary William Simon, without mentioning Venezuela by name, placed responsibility for the decision of the major U.S. oil companies to increase oil prices on the OPEC cartel and raised the possibility "that the United States might take economic and financial countermeasures if the 13 nation cartel of oil-producing nations raised prices again."[41] The specter of retaliation was again raised by Kissinger in subsequent Congressional testimony.[42] In September, in a note to Pérez, President Gerald Ford singled out Venezuela for specific criticism over its advocacy of oil price increases. In the same communication, Ford also voiced displeasure at Venezuela's verbal support for anti-imperialist and nationalist measures in Latin America, principally the Panama Canal issue.[43] Nevertheless, the executive branch has continued to actively oppose Venezuela's exclusion from the generalized tariff preferences of the 1974 U.S. Trade Act on the ground that it denies the U.S. "tactical flexibility" at the policy level.[44]

The Pérez regime, for its part, has gone out of its way "to avoid confrontation" with the United States of the sort that would signal a fundamental rupture in the relationship.[45] The limits of the Venezuelan position are reflected in the differing attitudes toward tariff preferences and oil supplies. On the one hand, Pérez is prepared to irritate U.S. policy-makers with an "open statement" to the *New York Times* declaring that Venezuela's exclusion from trade preferences "constitutes a clear act of economic aggression and political pressure."[46] On the other hand, Pérez has insisted that Venezuela will remain a reliable source of oil supplies for the United States and the industrialized capitalist world: "As far as Venezuela was concerned . . . the production of oil must take into account the needs of industrialized countries, as much as those of any other countries."[47] Pérez has opposed calls for a measurable reduction in the level of oil production which, in the opinion of some knowledgeable observers, "amounted to a clear recognition that the United States, in particular, could not be pushed too far, and is in line with Henry Kissinger's recent warnings to oil producers."[48]

The U.S. policy has been one of making tactical adjustments on specific issues, while attempting to maintain the "present [international] economic system." In the case of Venezuela, this has involved accepting certain modifications in the price of oil.

But beyond its success in relating oil prices and partially changing the terms of exchange, the Venezuelan government has basically supported in practice the U.S. contention that the "present economic system has generally served the world well."[49] That implies an acceptance of the premises that underpin the economic system, including expanding trade, unrestricted movements of investment capital and technology, reliable supplies of strategic raw materials.

## U.S. Policy: Interagency Conflict

The overall U.S. policy toward the bourgeois AD regime is one of accommodation and negotiated conflict. At the operational level the U.S. imperial state agencies share this common perspective, although different executive agencies play specific roles in realizing or pursuing it. Various agencies may have overlapping responsibilities, as well as separate interests rooted in functional institutional interests. Consequently, one finds a convergence of efforts side-by-side with the emergence of specific "bureaucratic conflicts." But these specific differences on particular issues are located within the framework of the larger consensus over policy goals. In the case of Venezuela, however, those differences have not challenged the common definition of what constitutes the larger interest of the United States.

The central "bureaucratic conflicts" are concentrated in three executive branch agencies: the Departments of State, Treasury, and Defense. One State Department official discussed the functional versus the institutional concerns of State and Treasury, out of which emerge their different priorities:

> Treasury tends to be more domestically oriented, more concerned about what to do about the high petroleum prices. Treasury is more ready than the State Department to take action on the high oil prices. Treasury tends to reflect the domestic conservative financial viewpoint and gives less weight to foreign policy than the State Department.[50]

Nonetheless, the same State Department official maintained that there was no strong interagency conflict over the U.S. policy of negotiated agreements with Venezuela, even in light of its role in OPEC: "I don't think that there are any strong disagreements between the State Department and Treasury [over Venezuela]."[51] The Defense Department, again reflecting specific institutional concerns, is critical of Treasury's refusal to authorize an increase in the level of foreign military sales credits to Venezuela because of its role in OPEC. Defense officials describe OPEC as Venezuela's "business" and criticize Treasury for its "very short-sighted objectives—tunnel vision" vis-à-vis the Pérez regime.[52] In their opinion, a confrontation with Venezuela over its activities in OPEC would be to substitute a short-term perspective for long-term political ties with the Venezuelan military. A recent U.S. government study observed that U.S. military personnel assigned to the Military Assistance Advisory Group in Venezuela during 1974 spent about half of their work time in "dialogue" activities:

> Dialogue consists of *influence*, representation, and information exchange. *Influence is generally described as a means to develop rapport so that the host military will more readily accept suggested improvements and the American way*; representation is generally regarded as a protocol function to establish or enhance working relationships; and information exchange swaps ideas and/or information with host military officials in matters not necessarily related to one's occupational specialty. (Emphasis added.)[53]

U.S. military personnel are heavily involved in creating important "liaison" groups within the Venezuelan military, preparing for any political eventuality. The primary ties established through "influence," "representation," and "information" exchange are strategic gains that will give the United States access at the critical moments that will sooner or later occur in the course of Venezuela's capitalist development. The conflict between the short-term exigencies of Treasury and State with the long-term views of the Pentagon is a struggle over the immediate and long-term interests of U.S. capital.

The executive agencies of the U.S. imperial state involved in the elaboration and implementation of its foreign policy function within a common political-economic framework. In the case of Venezuela, each agency focuses primarily on those political and economic factors designed to facilitate the ongoing conditions for capitalist accumulation and expansion. The tactics and evolution of each agency's position must be located within the context of overlapping interests. But the repetition of these basic concerns has also been paralleled by specific variations in positions taken by particular agencies, at different periods—reflecting their specific constituencies and unique institutional concerns.

## Notes

1. "Venezuela completes iron mines takeover," *Latin America Economic Report*, January 17, 1975, p. 9.
2. See "Venezuelan Compensation is Accepted," *New York Times*, October 19, 1975, p. 36; "Venezuelan Oil Takeover Still Faces Several Hard Tests," *Business Latin America*, November 5, 1975, pp. 353–54; " 'Good Manners' in Oil Nationalization," *Latin American Week* (Buenos Aires), November 21, 1975, p. 7.
3. Joanne Omang, "Venezuelan Oil: Troubled Bonanza," *Washington Post*, December 28, 1975, p. A23.
4. Ibid. See also "Exxon Reaches Venezuelan Pact on Oil Purchases," *Wall Street Journal*, January 7, 1976, p. 2.
5. Clive Jenkins, *Power at the Top* (London: MacGibbon and Kee, 1959).
6. Venezuela, Oficina Central de Coordinación y Planificación (CORDIPLAN), *Síntesis Organica de la Estrategia General del Desarrollo*, May 28, 1975, p. 33.
7. Organization of American States, CEPCIES, Ad Hoc Group on Venezuela, *Recent Developments in the Venezuelan Economy*, May 1975, p. 42.
8. *Business International*, March 14, 1975, p. 85.
9. *Business International*, February 5, 1975, p. 45.
10. *Business Latin America*, August 6, 1975, p. 254.
11. Interview with high official in CORDIPLAN, conducted by James Petras, Venezuela, Summer 1975.
12. Ibid.
13. Ibid.

14. *El Nacional* (Caracas), July 1, 1975.
15. Ibid., July 8, 1975.
16. Ibid., June 27, 1975.
17. Ibid., June 18, 1975.
18. Ibid.
19. See Meir Merhav, "Hacia una Política de Desarrollo Agrícola y de Cambio Estructural Orientada hacia el Exterior," Caracas, mimeo, 1974. For a statement of the entrepreneurial approach to agriculture, see René Dumont's (once described as a "socialist" critic of the Cuban Revolution) report, "Informe de René Dumont sobre la agricultura en Venezuela," *Resumen*, May 11, 1975, pp. 22–29. Whatever their "left" credentials, both writers clearly adapted to the exigencies of the Venezuelan capitalist class, designing development strategies to suit its needs.
20. *El Universal* (Caracas), December 28, 1974.
21. *El Mundo*, March 31, 1975.
22. Interview with official of the Venezuelan central bank, conducted by James Petras, Venezuela, Summer 1975.
23. Freddy Muñoz and Alonso Palacios, "Consideraciones Políticas en Torno a un año de Gobierno de Carlos Andrés Pérez," Part 11, Caracas, April 1975, p. 3.
24. *El Nacional* (Caracas), July 30, 1975.
25. Ibid., July 29, 1975.
26. Ibid., July 14, 1975.
27. Ibid., July 22, 1975.
28. Ibid.
29. Informal interviews with executive officer in U.S. Defense Intelligence Agency and senior officer in the Venezuelan armed forces, conducted by James Petras, Venezuela, Summer 1975.
30. Speech by Henry Kissinger, "Strengthening the World Economic Structure," Kansas City, Missouri, May 13, 1975 (U.S., Department of State: Office of Media Services, Bureau of Public Affairs).
31. Ibid.
32. "Kissinger on Oil, Food and Trade," interview in *Business Week*, January 13, 1975, p. 66.
33. U.S. State Department official, quoted in Robert M. Smith, "Ambassador Urged U.S. Take Role in Venezuelan Oil Talks," *New York Times*, June 30, 1975, p. 45.
34. Ibid.
35. Interview with U. S. Department of the Treasury official, conducted by Morris Morley, Washington, D.C., August 20, 1975.

36. Interview with official of the Chamber of Commerce of the United States, conducted by Morris Morley, Washington, D.C., August 6, 1975.
37. See U.S., Department of Commerce, Social and Economic Statistics Division, Bureau of the Census, *U.S. Foreign Trade, Exports, World Area by Commodity Groupings*, Annual 1970, 1971, 1972, 1973, 1974, 1975 (January-October).
38. Investment figures supplied by U.S., Department of Commerce, Bureau of Economic Analysis, International Investment Division, Research Branch.
39. Interview with U.S. Department of State official, Washington, D.C., August 7, 1975.
40. See Norman Gall, "The Challenge of Venezuelan Oil," *Foreign Policy* 18 (Spring 1975): 55, 56.
41. Edward Cowan, "Four Top Concerns Raise Gas Prices to 30 a Gallon," *New York Times*, July 2, 1975, p. 46.
42. Kissinger, "World Economic Structure."
43. See "Venezuela: Ford Weighs In," *Latin America*, September 26, 1975, pp. 298, 300.
44. See, for example, the speeches by Henry Kissinger, "The United States and Latin America: The New Opportunity," Houston, Texas, March 1, 1975, and "American Unity and the National Interest," Birmingham, Alabama, August 14, 1975 (U.S. Department of State: Office of Media Services, Bureau of Public Affairs).
45. Advisor to President Pérez quoted in "Caracas Shares Its Oil Wealth," *Washington Post*, December 28, 1974, p. A8.
46. "The Venezuelan Views," *New York Times*, January 26, 1975, p. 75. Also see "Letter of January 7, 1975 from Carlos Andrés Pérez, President of Venezuela, to all of the Latin American Chiefs of State," reprinted in Organization of American States, General Assembly, *Special Report of the Action Taken by the Permanent Council and Background Relevant to the United States Foreign Trade Act of 1974* (OEA/Ser. P, AG/doc. 544/75), April 9, 1975, Fifth Regular Session, May 8, 1975, pp. 345–47.
47. Quoted in "Venezuela: Prudent Audacity," *Latin America*, February 28, 1975, p. 65.
48. Ibid.
49. Kissinger, "World Economic Structure."
50. Interview with U.S. Department of State official, Washington, D.C., August 4, 1975.
51. Ibid.

52. Interview with U.S. Department of Defense official, Virginia, August 5, 1975.
53. U.S., General Accounting Office, Report to the Congress, *Assessment of Overseas Advisory Efforts of the U.S. Security Assistance Program* (ID-76-1), October 31, 1975, pp. 10, 11.

# 10

# CONTRADICTIONS OF COLONIAL INDUSTRIALIZATION AND THE CRISES IN "COMMONWEALTH" STATUS: THE CASE OF PUERTO RICO

*(with Juan Manuel Carrion)*

In January and February of 1976, the U.S. Congressional Committee on Interior and Insular Affairs held hearings on a piece of proposed legislation entitled, Compact of Permanent Union Between Puerto Rico and the United States.[1] The legislation centers on measures designed to find a political formula which would allow the colonial regime to overcome the economic impasse confronting the island's economy. Under the general notion of "greater autonomy," the idea is to allow the Puerto Rican government to lower wages, tax levels, and pollution control standards below those of the United States in order to compete successfully with other low-wage areas, while still maintaining the basic ties and subordination to the U.S. state. Thus, "autonomy" translates into greater incentives for the multinational corporations (MNCs) and continuing political "association" with the United States, i.e., subordination. The current debate about the "autonomist" tendencies in Puerto Rico can only be understood in light of the experience of colonial industrialization, the United States's stake in Puerto Rico, and the nature of the debate among sociopolitical forces in Puerto Rico.

## The United States' Stake in Puerto Rico

Given the growing economic and military importance of Puerto Rico to the United States, a solution to its chronic economic and political crisis has become imperative. Puerto Rico is economically important to the United States in several respects.

First, the amount of U.S. capital invested in the island is enormous. According to a report from the Commonwealth Government, U.S. capital investment in Puerto Rico totaled more than $14 billion in 1975, an increase of 870 percent since 1960. The direct industrial investment of U.S. firms, $6.11 billion in 1975, represents 5.5 percent of all direct U.S. investments worldwide.[2] These figures highlight the growing importance of Puerto Rico as a source of profits to U. S. capital. In 1975, profits leaving the island for the United States amounted to $1.37 billion, which is an increase of 1,083.2 percent since 1960. In 1975, Puerto Rico provided U.S. capital with 7 percent of all profits earned from its foreign capital investments. The island has always been a source of high profits for U.S. capital. It has been calculated that most United States companies' direct capital investments in Puerto Rico are recovered in just two years.[3] Moreover, certain industries key to the economy of the United States are located in Puerto Rico, including one of the biggest petrochemical complexes in the world, whose entire production is channeled to the east coast of the United States. In the largest of the several oil refineries in Puerto Rico, Commonwealth Oil Refinery Corporation (CORCO), capital investment has been calculated at $1 billion.[4] Yearly export of petrochemical raw materials to the United States is over $600 million, and total production in Puerto Rico represents between 20 percent and 30 percent of all petrochemical raw materials produced in U.S. territories and colonies. Some particular products, such as paraxilene, account for 40 percent of total U.S. production. The rate of profit in the petrochemical raw materials industries is more than 15 percent. They are able to accumulate profits at a yearly rate of $500 million.[5] Another factor not to be overlooked is the advantage for U.S. capital of having a captive market in Puerto Rico. Even before the colonial conquest in 1898, Puerto Rico had been one of the main markets for U.S. products. Today Puerto Rico ranks fifth in the world and second in the western hemisphere, after

Canada. On a per capita basis, Puerto Rico ranks first. Not only is Puerto Rico, for that reason, a huge source of profits for commercial interests and producers in the United States but, according to a 1974 United States Department of Commerce report, U.S. trade with Puerto Rico is also responsible for the existence of 139,000 jobs in the United States.[6]

A new factor has increased Puerto Rico's economic importance to the United States: since the 1960s, Puerto Rico has been known to have ample resources of copper, nickel, and other minerals, and in the early 1970s oil was added to that list. It has been calculated that the extraction of copper and other minerals will generate $20 billion in gross earnings during a span of more than 100 years.[7] In the case of nickel, which is not found in great quantities in the United States, Puerto Rico's deposits represent 40 percent of all U.S. reserves. In addition, Mobil Oil Company has concluded that an 85 percent probability exists of finding oil in exploitable quantities in Puerto Rico. The total amount of earnings these deposits could generate has been estimated at $20 billion and $13 billion in gross and net earnings, respectively. It has been calculated that the oil deposits in Puerto Rico are capable of producing 200,000 barrels of petroleum daily for twenty-five years.[8]

But the importance of Puerto Rico to the United States is not only economic: its strategic importance to the Pentagon should not be underestimated. Puerto Rico has always been a key military outpost in the Caribbean. At one time, 13 percent of the island's land was occupied by U.S. military bases. Today, some have been closed as part of the United States' general attempt to reduce or control military expenses and to reorganize its strategic posts because of advances in war technology. However, the atomic naval base at Roosevelt Roads (37,900 acres) on the east coast of Puerto Rico and other commands represent basic defensive points for the United States in the Atlantic and Caribbean arenas. With the increasing successes of socialist revolutions in Africa and constant social unrest and growing anti-imperialist sentiment in Latin America and the Caribbean, Puerto Rico has increased its military strategic value. It has been pointed out that the United States must consider the military importance of Puerto Rico in any change it may make in Puerto Rico's present colonial status.[9]

## "Operation Bootstrap" and the Current Crises

Between 1947 and 1974, Puerto Rico experienced an industrial boom. Its GDP increased from $500 million in 1947 to $8 billion in 1974. Almost all the impetus of this expansion involving new industries (1,406 between 1948 and 1967) came from U.S. companies, which controlled 90 percent of them.

The industrial expansion transformed the labor force from a primarily agricultural to an industrial/service workforce. Between 1950 and 1975, employment in agriculture declined from 214,000 to 50,000, while employment in manufacturing increased from 55,000 in 1950 to 155,000 in May 1974.[10] Along with the industrial expansion, average hourly wages of production workers rose from 28 percent of the United States average in 1950 to 53 percent in 1975.[11] The combined effects of unionization and industrialization created a steady growth in workers' income that set the stage, in part, for the current crisis. The whole program of industrial expansion was underwritten by a series of conditions that favored the large-scale invasion of corporate capital, including tax concessions (ten- and twenty-year tax holidays), cheap labor (surplus labor), and access to United States's markets. The continuing economic crisis in Puerto Rico and the political elite's current search for a new political formula centered on the notions of autonomy and statehood reflect the fact that incentives in Puerto Rico are no longer effective and that the corporations have no other commitment to sustain their activity in the island. The initial tax incentives that promoted investment have been exhausted; the cheap labor advantage has been undermined by the increasing power and organization of the working class. As Table 1 indicates, the average hourly earnings of production workers have increased faster in Puerto Rico than in the United States. Teodoro Moscoso, who administers Puerto Rico's

Economic Development Administration, testified before the Congressional committee on the vital necessity of "wage flexibility," meaning the capacity to reduce and cheapen Puerto Rican labor so that the island's colonial leaders can compete with other low-wage areas for corporate investment.[12] In apparel exports, Moscoso cited the displacement of Puerto Rico by Hong Kong, Korea, and Taiwan (see Table 2).[13] In support of the demand for greater autonomy, Moscoso pointedly stated:

> The public policy of the United States and of the Free Associated State is delared to be that the minimum wage in Puerto Rico be equivalent to the minimum wage in the United States as soon as the economic conditions so permit.
>
> The Free Associated State of Puerto Rico shall have exclusive jurisdiction over all matters pertaining to minimum wages and working hours, except for the shipping and aviation industries, which shall be covered by the appropriate federal laws, as may be determined by the Congress of the United States.[14]

To Moscoso, it is not essential that this legislation be achieved through the passage of the new compact, but, whatever the means, he wants wage flexibility restored. This issue has two interrelated aspects: (1) the flexibility to set different minimum wages for different industries, according to their competitive position and future prospects, and (2) flexibility as to the timing of increases so as to permit different rates of increase for each industry. The purpose is to undercut the advantages that currently accrue to other low-wage areas (see Table 3) from "island hopping," i.e., the tendency of corporations to shift operations from one island to another depending on where they can obtain the most profitable terms.[15]

The existence of a large surplus labor force is no longer an urgent necessity for some of the multinationals, since many of their operations require few workers. Hence, what was originally an incentive has become a huge welfare burden with dangerous political and social overtones. Finally, the close integration with the United States's economy and the access to the United States' market, which at first stimulated growth, have led to an amplification of the crises in Puerto Rico. The stagnation of the United

**Table 1**
**United States Minimum Wage and Average Hourly Earnings of Production Workers in Manufacturing Industries: Puerto Rico, the United States and Mississippi**
**(October 1950–1975)**

| Year | U.S. Minimum Wage ($4/hour) | Average Hourly Earnings, All Manufacturing Industries ($) | | | Puerto Rico as Percentage of | |
|---|---|---|---|---|---|---|
| | | Puerto Rico | U.S. | Mississippi | U.S. | Mississippi |
| 1950 | .75 | .42 | 1.50 | .97 | 28.0 | 43.3 |
| 1951 | .75 | .45 | 1.61 | 1.03 | 28.0 | 43.7 |
| 1952 | .75 | .45 | 1.70 | 1.09 | 26.5 | 41.3 |
| 1953 | .75 | .48 | 1.79 | 1.14 | 26.8 | 42.1 |
| 1954 | .75 | .50 | 1.81 | 1.18 | 27.6 | 42.4 |
| 1955 | 1.00 | .56· | 1.91 | 1.20 | 29.3 | 46.7 |
| 1956 | 1.00 | .66 | 2.02 | 1.29 | 32.7 | 51.2 |
| 1957 | 1.00 | .77 | 2.09 | 1.40 | 36.8 | 55.0 |
| 1958 | 1.00 | .83 | 2.14 | 1.51 | 38.8 | 55.0 |
| 1959 | 1.00 | .87 | 2.21 | 1.49 | 39.4 | 58.4 |

| | | | | | | |
|---|---|---|---|---|---|---|
| 1960 | 1.00 | .94 | 2.30 | 1.52 | 40.9 | 61.8 |
| 1961 | 1.15 | 1.00 | 2.34 | 1.56 | 42.7 | 64.1 |
| 1962 | 1.15 | 1.07 | 2.39 | 1.64 | 44.8 | 65.2 |
| 1963 | 1.25 | 1.14 | 2.47 | 1.69 | 46.2 | 67.4 |
| 1964 | 1.25 | 1.20 | 2.53 | 1.76 | 47.4 | 68.2 |
| 1965 | 1.25 | 1.26 | 2.64 | 1.82 | 47.7 | 69.2 |
| 1966 | 1.25 | 1.31 | 2.75 | 1.90 | 47.6 | 68.9 |
| 1967 | 1.40 | 1.43 | 2.85 | 2.03 | 50.2 | 70.4 |
| 1968 | 1.60 | 1.59 | 3.06 | 2.23 | 52.0 | 71.3 |
| 1969 | 1.60 | 1.71 | 3.24 | 2.33 | 52.8 | 73.4 |
| 1970 | 1.60 | 1.78 | 3.37 | 2.43 | 52.8 | 73.3 |
| 1971 | 1.60 | 1.91 | 3.59 | 2.57 | 53.2 | 74.3 |
| 1972 | 1.60 | 2.04 | 3.86 | 2.80 | 52.9 | 72.9 |
| 1973 | 1.60 | 2.17 | 4.14 | 3.02 | 51.4 | 71.9 |
| 1974 | 1.90 & 2.00 | 2.40 | 4.56 | 3.28 | 52.6 | 73.2 |
| 1975 | 2.00 & 2.10 (Sept.) | 2.59 | 4.89[a] | 3.59[a] | 53.0 | 72.1 |

[a] Preliminary.

Source: *Employment and Earnings*, U.S. Department of Labor, Bureau of Labor Statistics; Puerto Rico Department of Labor, Bureau of Labor Statistics.

**Table 2**
**U.S. Apparel Imports**

| Exporting Countries | 1961 $ Millions | 1961 % | 1968 $ Millions | 1968 % | 1974 $ Millions | 1974 % |
|---|---|---|---|---|---|---|
| Hong Kong, Korea, Taiwan | 46 | 12 | 313 | | 1,160 | 51 |
| Puerto Rico | 141 | 37 | 370 | | 363 | 16 |
| Other Countries | 191 | 51 | 543 | | 776 | 33 |
| | 378 | 100 | 1,226 | | 2,299 | 100 |

Source: *Employment and Earnings*, U. S. Department of Labor, Bureau of Labor Statistics.

**Table 3**
**Average Hourly Earnings in Manufacturing**

| Area | 1972 | 1973 | 1974 | 1975 |
|---|---|---|---|---|
| Barbados | $1.24 | $1.68 | | |
| El Salvador* | | | | $ .50 |
| Guatemala | $ .44 | $ .44 | $ .44 | |
| Mexico | | $ .60 | | $1.13 |
| Singapore | $ .98 | $1.08 | | |
| Taiwan* | | | | $ .25 |
| Puerto Rico | $2.04 | $2.17 | $2.40 | $2.59 |

* Unskilled labor.
Source: See note 1, vol. 1.

States economy has found expression in an absolute decline of manufacturing employment, which dropped from 155,000 jobs in May 1974 to 129,700 in July 1975.[16] What appeared as advantages propelling Puerto Rico's development have created the very forces which are now burdening the country, namely, the development incentives and their main beneficiaries, the MNCs. What seemed in the short run to be dynamic forces accelerating growth, employment, and income, have created a nightmare of unemployment, stagnation, and empty factories and offices. Because of the mobility of capital embodied in the multinational corporation and because of other countries' imitation of the Puerto Rican formula, which has caused the latter's competitive advantage to decline, Puerto Rico is in a chronic state of depression.

Some of the factors that have contributed to this crisis include the public debt, dependency, and the demise of agriculture. Long-term, heavy borrowing to finance growth has led to overexpansion at a time when production and demand are declining. Moody's Investor Service has lowered the rating on bonds issued by the majority of Puerto Rico's public corporations—a warning that the Commonwealth's debt is too large and growing too fast.[17]

Since multinational corporations control the bulk of production, increases in wage levels and the exhaustion of tax holidays have led to their migration to other Caribbean islands where costs are cheaper. Shifts to capital-intensive (petrochemicals, etc.) activities result in few jobs: millions are invested and few employed.

The demise of agriculture means that high-priced foodstuffs must be imported from the mainland at a time when industry and industrial exports are stagnating. The overall dependence of Puerto Rico on U.S. markets, imports, and investments, means that recession in the United States has multiple effects in Puerto Rico, with few, if any, of the reserves and state mechanisms available there to cushion the result and stimulate recovery. The result is long-term stagnation. As *New York Times* journalist David Vidal noted, "No one predicts an easy or quick solution for the troubles."[18]

## Consequences of the Crises

Since the mid-1970s, Puerto Rico has been passing through a profound crisis, which has affected every area of economic and social life, as is evident in a multitude of indicators. The economy is floundering: in 1975 it experienced a negative growth rate of 2.4 percent, and the country had a net loss of 19,300 jobs.[19] Unemployment hovers between 21 percent (official figures) and 40 percent (unofficial).[20] Over 50 percent of the population depends on federal food stamps to survive.[21] Consumer export industries, such as the garment industry, have declined precipitously from 37 percent of the total purchases by the United States to 16 percent in 1974 (see Table 2).[22]

The cost of living is skyrocketing (over 10 percent per year), while government economic policies are geared toward wage freezes, fiscal austerity, and budget cuts. As a result, there has been a steady decline in the real purchasing power of most wage and salaried groups, to say nothing of the vast army of unemployed. Given the size of the unemployed labor force, the duration of their separation from productive activity, and the dismal prospects, this strata can no longer be considered a *reserve* army but is, rather, a *permanent* army of unemployed, with little possibility of ever being effectively incorporated into the labor force. Even increases in production or expansion of the national income, based as it will be on highly capital-intensive investments, will have little or no effect on that branch of labor. Instead, increased income will tend to be concentrated in fewer hands, circulating between the island enclaves and the mainland, and may actually cause a deterioration of living standards by bidding up the price of goods and services. The crisis is multidimensional, involving social, economic, and political institutions and policies affecting the whole society. The incapacity of the government to finance basic services and to provide programs to promote industry is matched by industries' unwillingness to generate new growth to provide the fiscal revenues and employment opportunities that could finance government action and stimulate market demand. The result has been, in both United States and Puerto Rican ruling circles, a tendency to look back at the "golden age" of the 1950s and 1960s with nostalgia and, more seriously, to attempt to recreate the conditions that served big business so well in the past.

## Policy Directions for the Future: Washington and the Technocrats

Government officials and political leaders from both the opposition Popular Democratic Party and the New Progressive Party have fallen over themselves in providing more lucrative terms for the multinationals. The orientation of the current government is based on "investor confidence," as Moscoso's proposals to the U.S. Congress demonstrate:

1. Strengthen the family planning program.
2. Continue to promote high productivity and high-technology industries.
3. Create new incentives and more budgetary resources for industrial promotion.
4. Restore flexibility in setting the minimum wage.[23]

For fiscal 1977-1978 the Puerto Rican colonial legislature approved new tax incentives for United States mainland investors. The economic context in which these measures were taken reflect the continuing deterioration of the Puerto Rican economy: compared with the previous fiscal year, only half the number of government-promoted factories began operations, generating 32 percent fewer jobs at a time when large employers were laying off thousands of workers, causing the *official* unemployment rate for May 1977 to jump to 23 percent, compared with 16.8 percent the previous year.[24] Among the more recent economic areas adversely affected by the crisis are tuna processing, where almost half of the more than six thousand workers have been laid off;[25] tourism, where several luxury hotels are in financial trouble, and the American Hotel has closed leaving 450 workers out of work;[26] oil refining, where the Commonwealth Oil

Refining Company, the leading supplier of fuel and feedstock, is on the verge of bankruptcy;[27] and banking, where Governor Carlos Romero has asked the legislature for $60 million to rescue two banks (Obrero and Cooperative) from insolvency.[28] In the face of the continuing crisis, the legislature passed two measures to promote big business: (a) a reduction in the 10 percent tollgate tax on profits if 25 percent of them are reinvested in government bonds and (b) a 3 percent investment credit for expansion of Puerto Rican operations.[29] In addition, the legislature passed a measure allowing government agencies to contract with private companies for construction of buildings to be leased back to the government on a long-term basis.[30] These incentives, when added to the "typical" government subsidies to new investors, including location assistance and grants for setting up operations and installing equipment, construction of power stations, and personnel training, add up to a continuing shift in resources from the wage and salaried strata to the multinationals.

## Policy Directions for the Future: The Response of the Colonial Political Parties

Between 1972 and 1976, during the Popular Democratic Party (PPD) administration, the colonial leadership of the island increasingly came to realize that the economic crisis was not solely the reflection of the worldwide capitalist recession but that it was also rooted in the very type of colonial economic development that has typified Puerto Rico since the postwar years.

The PPD leadership attempted a short-range and a long-range strategy to deal with the crisis. Its short-range strategy was oriented to obtaining an increase in federal aid to Puerto Rico. Intensified lobbying efforts in Washington resulted in the extension of the federal food stamps program to Puerto Rico. The second feature of the short-range strategy was to increase the repression of the organized labor movement and of the patriotic organizations that favor independence. During Hernandez

Colon's administration (1972-1976), the "National" Guard was twice mobilized to crush strikes.

The purpose of the short-range strategy was to gain time to prepare a way out of a situation that increasingly had acquired the characteristics of economic stagnation. The colonial leadership gradually came to realize that the crisis was a result of the colonial relationship itself. Important sectors of the PPD's leadership understood that new political powers were needed to circumvent the crisis: not a complete rejection of the colonial connection but a renegotiation of the terms of colonial association. Hence, long-range strategy is seemingly focused on a search for more "autonomy." In fact, the U.S. government and its PPD clients promote the idea. Behind the search for "autonomy" is a new form of domination that is a way of thwarting the realization of Puerto Rico's independence. The compact of Permanent Union, or so-called New Compact, is no more than a smokescreen to confine the Puerto Rican working class and delude international opinion.

"More autonomy" thus translates into making wages even lower to make Puerto Rico "competitive" again in the arena of cheap labor, making it necessary to forestall any attempt to apply federal minimum wage standards to Puerto Rico. "More autonomy" is needed to be able to attract capital-intensive industries that are highly polluting and to avoid the application of federal environmental regulations to Puerto Rico. "More autonomy" is a means to find new sources of financial and industrial foreign investment and strengthen their control of Puerto Rico's economy. German and Japanese capital, among others, has been approached, ads are being published in foreign newspapers and magazines, offices of the Puerto Rican Economic Development Administration have been established in Germany and Japan—but all without success. New degrees of autonomy establish the basis for a new type of colonial economic development when the present one no longer seems to offer any future.

In the 1976 elections a pro-statehood party took control of the colonial administration with a narrow majority of the vote. Until very recently, the pro-statehood movement was dominated by that sector of the Puerto Rican bourgeoisie that had grown out of the sugar-producing establishment. As a political option, statehood promised access to the U.S. market for their raw sugar in an era when all of the Caribbean nations were sugar producers.

In 1967, a new sector under the command of millionaire Luis Ferré split from the old Republican Statehood Party and founded the New Progressive Party (NPP). In 1968, this party won the elections, but mainly because of a division within the ranks of the PPD. After its defeat in the 1972 elections, the more radically prostatehood sector was consolidated under the leadership of Romero Barceló. Concomitant with that shift, the ideology of the prostatehood movement changed. Now it presents itself as an anticolonial party, concerned with political equality and the modernization of the economic structure. Statehood is held to be in the interests of the poor, and the movement has re-dressed itself in a populist cloak. Romero Barceló has even written a book, called *Statehood Is for the Poor*.

But the goal of statehood needs the acceptance of the ruling class of the United States. Traditionally, statehood for Puerto Rico has never been desired by the U.S. government: Americanization and economic exploitation, yes, but not statehood. Although U.S. citizenship was imposed on Puerto Ricans in 1917 (when, incidentally, the United States entered World War I), the juridical classification of "nonincorporated territory" has been maintained. The Puerto Rican statehood advocates have had always to deal with the fact that Washington has little sympathy for their "ideal." Statehood faces two basic obstacles: the Hispanic culture of Puerto Rico and the difficulties in assimilating it, and the poor economic condition of Puerto Rico. In 1937, Theodore Roosevelt, Jr., a former governor of Puerto Rico, saw no possibility of the island ever attaining a stage of development that would permit it to contribute to the federal treasury; Puerto Rico as a state would be a burden to the U.S. government. Roosevelt preferred a "dominion status," and with the blessings of U.S. capitalists and the intervention of the U.S. government the Commonwealth was established in 1952.[31]

Today, the problem of Puerto Rico's Hispanic culture remains. And even if the United States is now less close-minded in its doctrine of cultural uniformity, "it would clearly require a generous measure of vision and non-dogmatism on the part of the U.S. Congress to acknowledge the uniqueness of Puerto Rico and to be willing to provide for the preservation of its cultural autonomy if it were to become a state."[32] To make things more fuzzy, the NPP is now at "odds" with its predecessor, rhetorically embracing the idea of saving Puerto Rico's culture and making that a "non-negotiable issue" in the face of growing Puerto Rican nationalism and anti-imperialist sentiment. Puerto Rico is still a poor country whose standard of living is lower than that of any state and whose unemployment rate is higher. But even without statehood, Puerto Rico is becoming a burden to the United States, and just before leaving office President Gerald Ford endorsed the idea of statehood.

The first question is: did Ford's declaration and the present warm relations between the Democratic Party and the pro-statehood leadership in Puerto Rico mean a change in U.S. policy? Is the U.S. government now endorsing statehood for Puerto Rico? And, if so, for what reasons? In Puerto Rico and in Latin America current speculation is that with statehood the United States could guarantee its possession of Puerto Rico's mineral and oil resources. But that does not explain why the United States could not do better economically by exploiting those resources under the existing colonial conditions. The main sectors of the Puerto Rican bourgeoisie that benefited from the colonial industrialization programs and the U.S. monopoly capital established in Puerto Rico are opposed to statehood. Not only do they benefit from their tax exemption (although that is an important factor), but they also have other advantages. For example, the existence of the huge petrochemical complex in Puerto Rico means that the price of domestic oil does not apply to them.

Five reasons have been cited as motivating the apparent trend in the U.S. government toward favoring complete annexation:

1. to extend the frontiers of the United States into the Caribbean, thus legitimizing U.S. intervention in all matters related to the area;
2. to guarantee U.S. heavy investment in Puerto Rico;
3. to guarantee control over Puerto Rico's natural resources;

4. to take the Puerto Rican case out of international forums, such as the United Nations, in their discussions about colonialism; and
5. to perpetuate the use of Puerto Rican territory for military purposes.

Statehood would require a fundamental change in the economic structure of Puerto Rico. In its present condition, Puerto Rico could only be a pauper, or "ghetto," state. Federal aid to Puerto Rico would have to be doubled, and already the increase in such aid is one of the reasons the "Commonwealth" has fallen from grace in Washington. The goal of the NPP is to find a way to develop economically that does not require the political structure of the "Commonwealth" or incentives such as tax exemption to increase sympathy for statehood and to discredit the PPD. Thus, its political strategy favors any measure that is directed toward greater integration with the United States. To secure that goal, the NPP is waging a campaign to obtain the right to vote in presidential elections, which would bring U.S. political party structures to Puerto Rico. It is also trying to develop measures to improve economic conditions in Puerto Rico, so that Puerto Ricans can eventually pay federal income taxes. And it is working hard to increase the flow of federal aid, arguing in Washington that Puerto Rico should be treated as any other state. But the NPP needs an economic strategy if it is to attain its goals. Its short-range strategy is the same as that of the PPD: to increase the flow of federal aid, but (for the time being) with less use of direct repression so as not to risk losing popular support. Its long-range strategy is more difficult to determine. The NPP is also searching for a way out of the crisis, but it currently has no coherent plan for economic development under statehood. Thus, the party seems to be attempting to duplicate the PPD's program of the 1950s, even down to its populist rhetoric. But the basic problem is that Puerto Rico's economic conditions contradict the NPP's political objectives: before the elections, as a step toward statehood, the party promised the immediate establishment of federal minimum wage standards, but after the elections that goal was postponed, as it was with the PPD, to the indefinite future.

## Notes

1. U.S., Congress, House, Subcommittee on Territorial and Insular Affairs, *Compact of Permanent Union Between Puerto Rico and the United States: Hearing*, 94th Cong., 2d sess., January 30–February 9, 1976.
2. Economic Research Group, Secretariat of Information and Propaganda, Puerto Rican Socialist Party (PSP), "The economic importance of Puerto Rico for the United States," *Latin American Perspectives* 10 (Summer 1976).
3. Ibid.
4. *Wall Street Journal*, September 23, 1977, p. 1.
5. Tomás Morales, *Recursos Naturales y Coloniaje Ambiental* (San Juan: Editorial Frente, 1977).
6. PSP, "Importance of Puerto Rico."
7. Neftalí García, "Los Recursos Naturales y la Coyuntura Económico Política Actual," *Punto Inicial*, no. 3 (1977).
8. Neftalí García, *El Estado Actual de la Exploración Petrolera en Puerto Rico* (San Juan: Proyecto de Educación Social, 1977).
9. C. Arthur Borg, "The Problem of Puerto Rico's Political Status" (Case study, Senior Seminar in Foreign Policy, U.S. Department of State, 1974–75).
10. Ibid., pp. 254–55.
11. Ibid., p. 259.
12. See Teodoro Moscoso, "Severe unemployment in Puerto Rico and the need for minimum wage flexibility" in Borg, "Political Status," pp. 251–71.
13. Ibid., p. 265.
14. Ibid., p. 299.
15. Ibid., p. 266.
16. Ibid., p. 259.
17. *New York Times*, February 15, 1976.
18. Ibid.
19. *New York Times*, February 15, 1976, p. 1.
20. Ibid.
21. Ibid.
22. Subcommittee on Territorial and Insular Affairs, *Compact of Permanent Union*, *Hearing*, 94th Cong., 2d sess., Jan. 20–Feb. 9, 1976, vol. 2, p. 287.
23. Subcommittee on Territorial and Insular Affairs, *Compact of Permanent Union: Hearing*, 94th Cong., 2d sess., Jan. 20–Feb. 9, 1976, vol. 1, p. 270.

24. *Business Latin America*, July 13, 1977, p. 219.
25. *Business Latin America*, May 11, 1977, p. 146.
26. Ibid.
27. Ibid.
28. Ibid.
29. *Business Latin America*, July 13, 1977, p. 220.
30. Ibid.
31. Theodore Roosevelt, *Colonial Policies of the United States* (New York: Doubleday, 1937).
32. C. Arthur Borg, "Political Status," p. 16.

# 11

# TOWARD A THEORY OF TWENTIETH-CENTURY SOCIALIST REVOLUTIONS

## Introduction

Twentieth-century socialist revolutions must be located within the *processes* by which societies are integrated into the world capitalist system.[1] The manner in which the "incorporation" takes place creates the conditions for the growth of large-scale social movements that transform society. Hence, what is crucial is less the economic position of a society within the capitalist world order (whether it is metropolis or periphery) at a given moment, but is rather the action/reaction of political and social forces—the reciprocal movements within and between social formations that alter social relations and the form and nature of state domination.

There is no fixed economic, political, or social *moment* that defines the "revolutionary period," such as early industrialization, national independence, global warfare, or periods of political decay.[2] All of these are *particular* settings, precipitating factors through which long-term, underlying forces act, but in no sense do those moments provide a *unifying* comprehensive explanation of twentieth century socialist revolutions.

The process of incorporation into the world capitalist system is not an initial and final act, but rather a constant process, renewed through "stages"—early or late capitalism—which finds expression in a variety of global forms, both peaceful and violent. The world capitalist system is indeed fraught with perpetual change: a system of constant expansion, aggressive competition, shifting alignments—all of which are accompanied by class conflict at the world and national basis. The manner by which societies are "integrated" into the capitalist system is never purely economic, political, or cultural. Historically, the pattern can incorporate a combination of economic expansion, military occupation, and the establishment of client regimes; the particular forms utilized to this end are endlessly varied, just as the constant need for capital to expand is perpetual.

Capitalist expansion and incorporation on a world scale has reproduced throughout the world, in strikingly uneven fashion, a series of class relationships juxtaposed with a variety of forms of state power within heterogeneous social formations.[3] The principal accompaniment of capital's incorporation has been war—colonial wars, world wars, civil wars, and the wars of foreign occupation. Without wars, the movement of capital would have been paralyzed: with war—as some of the cases indicate—capital and capitalists have been destroyed. The process which engenders capitalist incorporation has also led to the demise of capitalism.

The emergence of socialist revolutions in the twentieth century is thus a product of mature capitalism expanding on a world scale. Socialist revolution is the *outcome* of worldwide capitalist expansion, or what bourgeois writers choose to call "modernization"; revolution is not the precipitant of modernization.[4] The condition for continual expansion, the reproduction of capital throughout the world, has caused massive dislocations in previously precapitalist formations, exacerbating the levels of exploitation as the existing dominant classes attempt to convert from one mode of production to another. The entry of imperial capital into a social formation then leads to a multiple set of changes, finding expression in the creation of new productive forces, the destruction of old modes of production, and the intensification of exploitation within the "shell" of others. The conditions of exploitation combine the methods of primitive accumulation—mass deracination and genocide—with those of industrial capitalism proper (exploitation of labor). This combination of "stages" of capitalist development heightens the possibility of revolutionary union between social forces in the precapitalist or petty commodity sectors and those integrated within the modern capitalist sector. The multiple processes of exploitation occurring in the areas under primitive accumulation (land rent, taxation, increasing appropriation of the surplus as well as the means of production, labor requisitions, etc.) clear the way for large-scale, long-term movements of capital. In so doing, the rupturing of precapitalist communities and local bonds to precapitalist rulership creates a massive uprooted population: particular attacks on ties to land, ascriptive values, and kinship relationships are subsumed under a general offensive of capital, which threatens to destroy the very existence of the whole society.

One of the problems from the point of view of theorizing about socialist revolutions in the twentieth century is the relative importance which is imputed to "wars."[5] Most analysts consider wars as fortuitous events acting upon social structures. My position is that the wars are processes inherent to the social structure, extensions of the social-economic structures necessary to the accumulation activity of the dominant classes. Thus, wars are largely internal to the process of capital accumulation—creating conditions for the reorganization of societies to permit the process to go on unhindered by precapitalist formations or by advanced capitalist competitors. War is the extension of capital accumulation through noneconomic means.

The process of war-capitalism has the effect of homogenizing the social situation of all oppressed strata, dislocating traditional exploiters and national bourgeoisies and creating states which lack the traditions and bonds that make for effective rulership: an artifact of imperial forces, the "state," is sumperimposed on the society (whether it remains formally "independent" is a secondary question). The state rulers, lacking roots in the centers of productive activity, derive their power largely from the disintegrating precapitalist classes, from their linkages to imperial state power (loans, arms, etc.), and from the extension of the state bureaucracy itself.

The dynamic effects of imperial capital expansion undermine

the growth of a state linked to ruling classes exercising hegemony over society. Within the periphery, the growth of class antagonisms in the centers of capitalist production are not "mediated" by the state, but are repressed. Multiple waves of repression follow the waves of capital expansion: the condition for the continual reproduction of capital and its movement from the initial centers of production to the rest of the country requires that the workers in the centers be prevented from serving as detonators of national opposition.[6]

Despite massive and sustained repression, twentieth-century socialist revolutions have followed the movements of capital: the initial areas of imperial capital concentration have been the loci for the primary and determinant organization of the socialist revolutionary parties.

## Economic Development and Socialist Revolution

By examining changes in class relationships within the periphery, we are better able to explain changes in the nature and form of the external relationship as well as the possibilities for socialist revolutions implicit in the process of internal struggle.

Twentieth-century socialist revolutions are not a product of the underdeveloped areas of the periphery but are *initiated* in those areas most penetrated by the metropolis, where capitalist social relations predominate and where productivity exceeds that of the rest of the country. Likewise, the growth of nationalism in the periphery is not a product of dependency per se, but the result of a growing ability among the petty bourgeoisie to manage and control the productive forces under metropolitan domination. It is within this gap between capacity and control that petty-bourgeois nationalism emerges. The key issue in center/periphery relations, then, is the growing social and political differentiation and autonomy of class forces within economies under metropolitan domination and their ability to resist the exploitative drives of imperial capital. Conflict, therefore, is not between undifferentiated dependent countries against metropoles; much less is the anti-imperialist vanguard located in the traditional, poverty-stricken hinterland. The development of national and social revolutionary forces in the most productive sectors of peripheral society suggests that the struggle is less a product of underdevelopment and more a response to the conditions of imperial capital accumulation. In the case of the wage laborers, the relation is exploitative; in the case of the petty and national bourgeoisie, it is exclusionary, i.e., the imperial capitalists displace the local bourgeoisie as the locus of accumulation; in the case of petty commodity producers, imperial domination leads to a combination of exploitation, displacement, and appropriation of surplus.

In this way, we demystify the notion of dependence, which, as it has commonly been discussed, fails to take account of the different social formations within the periphery and the multiple sources of surplus appropriation located in the areas of direct metropolitan domination and in the surrounding productive forces that furnish labor and food supplies.[7] The initial formulation of the problem for the periphery is not external dependency but *imperial exploitation* located in the class structure of the periphery; and it is within this class structure and in the class struggles that ensue that this problem must be examined and eventually resolved.

If the principal contradiction between the periphery and metropolis is located in the technologically and economically advanced productive units of the periphery, the problem is not modernization but socialization or nationalization of those areas as instruments of liberation and growth. While the central contradiction is in the highly developed units, the conflict involves all the social forces directly and indirectly linked to them. In twentieth-century socialist revolutions, the original impetus, organization, leadership, and ideology of the revolutionary struggle *began* precisely in the more advanced sectors of the peripheral economy: in Russia, the Petrograd proletariat led by the Bolshevik Party; in China and in Vietnam, in the coastal cities; in Cuba, in Havana.[8] In all cases, however, the *success* of the revolution that began in the advanced productive units depended on joining efforts with the bulk of the social forces (peasants) located in the backward areas of the economy. The process of transformation in the periphery combines two distinct but interrelated experiences: the socialization of production in the metropolitan enclaves and the transformation of land tenure in the backward areas. The class struggle leading to the socialization of the economy is not based on an abstract notion of the level of productive forces, nor is it a creation of individual will, of transforming individuals' social consciences.[9] Revolutionary action is a product of the transformation of social relations under the aegis of imperial capital within the advanced industrial agricultural units and the extension of those sociopolitical changes to petty commodity producers, leading to the creation of organized political forces growing out of the working class and embracing masses of nonproletarian social forces. Capitalist development ("modernization") of the periphery under imperialism was essentially uneven and imposed through class relations of domination. The introduction of technology and organization was essentially a means of heightening the level of exploitation, increasing the absolute and relative rates of extraction of surplus value. This form of capitalist expansion (what liberal writers describe as "modernization from above and outside") led to the concentration, organization, and politicization of social forces, which then became the source of nationalist and socialist movements. The latter grew as a response to the exploitative and exclusionary nature of the total social situation. To continue to discuss the periphery as if the principal issue is one of "modernization" is to call for the continued and extended exploitative social relations that have already been established in the major productive units.

The modernization problem is an imperial project: it is based on the creation of political, social, and economic conditions which facilitate capital's introduction of new techniques and organizations to deepen and extend exploitative social relations throughout a country. To enter into that problem, to redefine its methods, is an effort at reformist politics: to ameliorate the conditions of capitalist accumulation without affecting the essential mechanisms.

The ultimate *success* of socialist economic effort depends not upon gaining control over the numerically important but backward semicapitalist or precapitalist areas, but upon capturing the commanding heights of the economy under the control of metropolitan capital. The modern and productive firms in the dynamic sectors of the economy are the enterprises that serve as the principal source for financing post-revolutionary economic expansion. Modernization theory, by locating the problem in the areas yet to be exploited, by focusing on the problems of economic backwardness, by examining the peasant or poverty or food problem isolated from imperial control of dynamic enterprises, obscures the essential sources of conflict between the periphery and metropolis, and the point of departure for national development.[10]

While the surplus extracted by imperial capital is concentrated in the most productive enterprises of the peripheral economy, the whole society (petty commodity producers and others) contributes directly and indirectly to sustaining and subsidizing the operation.[11] The resultant exploitative social relations of production have engendered antagonistic social classes—from the urban petty bourgeois through the urban proletariat to the rural petty commodity producers. The growth of productive forces concentrated in the advanced productive units and their backward linkages to petty commodity production has increased the breadth and scope of social forces in political and social combat, increasing their ability to contest imperial accumulation. Hence, while the main productive centers are the initial focuses of resistance, the *consummation* of a successful socialist transformation depends on forging links with the uprooted rural and urban petty commodity producers. The political formulation of this linkage between proletarian and petty commodity producers has not always been envisioned in the initial socialist efforts.

From the perspective of socialist revolution, the central issue in the periphery is not backwardness, and the answer therefore is not modernization. Nor is the *central* issue unequal exchange—an important but derivative problem. The central issues are imperial exploitative social relations and domination of the proletariat in the dynamic sectors of the peripheral economy and appropriation of the surplus from the petty producers, which provoke class confrontations and challenge the configurations of power dictating the terms of exchange.

## Capitalism and the Formation of the Proletariat in the Periphery

Capitalism requires labor that has been separated from the means of production in order to be in a position to exploit it. The process of separation of labor from the means of production can be based on economic, legal, and military methods. The alienation of the means of production from labor occurs in two forms: either the laborers' means of production are appropriated or the laborer is removed from access to them. They are then in a sense free to enter into a new set of labor relations with capital. The conditions under which labor enters into the relationship with capital varies from physical compulsion to wage payments, depending on the historical circumstances surrounding capital/labor relationships. The exploitation by large-scale agricultural and mining enterprises in peripheral regions that offered alternative sources of employment (farming) pressured capitalists to use coercive, noneconomic means and measures to control their labor force.

In England, the preemption of alternative sources of employment through the absorption of land via enclosures and the growth of commercial agriculture left the labor force without the means of production, without alternative ways to obtain it, and with two choices—emigration or entry into the industrial labor market. The abundance of labor, based on the disintegration of petty commodity production, created a condition in which the capitalist could enter into "exchange" relations with labor. There was no need to emphasize physical coercion to bring labor into a relationship with capital because there was an inner coercion—hunger.

In Europe, capital permeated the whole of society, so that the growth of commercial agriculture uprooted petty commodity producers and subsistence farmers and made them available for industrial capital in such a fashion and supply as to lead to wage payments.

The process in Africa, Asia, and Latin America was different.[12] Initially, the imperial powers seized and were able to exploit only limited areas—leaving substantial land open for alternative exploitation. As a result, means of production in land were available outside the imperial enclave. In the Third World, the commercialization of agriculture was accompanied by limited industrial expansion, requiring imperial capital to secure and maintain labor through physical compulsion.

The development of capitalism in Europe depended on a home market and thus created pressure for wage payments to solve the problem. Imperial capital, on the other hand, did not require an internal market, since the crucial element in its growth was the world market or the home market in the metropolitan country. Hence, there was no specific reason for capital to develop wage payments, as the principal exchanges were outside the locus of production. Thus, both the intensive, geographically restricted nature and the external orientation of imperial capital's exploitation contributed to the particular forms of capitalist exploitation in which physical compulsion and nonwage payments played a prominent role.

State coercion played a decisive role in fostering the cash nexus upon Third World countries in peaceful periods. During interimperialist wars the demands of imperial powers for raw materials and foodstuffs multiplied, and the process of surplus appropriation to sustain high profits for private industry and high levels of state expenditures led, in many cases, to the massive, forcible seizure of products and requisitioning of labor. The methods of primitive accumulation were applied by advanced capitalist social formations upon petty commodity producers in the Third World: pillage of peasant agriculture was directed by motorized columns.[13] The forcible seizure of surplus was accompanied by the massive uprooting of the peasantry; the source of surplus in local petty commodity production was divorced from the locus of accumulation in the imperial centers. Indeed, the transformation of surplus into imperial war industries through its transfer outside the social formation led to a situation in which petty commodity production was undermined, without a commensurate growth of alternative industrial activity. Hence, the advance of capitalism under conditions of imperialist war transformed peasants into landless laborers without any definite attachments to either capitalist or precapitalist production. The great mass of rural recruits to the Russian, Chinese, and Vietnamese revolutionary forces were precisely those *former* peasants, uprooted by the drives of imperial capital. The separation of rural labor from land and landlords means that the principal force in the revolutionary struggle was *not* peasants but ex-peasants; the principal conflict from which the bulk of the rural masses were recruited was not a socially specific, local landlord/peasant struggle but a confrontation with advancing imperial capital, upsetting *all* social relations in the precapitalist formation—subordinating or displacing local landlords. The main contradiction was between an uprooted landless mass and imperial capital; the separation from the means of production provides a concrete linkage between those rural masses and the working class ideology of the Communist Party.[14] The as yet incomplete proletarianization, found in the absence of incorporation in wage-paying industry, is, in the cases of China and Vietnam, compensated by the organization of this uprooted landless mass into various forms of cooperative agriculture in communist-occupied zones.

The Bolsheviks were most successful in winning over uprooted peasant conscripts into the army. The Chinese Communists recruited heavily among peasants forcibly inducted into labor gangs and military units and among others whose surplus had been appropriated or destroyed by Japanese imperialism and the Kuomintang. Similar processes occurred in Vietnam, where massive uprooting of peasants followed upon the large-scale entry of U.S. armed forces. The process of deracination in Cuba was a more prolonged, largely economic, process fostered by the United States' support for a local, coercive regime. The formaation of a proletarian class is hence largely the product of politicoeconomic forces, the tying of labor to capital through coercive measures, and the uprooting of peasants through military means. The state plays a central position in the formation of the peripheral proletariat through the mechanisms of coercion and deracination.

## Russian Revolution

In Russia, the center of capitalist expansion and imperial investment was in the area of St. Petersburg,[15] where great concentrations of factory workers in large, modern factories provided the social base of the Bolshevik party. St. Petersburg also contained the key organizing center of the soviets, which provided leadership and direction to similar organizations throughout the country. This industrial center became the pole of opposition to the tsarist and the transitory liberal-democratic regime of Alexander Kerensky. The economic linkages between the tsarist state and western imperial capital were matched by political and military alliances, which led to the tsarist state's participation in the war and the massive uprooting of millions of peasants and their transformation into a military force.[16] Thus the superimposition of Western capitalism onto the tsarist state led to exploitation of a modern proletariat, the harnessing of the Russian peasant to the conflicts of Western capital (via the tsarist state), and to efforts at capitalist development in the countryside. Thus, Russia's incorporation into the world capitalist system through large-scale industrial investments and loans, its involvement in the interimperial war, and the growing commercialization of agriculture combined to create a class-conscious proletariat and an uprooted peasantry. The former became the core of the revolutionary socialist organization which hegemonized the mass peasant movement that destroyed both the capitalist state and the underlying property relations.

The forms of incorporation into the capitalist world greatly influenced the particular role that different social classes played in the revolutionary process: the incorporation of labor via industrial investment provided the workers with the cohesion, discipline, and common basis from which to develop a "socialist consciousness"—the basis for the growth and success of the Bolshevik Party.

Contrary to the standard anti-Marxist accounts, which depict the Russian revolution as a coup engineered by a manipulative, disciplined, intellectual elite behind the back of the working class, a number of scholarly accounts clearly document that the Bolsheviks were successful because their principal goals coincided with those of the great bulk of the laboring population. The Bolshevik Party was able to win the key industrial cities in October 1917 because it had over the preceding decades been involved in many of the most important substantive struggles that affected the working class. Those struggles and the ties which had developed between the party and the class served as important points of entry later into the broader and more comprehensive movements for revolutionary change. The party itself was able to respond to the demands from below because, contrary to some writers, it was a party of debate, discussion, and differences—an open party subject to the exigencies of police repression. In large part, the great revolutionary upsurge was carried by nonparty organs—the soviets—which were arenas within which rank-and-file militant workers, Bolshevik Party members, and others debated policy and made the revolution. The revolutionary struggles—the massive day-to-day activities that carried the movement toward the social transformation—were products of those mass organizations in which the Bolsheviks were able eventually to win a democratic majority. The process of class organization and class struggle was accelerated by the intensification of exploitation under conditions of war-capitalism, leading to the concentration of social power in comprehensive and inclusive organizations of popular power; that political development was the underlying process that provided an opportunity for open and free confrontation between the Bolsheviks and the bourgeois parties, and under those open conditions the Bolsheviks were able to obtain the support of the majority.[17]

The incorporation of the ex-peasantry transformed into soldiers led to their uprootedness and turned them against the existing social order without developing in them any clear notion of an alternative. The peasants, incorporated through the growth of capitalist agriculture, turned against the emerging social order, but in the direction of petty commodity production. The convergence of these three forces was rooted in their opposition to the existing order, not in their common social location in the productive process. The post-revolutionary divergencies reflected the different sets of exploitative relations which had preceded the revolution and the different sorts of "solutions" inherent in each set.

## Chinese Revolution

The incorporation of China into the capitalist world was also through a combined process of investment, military-capitalist expansion, and the accentuation of surplus appropriation in the countryside.[18] The origins and growth of the Communist Party (CCP) coincided with a massive movement of students and workers responding to the exploitative relations located in the new commercial-industrial and railroad centers.[19] The ideology and organization of the party (cadres and leaders) were formed by the experiences of urban class conflict during the 1920s, culminating in the Shanghai massacre of 1927.[20] The losses in numbers and the shattering of the mass organizations did not, however, break the continuity of the revolutionary experience. Henceforth, the notions of socialism, class struggle, and anti-imperialism were transferred to the countryside, where substantial support was garnered among the increasingly proletarianized peasantry, a product of the growing commercial agricultural and capitalist class that was accumulating capital in the cities, towns, and villages. The initial urban-industrial experience of class struggle generated the central cadres and leadership, who were, in turn, the basis for the recruitment of the second circle of proletarianized peasants (1928-1935).[21] Both social layers (urban and rural proletariat) responded to the Communists' appeals against the imperatives of local and imperialist capital accumulation.[22] The third circle of party recruits was drawn largely from petty commodity producers and, in scattered cases, from so-called national capitalists overrun by the efforts of Japanese capital to crystalize a set of social relations for large-scale, long-term capital accumulation.[23] The displacement of petty and local capital by imperial capital—the process of uprooting and requisitioning—in effect, temporarily "proletarianized" these petty-bourgeois and bourgeois strata, setting in motion the process of attraction toward the Communist Party as the only source from which to work back toward a place in the social economy. The nationalist, antifascist political line of the CCP facilitated the movement of these strata. However, their incorporation was superimposed upon a substantial and longstanding noncapitalist core with which they stood in alliance only insofar as the movement of Japanese capital could not successfully incorporate them into its economic project. The effort by Japanese capital to substitute military means of incorporation in place of searching for mechanisms by which to articulate local Chinese capital to imperial capital was dictated by the exigency of the interimperialist war with the United States.[24] Where the efforts to incorporate Chinese capital were successful, there were few contradictions between national and imperial capital. The problem of incorporating Chinese capital, however, was not only a product of the war conditions between rival imperialisms (and the needs to requisition labor and appropriate capital) but was also, in part, a result of the disadvantageous position of Chinese capital vis-à-vis Japanese capital—in terms of capital, resources, technology, and other needs. The preponderance of state backing for Japanese capital wiped out any chance of a durable coprosperity alliance.

The result was a revolutionary movement of singular breadth, combining layers of cadres tempered by working-class struggle, proletarianized peasants, deracinated petty producers, and uprooted petty and local capitalists. All were responding to the different aspects of imperial capital accumulation and the particular transformations that it wrought within the heterogeneous Chinese social formation. The early worker-based Communist ideology merged imperceptibly with the populism of the second layer of rural proletarians and later with the nationalism and antifascism of the petty commodity producers and local capitalists. The mass base and geographic locus of the revolution (rural) was juxtaposed with its origins and leadership, which was rooted in the urban working class's past and legitimized by a veneer of nationalism and antifascism reflecting the last and least consequential strata in the revolutionary process—the petty commodity producers and local capitalists.

In summary, the initial revolutionary socialist movement was generated by the advanced forms of imperial capitalist expansion in the coastal cities; the impact was to dislocate traditional artisan and handicraft industries, creating a nationalist movement among the backward local capitalists and a revolutionary socialist movement led by the Communist Party. In the struggle for power, the national movement sought to come to terms with imperialism, demarcating spheres of economic activity; in order to bargain, it first allied with and then subdued the burgeoning workers' movement. The latter, basing itself on a conception of China as a precapitalist social formation articulated with imperialism, lost sight of the crucial linkages between local and foreign capital, which overlaid their immediate conflict. Hence, the schema of a two-stage revolution (bourgeois preceding socialist) based on an alliance of classes informed the tactical and strategic thinking of the Communist Party.

The political victory of the Kuomintang-led bourgeoisie forced the rapid expansion of a bourgeois state authority, yet it was one that interpenetrated with the local landlords and commercial classes that were expanding under the impetus of commodity exchanges. The bourgeois regime partially united the several regions, heightened the exactions from the rural labor force to the central government and accelerated the extraction of surplus from the countryside. Without a firmly rooted and overpowering industrial class capable of appropriating the surplus, it was squandered by a ruling stratum composed of nonproductive financial, commercial, and bureaucratic fractions.[25] Moreover, the expansion of Japanese imperialism preempted the key industrial centers, and the Japanese occupied and requisitioned means of production and surplus in rural areas, further aborting efforts at national capital accumulation. The result was that the national regime, due to its internal heterogeneity and because of external constraints, was not able to complete the consolidation of its social power. Born in the midst of a civil war against the working class, the bourgeoisie was never able to carry the popular masses along with its class-specific demands; the imperial invasion and the assimilation of nonindustrial invasion and the assimilation of nonindustrial classes within the regime effectively undercut efforts to enlist the support of rural petty commodity producers. The end of the 1927 civil war and its aftermath was a bourgeois regime without a significant mass social base. The existence of a heterogeneous rural mass provided a base within which the displaced Communist Party could begin to rebuild its organization. The Chinese revolution occurred neither in a fully capitalist society nor in a precapitalist society but, rather, in a country which combined advanced forms of capitalist exploitation with the most rudimentary beginnings of the process of capital accumulation through wholesale appropriation of surplus from the countryside. The long-term effect was to create the ingredients for a revolutionary movement torn in two directions: one rooted in the earlier experience of workers seeking the transformation of the social relations of production; the other in rural petty commodity exchanges oriented toward the development of the market forces. The prolonged process of struggle in the countryside was evident in the post-revolutionary development, where party leaders made a clear determination to subordinate workers' rule to centralized bureaucratic control and local rural autonomy. The proletarian nucleus fed the efforts at large-scale collectivization in rural and urban areas; that residual influence, however, was insufficient to shape the central political institutions that dictated policy. The great mass of uprooted peasant military forces were, in turn, susceptible to collectivist organization but imposed their localist orientation in the form of decentralized productive units. The heterogeneous social forces which made the revolution indirectly found expression in a complex pattern of rulership through indirection: the forms of property took a collectivized form, while the units of local governance were decentralized.[26] The revolutionary process, which began in the early 1920s, effectively ended in the mid-1950s with the collective forms of property—a period that sets the stage for new forms of conflict between rival bureaucratic factions anchored in different economic sectors and reflecting competing class interest and development strategies.[27] Those struggles continue because, unlike the Soviet Union, the social transformation in China has not been accompanied by the massive purges that have so depoliticized the population and left so few traces of the original Bolshevik-led workers' revolution.

## Cuban Revolution

In Cuba, the revolutionary process has several possible beginnings: (1) the 1860s, when the first nationalist uprising was launched; (2) the independence struggle in the 1890s, when the Cuban nationalist forces were on the verge of displacing Spain and were subjected to U.S. intervention and occupation; (3) the 1933 national social revolution, which overthrew the Machado dictatorship and led to massive worker-led industrial factory occupations; (4) the 1952 launching of the 26th of July Movement, when the political leadership that forged the new revolutionary regime initiated the armed struggle; or (5) the 1959 overthrow of Zaldívar Batista and the assumption by the revolutionary leadership of the key positions in and around the governmental apparatus.[28]

All of these processes and events have some bearing on the revolutionary struggle in Cuba. Clearly, the uprisings and conflicts in the nineteenth century and at the turn of the century created a strong nationalist tradition and provided a sense of national identity that was consciously taken up by the post-1959 revolutionary leadership. Nevertheless, the 1933 revolution marks the key point of departure for the *socialist* revolutionary process.[29] That period witnessed the first massive entry of the working class into clearly anticapitalist, as well as economically consequential, anti-imperialist struggles. The workers' uprising of 1933 was massive and national, and it contributed to the growth of an anticapitalist working-class tradition. Moreover, the uprising of 1933, by fusing the social and national struggles into one common movement (albeit without a revolutionary socialist leadership), foreshadowed the revolutionary process of the 1950s and 1960s. The events leading up to the 1933 uprising and the experiences and organization that grew out of it clearly reflected the intense class polarization of the period. Despite the sharp turn toward class collaborationist politics by the Communist Party trade union leadership in the late 1930s and 1940s, the underlying basis of class-based struggles persisted and re-emerged with increasing intensity in the late 1950s and early 1960s.[30] The 1933 revolutionary struggles opened the possibilities of a socialist revolution by providing a working class socialized in the anticapitalist struggle and capable of providing the mass base for historical moves in that direction.

On the other hand, the 1933 revolution also provided a set of negative experiences regarding the possibilities of a bourgeois-democratic revolution: the inability of the Ramon Grau government to consolidate a nationalist transformation; the impossibility of negotiating a settlement acceptable to both the Cuban masses and U.S. government and business; the inconsequential nationalist commitment of the local bourgeoisie and petty bourgeoisie when confronted with imperial power; and the incapacity of the nationalist-democrats to realize mass democratic rule within the existing state structure, i.e., with the old military apparatus intact.[31] The upshot was that 1933 was the crucial reference point for the development of the socialist revolution: the failure of national-democratic capitalism precluded any effort to follow once again a two-stage revolutionary schema. The positive experience of a popular uprising provided a socialized mass base and an example of the revolutionary possibilities inherent in mass mobilization and struggle.

The existence of a common anticapitalist tradition among the mass of workers and the presence of the Communist Party, with its experienced cadres and militants, provided the material basis for the consummation of the socialist revolution *after* 1959. Without those key elements, no amount of revolutionary will on the part of leadership would have propelled the process to a successful end.

The first major component of the socialist revolution, then, was neither the petty bourgeoisie or the 26th of July Movement but was rather the workers' movement that had initiated the revolutionary struggle in the 1930s. This movement and experience provided the political and social framework within which the 26th of July Movement could function and hope to succeed. It was within this anticapitalist political culture that Fidel Castro's forces were radicalized and it was the Communist Party, which in distorted collaborationist form carried the earlier tradition embodied in its working-class militants. The socialist and working-class roots of the Cuban revolution go back to the 1930s revolution: the 1959 overthrow of Batista picks up where that impetus left off.

The reason why the Cuban revolutionary struggle of the guerillas succeeded, whereas in the rest of Latin America such struggles failed, was because Cuba had a revolutionary past, a working class to which appeals could be directed, and a national constituency that could understand and respond to its anti-imperialist and social reform appeals. Castro's appeals were part of that tradition, and consciously so. In Latin America, there was no similar tradition, no mass communist parties that had engaged in insurrectionary activity. Hence, in Latin America (unlike Cuba), the guerrillas' appeals could not draw on the prior socialization of workers in class struggle but had to engage in the struggle that would create the base—while isolated in rural areas away from the main concentrations of workers and peasants.

The 26th of July Movement drew support from a number of socially oppressed classes: the provincial working class and petty bourgeoisie, which had embodied the earlier traditions of struggle (Santiago de Cuba); the small coffee farmers of the Sierra Maestra, who retained their hostility toward the sugar corporations which had displaced them; and the urban labor force of the capital city, exploited and coerced by the regime.[32] Although the locus of direct struggle occurred primarily in the countryside in the initial period, the urban resistance was not a negligible factor. As the revolution progressed, it increasingly drew mass support from the urban poor and working class, as well as from the liberal professions and fractions of the bourgeoisie. The original core of the revolution, shaped by the experiences of the 1930s and drawing support from the oppressed rural population, proceeded to develop closer links with the provincial urban working class: the mass character of the 1959 overthrow of Batista was a conjunctural phenomenon sandwiched between two sets of working-class experiences. The origins and determinants of the socialist revolution were drawn from the experiences of the 1930s and the increasing social weight of the urban and rural proletariat in the struggles after 1959.

The 1959 overthrow of Batista was one *moment* in the historical process—a moment in which the bourgeoisie and petty bourgeoisie were temporarily incorporated into the ongoing revolutionary movement. The period immediately after the overthrow witnessed a sustained and consequential effort by the revolutionary leadership to strengthen the working-class core within the revolutionary movement through a series of measures:[33] (1) the old state apparatus was dismantled; (2) agrarian and urban reform were decreed; (3) workers and peasants were armed and organized in militias; (4) urban and rural masses were mobilized independently of and against the efforts of the bourgeoisie to restore the old order and against the bureaucratic sectarian designs of a faction of the Communist Party. The net effect of these measures and struggles that ensued was to tip the balance of power in favor of masses against the landlords, imperial firms and the petty bourgeoisie.

The Cuban revolution first began in 1933, was revived in 1952, overthrew the Batista regime in 1959, and proceeded to transform the social system by 1962. The concentration of working-class forces within the regime (in the militias and the organizations of mass mobilization) and the prior socialization of the class explain in part the rapidity of the transition to socialized production and the relatively weak opposition from procapitalist classes. No other revolution has moved so far and so fast toward socialization as did the Cuban. That phenomenon, juxtaposed with the fact that the Communist Party was not the leading party, is not paradoxical—if we keep in mind the fact that the socialized working class provided the main impetus and base of support after 1959.

Cuba's socialist revolution did not reflect the backwardness of capitalism.[34] On the contrary, the main centers of revolutionary ferment in Cuba during the 1930s were those of imperial capitalist exploitation—the sugar plantations. The process of imperial capital accumulation created a large reserve army of seasonal laborers and an agrarian proletariat, exercised hegemony over local capital, and displaced petty commodity producers to the highlands of the interior. The worldwide expansion of capitalism created new centers of exploitation in sugar, thus leading to stagnation and periodic crises, which affected production in Cuba. The subordination of Cuban production to the world market and the capacity of U.S. sugar industrialists to determine optimal production within any given social formation led to the long-term stagnation and perennial unemployment that characterized the Cuban sugar industry. Thus, the complete subordination of Cuba to the world capitalist market through the U.S. multinationals had an adverse effect generally on the process of locally based capital accumulation and a specific dislocating effect on the labor force: it generated capitalist relations of production without incorporating and disciplining the labor force on a stable basis. Class struggle and class politics were the resultant expression of a labor force confined to a social situation of limited mobility and permanent economic insecurity.[35] The durability of anticapitalist sentiment among the mass of the working class was sustained by the social consequence of world capitalist integration. The unevenness of capitalist development, both in regional and sectorial terms, combined with the process of proletarianization of the labor force to create a volatile agrarian and urban population concentrated in geographical as well as occupational centers.

Cuba experienced the typical form of imperial exploitation, in which the source of capital accumulation is not the locus of accumulation. The transfer of surplus from Cuba to the United States was matched by inflows of investments into particular service sectors and areas of Cuban economy that accentuated social and regional inequalities. The reserve army of labor in the countryside shifted toward the city. This urbanization was accompanied by the growth of tertiary employment, embodied in a vast network of administrative, financial, and other occupational services.[36] Thus, while the historic result of capital flow from Cuba to the United States created an underindustrialized society, the flow from the United States to Cuba created a substantial network of white-collar workers within the boundaries established by Cuba's subordination to the world capitalist system. Hence, the growth of white-collar radicalism was grafted upon the previously organic ties of social solidarity established among agricultural workers by the expansion and stagnation of imperial capital in agribusiness. This pattern of imperial capital expansion generated several centers of opposition differentiated by their inclusion in different waves and forms of imperial investment but united in their opposition to the regime that embodied the common enemy. Hence, the Cuban revolutionary movement, which began in the countryside in 1933, re-emerged in the urban white-collar centers during the 1950s, converged toward class alliances during the late 1950s, and was polarized during the social revolutionary effort of the 1960s.

The accretions and losses in the latter period reflected the internal differentiation among the urban classes: the intensification of class polarization led to divisions within the urban labor force, with large-scale additions to the revolutionary socialist movement from the industrial and rural labor force and defections from the professional and semiprofessional strata.[37] These divisions within the urban centers reflected less the unevenness of capitalist development and more the different positions occupied within imperial-structured capitalism. In a word, the extension of the class struggle to the cities was possible through the mobilization of labor which included hidden or passive strata (from the empirical perspective of the early 1950s period of struggle) located in the interstices of imperialism—the slum dwellers, underemployed, unemployed—while the initially visible and vocal student and petty-bourgeois strata increasingly defected. This process of class polarization reflected the intricate and elaborate linkages that bound even seemingly radical strata—including revolutionary students—to the imperially constituted class order. Only the mass working class remained to sustain the revolutionary movement once it began to uproot the imperial system: the mass of intermediary strata began to experience or perceived that they would experience some loss.

The socialist nature of the revolution grew directly out of the closely entwined interests of local and foreign capital—leaving no possibility of alternative paths to development. The epicenter of social revolutionary activity from 1960 onward was the urban and rural masses located in the productive sectors: the service employees and the remaining loyalist petty-bourgeois strata increasingly formed the rearguard, supporting a process they no longer could control. The transformation of Cuba was a reflection of a revolutionary socialist process within an advanced capitalist social formation, with its peculiar retrograde features imposed by the overdeterminant role of imperialism. The classes most directly involved in the socialization of production were those most actively exploited by imperialism. To the degree that the revolution has survived and moved in the direction of collectivization, it has always done so with the support and backing of the working class. The profound and rapid uprooting of capitalist property relations reflected the ripeness of the society—the relatively high levels of anticapitalist consciousness within capitalist development. The driving force of Cuban socialism was the rural and urban working class struggling to eliminate exploitation and to promote the growth of egalitarianism within a radically collectivized society, in which social solidarity replaced individual mobility and competition.

The presence and active role of a radicalized working class in the decisive anticapitalist struggles was not sufficient to consolidate a body of institutions through which the workers could legislate and execute measures on their behalf. The amorphousness of the political organizations, the primacy of military actions and organizations taken up with the tasks of defending the revolution against imperialist-directed assaults, and the ideological weakness of the revolutionary leadership on the particular issue of institutionalizing direct workers' power created a layer of political officialdom distinct from the working class, though dependent on it and influenced by its historic needs.[38] That process of differentiation was nurtured by the presence of a substantial white-collar faction within the revolutionary movement and the presence of post-revolutionary technicians deriving authority from economic models from other noncapitalist countries. The consolidation of the post-capitalist society has thus eliminated classes, but not politically significant social differentiation. As in the cases of the Soviet Union and China, but with substantial differences of degree and kind, Cuba has experienced the reemergence of nondemocratic forms of political representation based on the coming together of new and old sectors of white-collar strata. This problem, of great importance in defining the present and future course of the revolution, is beyond the scope of this essay, which is devoted primarily to the socialist revolutionary process, not how a revolutionary socialist regime consolidates itself.

## Vietnamese Revolution

The Vietnamese socialist revolution was the first to begin within a strictly colonial setting and to succeed by overthrowing a neocolonial regime and defeating a massive U.S. occupation army. This historical victory can only be understood through an analysis of (1) the accumulation of social forces in the class and national struggle, which propelled the revolutionary movement, and (2) the development of capitalist forces on a world scale and the U.S. commitment in this momentous struggle.

The initial formation of the Vietnamese Communist Party took place in the major urban areas of Saigon and later spread to the outlying areas of capitalist mining and plantation activity.[39] The centers of imperial capitalist domination became the sources for recruitment for socialist revolution. The implantation of the Communist Party and its ideology and the recruitment of the initial cadres and militants coincide with the initial intervention of the Communist Party in the first major class struggles in the region. The growth and expansion of communist influence coincide with the expansion of the class struggle throughout the 1930s, increasingly enveloping regions of petty commodity producers. From a movement of class mobilization there emerged a mass mobilization involving small producers, traders, school teachers, civil servants and others. The working-class movement served as the detonator for a larger movement but remained, through the Communist Party, the ultimate determinant of the political direction which the social struggle would take.[40]

In the post-World War II period, with the consolidation of the centers of capitalism in Western Europe and Japan, the United States and its reconstructed allies moved to recreate the conditions for imperial expansion throughout the periphery.[41] In Vietnam, the reconstitution of the social order was centered on the organization of the state; the human materials from which the state could be constituted drew largely on the colonial classes, their immediate followers and those nationalist forces opposed to large-scale, long-term social changes.[42] The conservative criteria for selection led to the recruitment of a mixture of colonial and post-colonial forces—regrouped to forcibly repress mass movements, which had developed through the merger of revolutionary socialist rural and urban workers and nationalist petty-bourgeois forces. The long-term outcome of a socialist revolution, which transcended changes in the type and pattern of imperialist domination, reflects the essential continuity in ideology, leadership, and core supporters of the Vietnamese revolutionary movement—embodied in the Communist Party.

The Vietnamese revolution occurred in the context of three intersecting imperial powers: a declining European imperialism (France) and a rising Asian and North American imperialism (Japan and the United States), each competing with the others. Each essentially reorganized Vietnamese society in the image of its own needs. French imperialism, basically oriented toward the economic exploitation of the region through the implantation of commercial agriculture and mining, created a rural and urban proletariat, which served as the original nucleus of the Communist Party. The initial integration of Vietnam into the capitalist world was essentially through the process of capital export, which also served as a source of surplus extraction. Nevertheless, the weakness of French imperialism prevented it from affecting the bulk of petty commodity producers who, in large areas, subsisted side by side with the expanding capitalist mode of production.[43] The attempts of Japanese imperialism to fuel its continental expansion—indeed to subordinate Asia to its effort to accumulate capital on a world scale—led to excessive exactions of surplus from petty commodity producers, to the requisition of resources from local producers and the superexploitation of labor, thus creating a broader basis of resistance.[44] The scope and depth of Japanese imperialist expansion, products of the greater dynamism of Japanese capital (and its more limited internal resources), led to a substantial transformation of the Vietnamese countryside. The uprooting of populations and the appropriation of surplus brought new and wider strata into antagonistic relations with capital. To accommodate this historical conjuncture, the Vietnamese Communist Party created a new form of political organization (the Vietminh), which could incorporate the mass of petty commodity producers who were increasingly coming under the oppressive rule of capital.[45] The movement from the working class to the petty commodity producers was accompanied by a continuity of program and leadership rooted in the working class: the rural masses were incorporated through tactical, programmatic adaptations, which included their immediate interests with the long-term goals defined by the original collectivist goals championed by the working-class cadres. The national character of the revolution was real, but must be understood in sociologically concrete terms: the multiple classes subject to the massive demands of Japanese capital were under the direction and leadership of the original core group of Communists, disciplined and decisively influenced by the working-class struggle.[46]

The defeat of Japanese imperialism furthered the position of the Vietnamese revolutionary socialists, allowing them to establish de facto political power in the cities as well as in the countryside. The reinsertion of French imperialism, facilitated by the Soviet-Western alliance, precipitated a renewal of class conflict. The efforts of the French to transform the war into a civil war largely failed because of the numerical strength and political-military organization of the Communist Party. The final demise of French imperialism in Vietnam overlapped with the rise of U.S. hegemony in the capitalist world. As the center of imperial expansion, the United States sought to level all obstacles to worldwide accumulation and trade; the particular targets were mass revolutionary socialist movements, such as in Vietnam, which, through their success, opened the possibility of extending socialist revolution from the Chinese subcontinent to the rest of southeast Asia.[47] The nature of the commitment of the United

States to war was, in an *immediate* sense, political: to destroy the revolutionary socialist movement/state in order to extend and consolidate its historic interests in the rest of the capitalist-dominated countries of the Third World. The scope and depth of the political goals (destruction of a mass popular movement) and the lack of profound direct economic ties—that is, the absence of an imperative to accumulate capital in the immediate context of Vietnam—loosened all constraints on politico-military warfare.[48] The fact that the United States did not seek to secure a surplus in Vietnam allowed it to destroy the productive forces—land, factories, and labor. The process of unlimited warfare guided by global political concerns led to the massive uprooting of population throughout the country, *cutting across class boundaries*. The total war effort, unleashed by the most dynamic imperial power, greatly reduced centuries of disparities and conflicts between regions, classes, clans, and ethnic groups. The indiscriminate bombing accelerated the movement of commodity producers from local bondage to communist activism in the course of a decade. Western accumulated wealth, product of centuries of oppression, was concentrated and transformed by U.S. imperialism into the lethal weapons of warfare. Centuries of historical development were telescoped into a decade: the Vietnamese conflict moved millions of peasants from subsistence (prefeudal) production to socialist revolution.

The grounding of the revolutionary party in the activities of the proletariat, the diffusion of its ideas and programs into the countryside, the incorporation of the uprooted peasantry into a revolutionary army, and the convergence of the two social forces in the final victory in Saigon and the unification of the country, describe the dialectical movements between city and countryside in the making of the socialist revolution in Vietnam.[49] The final consummation of the socialist revolution rested on the organization of the proletariat linked to the revolutionary army. The revolutionary regime is recreating the productive forces destroyed by the imperialist forces, first and foremost by restoring the great floating masses in Saigon to their former status as peasants and proletarians. The process of the socialization of production is still at the beginning stages because of the enormous physical losses and dislocation. But the political power of the Communist Party, which is based at least in part on the working class, serves as a guarantee that there will be a continuous process of transformation, independent of any conjunctural agreements with local or foreign capital.[50]

The case of Vietnam illustrates the proposition that the movement for revolution grows out of the most dynamic encounters with world capitalism. The process of class transformation based on exploitation anchored in capital accumulation under France, the forced requisition and selective displacement under Japanese imperialism, the massive destruction and uprooting of rural and urban workers under U.S. imperialism—each in its turn created a greater and more dynamic anticapitalist force, propelling petty commodity producers as well as some capitalist forces into the maelstrom of revolutionary activity. The progress of capitalism at the international level increasingly destroyed the social bonds of the existing order, thus undermining those social forces, which, in other times and places (when imperial capital was less potent), might have served as allies. The artificial supports of imperialism—local satraps, bureaucrats, military officials, contractors, retailers, speculators, etc.—were ill-suited to command an army, let alone secure the consent of a population from which they had to recruit a coercive force.

The Vietnam confrontation embodied, in pure form, the unmitigated power of imperialism; it represented the outcome of a social system that would subordinate a whole people to world capitalist expansion. To the degree that local capital accumulation became secondary and strategic political goals and global accumulation became primary, total warfare emerged as the final answer.

The defeat of U.S. imperialism in the Vietnamese class struggle is visible in two historical moments: the losses upon entering the class war and the losses resulting from efforts to recuperate after the war. In this conjuncture, the limitations on massive and direct U.S. involvement are evident and the opportunities for other revolutionary countries (Angola) to follow are exceptional. It is in this sense that the Vietnamese revolution has had world historic significance within the present conjuncture.

## Conclusion

Socialist revolutions are not products of backwardness; rather, revolutionary movements have developed with the spread of capitalism and in opposition to the exploitative relations it engenders.[51] Within the process of capital expansion, the formation and exploitation of an industrial labor force have laid the basis for the emergence of revolutionary parties.

As a result of capitalist expansion, the displacement and disarticulation of peasant agriculture have provided recruits to revolutionary movements. Recruits from the rural labor force have come from two sources—peasants turned into landless laboreres and impoverished small holders. The process of capital accumulation within the interstices of a commercial-bureaucratic society has accentuated the exploitation of the peasantry. The development of commodity production has hastened the process of land concentration, usurious practices, and speculative activity. The growth of money exchanges has heightened the exploitative relations between peasant and landlord, peasant and tax collector. Peasant rebellions historically were essentially incapable of terminating the organized forms of exploitation; they might eliminate a particular individual expression of exploitation, but never the social forms through which it was expressed. Led and directed by peasants or members of exploitative classes, the massive peasant rebellions were incapable of reorganizing society. The ideology of peasant rebellion contained elements of messianic vision, populism, and local vindictiveness, but not a clear and consequential vision of the state and an alternative form of organization.[52] In the twentieth century, rural revolts have led to a reorganization of the social form of agricultural production under conditions of large-scale uprooting and transformation of petty commodity production. This has predisposed the dispossessed to accept the party, leadership, and ideology derived from urban working movements and has led to the seizure of state power and the application of socialist ideology to the collectivization of society.

The growing concentration of capital, product and source of the extension of capital on a world scale, has internationalized domination and class struggle: each socialist revolution has grown out of an international civil war or into an international confrontation. The counter-revolution in Russia counted on the support of twenty capitalist countries; the Chinese revolution faced Japanese and later U.S. imperialism (indirectly in China through the Kuomintang and later directly in Korea). Cuba faced U.S.-directed aggression for almost two decades. Vietnam experienced the military occupation by the French, Japanese, and U.S. imperial powers. The struggle for a socialist transformation has pitted the revolutionary workers and peasants against the imperial state and its allied and dependent political and social forces within each formation.

The primary result of the acceleration of capitalist accumulation on a world scale is not modernization, development, underdevelopment, dependency, or industrialization, but the intensification of exploitation. Within a multiplicity of forms—including production, rent, taxation, usury, and exchange—the central problem, from the point of view of the class struggle (the historic viewpoint of the exploited classes) is the appropriation of the surplus by a capitalist ruling class, which controls and wields state power. The manner by which surplus is appropriated and the form it takes are related to the degree of integration of the world capitalist system, an integration mediated through a whole series of institutions and classes, beginning with family and kinship groups and continuing through to international ruling classes and their state.

The foundation of the current world order, the configuration of social forces, is largely the product of wars and revolutions. The very formation of territorial units, the framework within which the productive forces grow, has been the product of national or, more specifically, imperial wars. The United States is a prime case in point: at each crucial moment in the process of capital accumulation, the obstacles to further development have been overcome through violent action. The growth of capital through war and conquest suggests that those processes form an integral part of the ongoing political economy of capital. The imposition by force of coercive regimes and ongoing noneconomic bonds that characterize much of capitalist expansion are the inherent consequences of systemic needs for surplus labor power disciplined to the imperatives of profit maximization within a competitive world system. The mode of production cannot be abstracted from the exigencies of world expansion and domination and defined a priori through tendentious analogies to a particular set of experiences defined by countries in the process of becoming imperial states. Due to its nature and form in the context of competing imperial states and revolutionary challenges, capital, in expanding, imposes coercive forms of social relations as a means of extracting the maximum surplus to meet its immediate needs, while denying competitors access to the sources of surplus. State power, then, permeates all levels of society in the dominated countries. All aspects of social, political, and cultural life are politicized to provide an entry for capital. Precapitalist forms are instrumentalized for imperial expansion or, if they block entry, are literally destroyed, along with the productive forces and the labor force. This mode of penetration and transformation of society by capital is characteristic of the dominated countries. The external imposition of generalized conditions of exploitation interpenetrates with a massive politicization, provoking a direct mass response against the state—be it nominally independent or formally colonial. The commonplace response of imperial policy-makers and their academic advisers is to seek a strong state, a depoliticized (technically oriented) population, and civic actions and corporate structures that act as prophylactics against socialist revolutions.[53]

The objective basis and the realization of socialist revolutions have been less determined by fortuitous circumstances or by the inner rot of capitalism, than precisely by its continuing expansion. It is in its historical destructive role in pursuit of greater markets, resources, and sources of labor that capitalism, in its imperial form, has provoked the mass social movements, which have, in turn, overthrown it. The precise configuration of forces and conditions within this process of capital accumulation and destruction that has generated socialist revolution is the further subject of this study.

## Notes

1. Among the earlier writers on the process of capital accumulation on a world scale, see Nikolai Bukharin, *Imperialism and World Economy* (New York: Monthly Review Press, 1973), especially parts I and III; Rosa Luxemburg and Nikolai Bukharin, *The Accumulation of Capital* (New York: Monthly Review Press, 1968), especially section 3, "The historical conditions of accumulation"; and V. I. Lenin, *Imperialism: The Highest Stage of Capitalism* (New York: International Publishers, 1939). During the 1920s and 1930s, with the growth of Stalinism and nationalism, the world-historic approach virtually disappeared, re-emerging in the 1960s and 1970s. An excellent account of the degeneration of the communist movement can be found in Fernando Claudín, *The Communist Movement: From Comintern to Cominform* (New York: Monthly Review Press, 1975). Among the contemporary works which are relevant, see Ernest Mandel, *Marxist Economic Theory* (New York: Monthly Review Press, 1968), especially vol. 1, chap. 4, and vol. 2, chap. 13; Ernest Mandel, *Late Capitalism* (London: New Left Books, 1975), chaps. 2 and 11; and Samir Amin, *Accumulation on a World Scale* (New York: Monthly Review Press, 1974). A summary statement of Amin's model can be found in his "Accumulation and development: a theoretical model," *Review of African Political Economy* 1, no. 1 (1974): 9–26. Also see Andre Gunder Frank, *Capitalism and Underdevelopment in Latin America* (New York: Monthly Review Press, 1969); Immanuel Wallerstein, *The Modern World-System* (New York: Academic Press, 1973); Roger Owen and Bob Sutcliffe, eds., *Studies in the Theory of Imperialism* (London: Longman, 1972); Paul Sweezy, *The Theory of Capitalist Development* (New York: Monthly Review Press, 1956), in which see especially part 2 on the accumulation process and part 4 on imperialism; and Pierre Jalée, *The Pillage of the Third World* (New York: Monthly Review, Press, 1968).
2. My approach thus rejects theories arguing that revolution first has to occur in "advanced" capitalist centers. For example, in some of his journalistic writings Marx emphasized the positive role that imperialism would play in the periphery by destroying the old social order and establishing capitalism as a prelude to revolution. See Karl Marx and Frederick Engels, *On Colonialism*, 4th ed. (Moscow: Progress Publishers, 1968), especially pp. 81–87; and Saul Padover, ed., *Karl Marx on Revolution* (New York: McGraw-Hill, 1971). The more commonplace contemporary view argues that revolutions can

occur only in "Underdeveloped" societies. See John H. Kautsky, "An Essay on the Politics of Development" in John H. Kautsky, ed., *Political Change in the Underdeveloped Countries* (New York: John Wiley and Sons, 1962); Barrington Moore, *Social Origins of Dictatorship and Democracy* (Boston: Beacon Press, 1966). Both notions depend on a rather simplistic relationship between technico-economic levels and political action. Further, both approaches tend toward a unilinear, static conception of history, which stresses "location" in the world capitalist system rather than the dynamic processes inherent in the capitalist mode of production (class formation, exploitation, class consciousness, and struggle).

3. On the revolutionary possibilities involved in uneven development, see Leon Trotsky, *Permanent Revolution* (Calcutta: Gupta Rahmanand Gupta, 1947); V. I. Lenin, *Development of Capitalism in Russia* in *Collected Works*, vol. 3 (Moscow: Foreign Languages Press, 1960); and Jean Chesneaux, *The Chinese Labor Movement 1919-1927* (Stanford: Stanford University Press, 1968). In recent times the notion of "uneven" development has been dubbed "internal colonialism" and the revolutionary possibilities of it have been analyzed in a variety of contexts. For Mexico, see Pablo Gonzáles Casanova, "Internal colonialism and national development" in *Latin American Radicalism*, eds. Irving Horowitz, Josué de Castro, and John Gerassi (New York: Random House, 1969), pp. 118–39; for Great Britain, see Michael Hechter, *Internal Colonialism: The Celtic Fringe in British National Development 1536–1966* (Berkeley: University of California Press, 1975). Discussions that elaborate on the complex class and state relations in heterogeneous social formations in contemporary peripheral countries include: Harold Wolpe, "Capitalism and cheap labor power in South Africa: from segregation to apartheid," *Economy and Society* 1, no. 4 (1972): 425–56; Hamzi Alavi, "The Post-Colonial State," *New Left Review* 74 (1972); and Mahmood Mamdani, *Politics and Class Formation in Uganda* (New York: Monthly Review Press, 1976), especially chap. 5 on the colonial state and the articulation of modes of production.
4. The use of terms like "modernization" and "modern world" by writers like Barrington Moore obscures the precise nature of the social processes and social classes which are involved. This lack of precision in turn results in a failure to identify the major social forces involved in shaping and directing the process of revolutionary socialist transformation. Thus, it is not surprising that the goals and demands of the revolutionary forces are submerged into the

amorphous notion of "modernization." See, for example, Moore, *Social Origins*. The same terminology is found in Cyril Black, *Comparative Modernization* (New York: Free Press, 1976) and John Kautsky, *Political Consequences of Modernization* (New York: John Wiley and Sons, 1972).

5. The classic position separating war from the development of capitalism is found in Joseph Schumpeter, *Imperialism and Social Classes* (New York: Meridian Press, 1955). On the other hand, the notion that historical circumstances (i.e., war) have provided the opportunity for revolution is found in Chalmers Johnson, *Peasant Nationalism and Communist Power: The Emergence of Revolutionary Power 1937-1945* (Stanford: Stanford University Press, 1962, and Boston: Little, Brown & Co., 1966). While the former account blinds itself to the predominant forces acting in society by resorting to "residual" features from bygone eras, the latter begs the questions entirely: why do "historical circumstances" arise, and who do they lead to mass revolutionary action?
6. This phenomenon of "waves" of capital expansion helps to explain the "recurrence" of dictatorial regimes or practices in Third World countries that are seemingly pursuing their economic "take-off." No end of discussion is mystified by the so-called "gap" between economic growth and political democracy. To offer "retarded" or "uneven" development as a solution or explanation is to create a new form of circular argumentation. The histories of Cuba, Vietnam, Russia, and China all evidence the waves of economic expansion, class formation, and conflict "waves of repression." On the waves of repression in China in the 1920s, see Chesneaux, *Chinese Labor*. For the later period, see Nym Wales, *The Chinese Labor Movement* (New York: John Day, 1945). On the Cuban case, see Maurice Zeitlin, *Revolutionary Politics and the Cuban Working Class* (Princeton: Princeton University Press, 1967). On the waves of repression, see Samuel Farber, *Revolution and Reaction in Cuba, 1933–1960* (Middletown, Conn.: Wesleyan University Press, 1976). For a summary of repressive conditions in Russia between revolutions, see Tony Cliff, *Lenin*, vols. 1 and 2 (London: Pluto Press, 1976).
7. The dependency perspective is fully presented in "Dependence and Undervelopment in the New World and the Old," *Social and Economic Studies* 22, no. 1 (March 1973). The contributers include Norman Girvan, Aníbal Pinto, Celso Furtado, and Osvaldo Sunkel, among others. Other examples of the dependency approach can be found in Fernando Cardoso, "Dependency and Development in Latin

America," *New Left Review* 74 (1972); Celso Furtado, "Development and Stagnation in Latin America," in Irving Horowitz et al., *Latin American Radicalism;* and Raul Prebisch, "A Critique of Peripheral Capitalism," *CEPAL Review*, first semester 1976, pp. 9–76. For a discussion of how "noncapitalists" are integrated into and exploited by the capitalist and imperialist systems, see Wolpe, "Cheap labor"; and Oliver LeBrun and C. Gerry, "Petty Producers and Capitalism," *Review of African Political Economy* 3 (1975): 20–32. On the capitalist draining of peasant surpluses, see Rodolfo Stavenhagen, *Social Classes in Agrarian Societies* (New York: Doubleday & Co., Anchor Books 1975), especially pp. 224–33 and the epilogue; and NACLA, *Guatemala* (New York: NACLA, 1974).

8. For Russia, see Alexander Rabinowitch, *The Bolsheviks Come to Power* (New York: W. W. Norton & Co., 1976). On China, see Chesneaux, *Chinese Labor*. On Cuba, see Zeitlin, *Cuban Working Class*. On Vietnam, see I. Milton Sacks, "Marxism in Vietnam" in *Marxism in Southeast Asia*, ed. Frank Trager (Stanford: Stanford University Press, 1959), pp. 102–170. The alternative perspective, which emphasizes the notion of "peasant revolutions," is found in Eric Wolf, *Peasant Wars of the Twentieth Century* (New York: Harper and Row, 1969), see especially, chaps. 2–4 and chap. 6. Also see Frantz Fanon, *The Wretched of the Earth* (New York: Grove Press, 1963); Norman Miller and Roderick Aya, *National Liberation Revolution in the Third World* (New York: Free Press, 1971); and Moore, *Social Origins*. A good compilation of studies is found in Douglas Deal, "Peasant Revolts and Resistance in the Modern World: A Comparative View," *Journal of Contemporary Asia* 5, no. 4 (1975): 414–45.
9. A critique of the level of "productive forces" as a determinant of revolution is implicit in V. I. Lenin, *State and Revolution* (New York: International Publishers, 1932); Leon Trotsky, *1905* (New York: Vintage Books, 1972); and Charles Bettelheim, *Class Struggles in the USSR, First Period 1917-1923* (New York: Monthly Review Press, 1976).
10. Despite variations in emphasis and in the agencies of diffusion, the following modernization theorists follow this schema: Daniel Lerner, *The Passing of Traditional Society: Modernizing the Middle East* (New York: The Free Press, 1964); W. W. Rostow, *Politics and the Stages of Growth* (London: Cambridge University Press 1972): David Apter, *The Politics of Modernization* (Chicago: University of Chicago Press, 1965).
11. A discussion of the contribution of petty commodity producers to

capitalist production is found in Stavenhagen, *Agrarian Societies*; LeBrun and Gerry, "Petty Producers"; NACLA, *Guatemala*; Wolpe, "Cheap labor"; and Mamdani, *Class Formation in Uganda*.

12. On the mechanism of surplus extraction in Latin America see Andre Gunder Frank, *Latin America: Underdevelopment or Revolution?* (New York: Monthly Review Press, 1969). On Africa, see Walter Rodney, *How Europe Underdeveloped Africa* (Bogle: L'Ouverture Publications London, 1972). The most influential account has been Paul Baran, *The Political Economy of Growth* (New York: Monthly Review Press, 1957). The rather one-sided view that emphasizes exchange transactions as the vehicle of exploitation can be found in Arghiri Emmanuel, *Unequal Exchange: A Study of the Imperialism of Trade* (New York: Monthly Review Press, 1972). The most cited article, which best exemplifies the mechanical transposition of particular forms of capitalist social relations into a universal type, is Ernesto Laclau, "Feudalism and Capitalism in Latin America," *New Left Review* 67 (May-June 1971): 19–38. For a discussion of these theories, see the first piece in this volume.
13. The notion that the spread of capitalism through peaceful means is a product of maturity is one of those Rostovian myths that embellishes more than it explains. Indeed, the whole argument that visualizes "brutality" with the "early stages" of capital accumulation—in short, that envisions "primitive" accumulation (the forcible usurpation of resources to further capital reproduction) as a static early state—fails to account for the aggressive behavior that continues to accompany Western expansion. Recent European, U.S., and Japanese economic history is rife with examples of "recurring stages" of "primitive accumulation," i.e., expansion, pillage, and violence. Soon after Vietnam, discussion among U.S. policy-makers focused on possible "seizures" of oil: where conflicts with the need for accumulation cannot be dealt with through a "normal" flow of exchanges, the other, the "primitive," force of capital appears. Historically, the principal conjuncture for the use of primitive accumulation methods has been largely the global contests between competing imperial capital for global hegemony. In those conflicts, the ultimate logic of capital is manifested: everything is subordinated to the elements of production without mediating forces. The repetitive use of force accompanying U.S. expansion in the nineteenth century can be found in Walter LaFeber, *The New Empire: An Interpretation of American Expansion 1860-1890* (Ithaca, N.Y.: Cornell University Press, 1969). On interimperialist rivalries, see Gabriel Kolko,

*The Politics of War: The World and U.S. Foreign Policy 1943-1945* (New York: Random House, 1968). On U.S. intervention in revolutionary processes, see David Horowitz, *Containment and Revolution* (Boston: Beacon Press, 1967). The recurring or perpetual nature of the "crises" in U.S. capitalism is discussed in Gabriel Kolko, *Main Currents in Modern American History* (New York: Harper and Row, 1976), especially in chap. 10.

14. The notion of "uprootedness" as the basis of revolutionary action is clearly differentiated from the notion of exploitation. In the latter, labor tied to the productive process continues to produce surplus value. In the former, the worker is separated from the means of production, and labor is prevented from selling labor power (conscription and requisition being the forms of coerced labor). While these processes defy an analysis that focuses on identifying labor through its relationship with individual capitalists, the conditions of uprootedness are products of the collective behavior of all capitalists acting primarily through the state. The collective responsibility of the imperial state is reflected in the mass opposition of the uprooted; and the loss of productive forces, position in the labor force, and the coerced nature of work all contribute to a total rupture between the intruding state and the uprooted population. Hence, "uprootedness" is potentially an even more revolutionary force than exploitation.
15. Leon Trotsky, *The History of the Russian Revolution* (Ann Arbor: University of Michigan Press, 1957), especially chaps. 1–3, 9–11, 13, 20–22.
16. E. H. Carr, *The Bolshevik Revolution* (Baltimore: Penguin Books, 1966), see parts 1 and 2 of vol. 1.
17. The conspiratorial account can be found in Leonard Schapiro, *The Origins of the Communist Autocracy* (Cambridge, Mass: Harvard University Press, 1955) and Merle Fainsod, *How Russia is Ruled* (Cambridge, Mass: Harvard University Press, 1963). The standard distortion of the "Leninist" Party is found in both liberal and Stalinist sources. See Alfred Meyer, *Leninism* (New York: Frederick A. Praeger, 1967); and Stalin, *The Foundations of Leninism* (New York: International Publishers 1932). The best single recent account of the popular basis of the Bolshevik revolution is Alexander Rabinowitch, *The Bolsheviks Come to Power* (New York: W. W. Norton, 1976). The Bolshevik Party, as Cliff has shown, developed over time into an overwhelmingly working-class party, tightly integrated with the working class and playing an important role in the evolution of working-class institutions (trade unions and soviets), especially in

the period between the 1905 and 1917 revolutions. There is no basis for conceiving of the revolution as an elitist coup carried out behind the backs of the workers; even less reason is there to argue that the revolution was conceived of by the great majority of its participants as an instrument of modernization at the expense of the working class. See Cliff, *Lenin*, vols. 1 and 2. Other useful descriptions of the revolutionary role of the workers and "peasants" in the Bolshevik Revolution can be found in Carr, *Bolshevik Revolution;* Trotsky, *Russian Revolution*; N. N. Sukhanov, *The Russian Revolution 1917* (New York: Harper and Row, 1962); Bettelheim, *Class Struggles in the USSR*; and Victor Serge, *Year One of the Russian Revolution* (New York: Holt, Rinehart and Winston, 1972). Useful documents on mass organizations can be found in James Bunyan and H. H. Fisher, *The Bolshevik Revolution 1917-1918* (Stanford: Stanford University Press, 1934). On the party meetings during the revolutionary period, see *The Bolsheviks and the October Revolution*, Central Committee Minutes of the Russian Social-Democratic Labor Party Bolsheviks, August 1917–February 1918 (London: Pluto Press, 1974). On the open nature of Lenin's Marxism see Cliff, *Lenin;* Victor Serge, *From Lenin to Stalin* (New York: Pioneer Publishers, 1937); Roy Medvedev, *Let History Judge* (New York: Vintage Press, 1973); and Valentino Gerratano, "What Was the Origin of Leninism," *New Left Review* 103 (May–June 1977): 59–71.

18. Harold Isaacs, *The Tragedy of the Chinese Revolution* (Stanford: Stanford University Press, 1951); Jean Chesneaux, *Peasant Revolts in China 1840–1949* (New York: W. W. Norton & Co., 1973); Chesneaux, *Chinese Labor*.
19. Chesneaux, *Chinese Labor*; Isaacs, *Chinese Revolution*.
20. Chesneaux, *Chinese Labor*; A. Neuberg, *Armed Insurrection* (New York: St. Martin's Press, 1970), especially chaps. 5 and 6, pp. 105–150, and Wales, *Chinese Labor Movement*. For a good critique of the events leading to the 1927 massacre, see Leon Trotsky, *Problems of the Chinese Revolution* (Ann Arbor: University of Michigan Press, 1967).
21. Chesneaux, *Peasant Revolts;* Lucien Bianco, *Origins of the Chinese Revolution 1915-1949* (Stanford: Stanford University Press, 1971), especially pp. 75 passim. The long-term process of pauperization and proletarianization is described in R. H. Tawney's *Land and Labor in China* (New York: Octagon Books, 1964).
22. Chesneaux's study of labor and the peasantry underlines the socioeconomic basis of radicalization. It is hard to understand how

the notion of "peasant nationalism" would make any sense when (1) most peasants were literally not part of a "nation" and (2) they are overwhelmingly concerned with local economic issues. The opposition to Japanese encroachments followed similar protests against the *local* requisition of wealth. The peasant opposition to Japan had little to do with "nationalism" but was rather a response to the process of a massive forcible appropriation of surplus. "Nationalism" is an inaccurate "catch-all" term, which encompasses a broad opposition movement to the despoliation of petty commodity producers. On "peasant nationalism," see Johnson, *Peasant Nationalism*.

23. Most writers who discuss the Chinese Revolution as a "peasant" revolution or who discuss the "originality" of Mao Tse-tung focus on this period. See Benjamin Schwartz, *Chinese Communism and the Rise of Mao* (Cambridge, Mass.: Harvard University Press, 1951); Edgar Snow, *Red Star Over China* (New York: Random House, 1944); and Mark Selden, *The Yenan Way in Revolutionary China* (Cambridge, Mass.: Harvard University Press, 1974).
24. O. Tanin and E. Yohan, *When Japan Goes to War* (New York: International Publishers, 1936), especially chap. 3 on strategic materials and chap. 4 on the economic strains. The political basis for these policies is found in Jon Halliday, *A Political History of Japanese Capitalism* (New York: Pantheon, 1975), chaps. 4–6. On the interimperialist rivalry, see Noam Chomsky, *American Power and the New Mandarins* (New York: Pantheon, 1969), especially the chapter entitled, "The Revolutionary Pacifism of A. J. Muste."
25. On the Kuomintang, see Moore, *Social Origins*, pp. 187 passim, and Isaacs, *Chinese Revolution*.
26. Livio Maitan, *Party, Army and Masses in China* (London: New Left Books, 1976).
27. Ibid.
28. The most detailed account of Cuban revolutionary history is Hugh Thomas, *Cuba: The Pursuit of Freedom* (New York: Harper and Row, 1971); on U.S.-Cuban relations, see Robert Freeman Smith, *The United States and Cuba* (New York: Bookman Associates, 1961), and Philip Foner, *A History of Cuba and Its Relations with the U.S.* (New York: International Publishers, 1962–1963), vols. 1 and 2. On prerevolutionary Cuba, see Lowry Nelson, *Rural Cuba* (Minneapolis: University of Minnesota Press, 1950). A general historical survey is found in Wyatt MacGaffey and Clifford Barnett, *Twentieth Century Cuba* (Garden City, N.Y.: Doubleday & Co., Anchor Books, 1965). On the 1933 period, see Luis E. Aguilar, *Cuba 1933:*

*Prologue to Revolution* (Ithaca, N.Y.: Cornell University Press, 1972).

29. See Zeitlin, *Revolutionary Politics;* Aguilar, *Cuba 1933;* Charles Page, "Communism and the Labor Movements of Latin America," *Virginia Quarterly Review* 23 (Summer 1959); and Vania Bambirra, *La revolucion Cubana: una interpretacion* (Mexico City: Editorial Nuestro Tiempo, 1974).
30. On communist collaborationism, see Farber, *Revolution and Reaction in Cuba*. On the military of the 1950s, see Zeitlin, *Revolutionary Politics;* and Ramon Bonachea and Marta San Martín, *The Cuban Insurrection 1952-1959* (New Brunswick, N. J.: Transaction Books, 1974).
31. See Smith, *United States and Cuba;* and Aguilar, *Cuba 1933*.
32. Bonachea and San Martín, *Cuban Insurrection;* Zeitlin, *Revolutionary Politics;* Ernesto Che Guevara, *Reminiscences of the Cuban Revolutionary War* (New York: Monthly Review Press, 1968); Leo Huberman and Paul Sweezy, *Cuba: Anatomy of a Revolution* (New York: Monthly Review Press, 1961).
33. Régis Debray's portrayal of the revolution as largely a product of a rural focus is as much a gross distortion of the actual historical process as many of the conservative and liberal descriptions of the mass social transformation were a product of Castro's "manipulation." A more plausible interpretation, which stresses the mass efforts from below, is found in Bambirra, *La revolucion Cubana*, and Simón Torres and Julio Aronde, "Debray and the Cuban Experience," in *Régis Debray and the Latin American Revolution*, eds. Leo Huberman and Paul Sweezy (New York: Monthly Review Press, 1967). The "manipulation" theory is found in Theodore Draper, *Castro's Revolution: Myths and Realities* (New York: Frederick A. Praeger, 1962). The early revolutionary measures are discussed in Huberman and Sweezy, *Anatomy of a Revolution* and Edward Boorstein, *The Economic Transformation of Cuba* (New York: Monthly Review Press, 1968).
34. The best account of stagnant capitalism is James O'Connor, *The Origins of Socialism in Cuba* (Ithaca, N.Y.: Cornell University Press, 1970).
35. Zeitlin, *Revolutionary Politics*.
36. Farber, *Reaction in Cuba*.
37. See Richard Fagen, *The Transformation of Political Culture in Cuba* (Stanford: Stanford University Press, 1969); Carmelo Mesa Lago, ed., *Revolutionary Change in Cuba* (Pittsburgh: University of

Pittsburgh Press, 1971), especially chap. 12; James O'Connor, *Socialism in Cuba*; chap. 7; Dudley Seers, et al., *Cuba: The Economic and Social Revolution* (Chapel Hill, N.C.: University of North Carolina Press, 1964); Rolando Bonachea and Nelson Valdés, eds., *Cuba in Revolution* (New York: Doubleday & Co., Anchor Books, 1972), especially pp. 1–110 and 154–224. Theodore Draper's thesis of a "revolution" betrayed is premised on a series of historic distortions and misconceptions: (1) he totally obliterates the history of anticapitalist struggle preceding and accompanying the Cuban revolution; (2) he exaggerates the role of the "middle class" (a formulation which includes everything from low-paid salaried employees to large corporate capitalists—strata whose interests are not usually compatible); (3) he identifies the revolution with a particular event, the downfall of Batista, rather than a process; and (4) he identifies the "goals" of the revolution with the pronouncements of political leaders at a given moment rather than as products of an ongoing social struggle between conflicting shifts in programmatic emphasis. See Draper, *Castro's Revolution*.

38. On the incipient bureaucratism see Leo Huberman and Paul Sweezy, *Socialism in Cuba* (New York: Monthly Review Press, 1969), especially chaps. 9 and 11. An overdrawn and distorted account of the same process is found in René Dumont, *¿Cuba es Socialista?* (Caracas: Editorial Tiempo Nuevo, 1970). See also Maurice Zeitlin, *Revolutionary Politics and the Cuban Working Class* (New York: Harper and Row, Harper Torchbook, 1970). On the process of institutionalization, see Nelson Valdés, "Revolution and Institutionalization in Cuba," *Cuban Studies* 6, no. 1 (January 1976): 1–38. Two views on the extent of influence of the Russian model can be found in Carmelo Mesa Lago, *Cuba in the 1970s* (Albuquerque: University of New Mexico Press, 1974) and Frank Fitzgerald, "A Critique of the 'Sovietization of Cuba' Thesis," *Science and Society* 42, no. 1 (Spring 1978): 1–32. For a descriptive survey of some of the issue conflicts, see Donald Bray and Timothy Harding, "Cuba," in *Latin America*, eds. Ronald Chilcote and Joel Edelstein, (Cambridge, Mass.: Schenkman, 1974).
39. I. Milton Sacks, "Marxism in Vietnam."
40. See Bernard Fall, *Ho Chi Minh on Revolution 1920-1966* (New York: New American Library, Signet, 1967). Many scholars have erred when, in emphasizing the mass peasant base of the 1940s and 1950s, they have dismissed communist references to working-class leadership, attributing the latter to the need for the "orthodox" to pay lip

service to communist dogma while assuming a more pragmatic posture. Such attributions seem to me to play too fast and loose with the positive commitment of communist leaders to the working-class movement; but more important they erroneously underestimate the fundamental importance of the initial working-class struggles in the formation of parties, cadres, and individual consciousness—in Vietnam and elsewhere. See Wolf, *Peasant Wars*; and Jeffery Paige, *Agrarian Revolution* (New York: Free Press, 1975), especially chaps. 1, 2, 5, and 6.

41. Richard Barnet, *Intervention and Revolution* (New York: World Publishing Co., 1968), especially chap. 9, pp. 181–224; Philippe Devillers and Jean Lacouture, *End of a War: Indochina 1954* (New York: Frederick A. Praeger, 1969); Kolko, *Politics of War*.
42. See John T. McAlister, *Vietnam: The Origins of Revolution* (New York: Alfred A. Knopf, 1965); Wilfred Burchett, *Vietnam Will Win* (New York: Guardian, 1970).
43. Ellen Hammer, *The Struggle for Indochina* (Stanford: Stanford University Press, 1954), chap. 3, pp. 67–71; McAlister, *Vietnam*, chap. 6.
44. Most treatment of the Japanese occupation gives sparse attention to this process except to mention its "cruelty." See Joseph Buttinger, *A Dragon Defiant* (New York: Frederick A. Praeger, 1972), pp. 74–75.
45. Bernard Fall, *The Viet-Minh Regime* (New York: Institute of Pacific Relations, 1956).
46. The issue of communist leadership has of couse been one of contention, overlain by polemical concerns. For the Left, the Vietminh was presented, especially at the time of its gestation, as an association of patriotic and democratic agrarianists; on the other hand, U.S. Cold War writers presented it as a cold-blooded and devious "front" manipulated by communist totalitarians. A reasonable account would recognize that the Vietminh was largely organized by social forces—workers, intellectuals, and salaried employees—linked to the Communist Party, which successfully combined forces with petty-bourgeois and other nationalist social forces because they shared a common adversary whose depredations overshadowed their differences. The notions of "deception" and "manipulation" as characteristics of the internal relationship are hardly tenable—as most of the political forces involved were hardly unaware of the political background of the other participants. What seems to me more interesting is to note the long-term (historic) importance that the previous working-class struggles had in etching upon the com-

munist cadre a collectivist perspective, one that endured the pressures and tactical retreats which were inherent in the multiclass alliance. The eventual shift from anticolonial struggles to social transformation attests to the enduring ties that bound the Communist Party to the working-class struggles. The latter point is crucial for understanding the historic trajectory of the party: no other classes or set of classes embraced and sustained in a coherent and consequential fashion the notion of collectivization of production. Neither the intellectuals nor the peasants (apart from individuals) thought in terms of egalitarian norms and socialized production—though through party influence conversions were made. What makes the impact of working-class politics especially significant in the case of Vietnam is that despite the long tortuous history of the party, involving multiple alliances, shifts to overwhelmingly "national" and even antigenocidal positions embracing extremely diverse strata, when the commanding positions of power were won, the revolutionary regime began to clearly and perceptibly develop policies tied specifically to a working-class-based collectivist position.

47. Barnet, *Intervention and Revolution*, emphasizes the "political" considerations, while Horowitz, *Empire and Revolution*; and Gabriel Kolko and Joyce Kolko, *The Limits of Power* (New York: Harper and Row, 1972) emphasize the more fundamental economic processes.
48. A good account of the destructiveness of U.S. involvement is found in the *International War Crimes Tribunal: Stockholm and Roskilde 1967* (New York: Bertrand Russell Peace Foundation, 1968). Numerous novels, news, and other reports deal with individual experiences or particular situations. A thorough history integrating all facets of the destruction has yet to be written. See, for example, Frances Fitzgerald, *Fire in the Lake* (Boston: Little, Brown & Co. 1972).
49. This summary statement of the overall reciprocal movement of social forces between city and countryside is meant to highlight the rather sterile attempts to isolate and analyze "sectors" as disparate elements acting as independent forces. For an account of the convergence of forces in the final stages of the revolution in South Vietnam, see General Van Tien Dung, *Our Great Spring Victory* (New York: Monthly Review Press, 1977); and Tiziano Terzani, *Giai Phong: The Fall and Liberation of Saigon* (New York: St. Martin's Press, 1976).
50. The movement toward collectivization accelerated during the sec-

ond and third years, thus confirming the socialist direction. In August 1977 increasing pressure was evidenced in efforts to collectivize agriculture (*New York Times*, August 27, 1977). The collectivist process will, in turn, increasingly depend on support among the working class.

51. See Moore, *Social Origins*; and Kautsky, *Political Consequence of Modernization*.
52. Eric Hobsbawm, *Primitive Rebels* (Manchester, Eng.: Manchester University Press, 1959); and Chesneaux, *Peasant Revolts*.
53. Probably the classic account is found in Samuel Huntington, *Political Order in Changing Societies* (New Haven, Conn.: Yale University Press, 1968).